Advance Praise for *When Truth Mattered*

Robert Giles has crafted an absorbing and meticulous story of how one newspaper — The *Akron Beacon Journal* — told the truth about a national tragedy in a time, like our own, when Americans were deeply divided. I've never seen a better demonstration of why good journalism matters.

JAMES TOBIN, author of *Ernie Pyle's War: America's Eyewitness to World War II*; professor of journalism, Miami University

• • •

From the editor who led his newsroom through one of the nation's saddest moments comes this story of a painstaking pursuit of the truth — and a searing reminder of how sorely we lack it today.

GENEVA OVERHOLSER, Pulitzer Prize-winning editor, journalism consultant and advisor

• • •

When Truth Mattered is a newsroom thriller that truly uplifts and educates. Giles' genius as the consummate reporter and brilliantly paced storyteller offers us a front row seat to an American tragedy. We see news — truth — reported as history is being made. Giles' reflections on a lifetime spent reporting and editing offer all of us lessons on reading today's headlines. This is an essential and dramatic book.

DOUG STANTON, #1 *New York Times* best-selling author

• • •

Robert Giles forged his status as one of the legendary newspaper editors in modern American history on May 4, 1970, with his steady stewardship of the *Akron Beacon Journal* on the day of the Kent State shootings. This never-before-told account will take you inside the turmoil and drama of the newsroom, the campus of Kent State and the city of Akron. At a time when journalists are under attack from the very highest levels of government, this book is a reminder of why journalism — especially local journalism — is one of the last great guarantors of our democracy.

GUY RAZ, host, creator of NPR's TED Hour and How I Built This

"Four dead in Ohio" still rings in our ears because Bob Giles and his team at the *Akron Beacon Journal* got the story and got it right. Now Giles delivers the backstory with the same attention to detail, accuracy and history. In an era when journalism is under attack, Giles delivers a crisp, punchy narrative of a little-known turning point in American history—and a call to understand just how key good journalism is to a healthy democracy.

BETH MACY, author of *Dopesick: Dealers, Doctors, and the Drug Company That Addicted America*

• • •

Fifty years after Ohio National Guardsmen killed four Kent State students, the then-managing editor of the *Akron Beacon Journal* scratches a nagging itch: He revisits his newspaper's Pulitzer Prize-winning coverage of the local story that became a national flashpoint in 13 seconds of gunfire. *When Truth Mattered* shows a small, assertive newsroom (large by today's standards) operating full-tilt, around-the-clock for days, then weeks, then months, even years in pursuit of an elusive truth: Who fired? And why? More importantly, Bob Giles asks how a local newsroom, now stripped of staff and resources, could possibly respond today.

HANK KLIBANOFF, director, Georgia Civil Rights Cold Cases Project at Emery University, author of Race Beat and winner of the 2007 Pulitzer Prize in history

• • •

When Truth Mattered is an important reminder that in today's digital age, meticulous reporting and the quest for truth are even more powerful together. Then and now, journalism served as a tool for accountability. It is a timeless story that resonates today.

FREDDY CORCHADO, Mexican bureau chief, *Dallas Morning News*, author of *Midnight in Mexico*

• • •

This book harkens to a time when journalists were respected, and troubling stories could not simply be dismissed as "fake news." If you care about history, journalism, great storytelling, or simply the truth, you'll devour *When Truth Mattered*.

JOHN U. BACON, *New York Times* best-selling author

Building a full, truthful picture was the responsibility of the *Akron Beacon Journal*. It would require deep sourcing and rigorous reporting, day after day, one fact built on another, to tell the story of what had happened, how and why. Fifty years later, it is a story that demands to be more deeply retold. Robert Giles, the *Beacon Journal* managing editor at the time, was the right leader through those days and is uniquely suited today to put the events of that horrific week in the context of Kent State's history of protest. His is a probing, honest, insightful portrait of a newspaper facing its greatest challenge in an era when the print newspapers were the essential news source in every community.

SANDY ROWE, former editor of *The Oregonian* and board chair of the Committee to Protect Journalists

• • •

Robert Giles has crafted a powerful memoir of the tragic Kent State shooting. This is a heart-pounding story, where readers will hear the crack of rifles on the sunny college campus as well as feel the stress reporters and editors faced sorting fact from fiction in a race against deadlines, all the while under pressure from readers, the FBI, and even the president. *When Truth Mattered* shines a light on the vital role journalism plays in our democracy, a role that is increasingly under threat in today's world of social media and so-called fake news.

JAMES M. SCOTT, Pulitzer Prize finalist and author of *Target Tokyo* and *Rampage*

• • •

Journalist Robert Giles makes history come alive in this compelling and authoritative account of the Kent State tragedy. Giles weaves together the tension and turmoil at Kent State with the professionalism and dedication that led a medium-sized newspaper to win the Pulitzer Prize for its fearless coverage. His account needs to be heard by generations new and old, not only to better understand what happened that fateful day, but also to appreciate how and why courageous journalists do what they do to teach us the truth of our times.

AMY GAJDA, The Class of 1937 Professor of Law, Tulane University Law School. Author of *The First Amendment Bubble*

When Truth Mattered: The Kent State Shootings 50 Years Later
By Robert Giles

Mission Point Press
2554 Chandler Road
Traverse City, Michigan 49696
www.MissionPointPress.com
231-421-9513

Cover photograph by John Darnell

Title page photo by John Filo

ISBN: 978-1-950659-42-5 (softover)
ISBN: 978-1-950659-39-5 (hardcover)
Library of Congress Control Number:
2019920592
Printed in the United States of America

THE KENT STATE SHOOTINGS
50 YEARS LATER

WHEN TRUTH MATTERED

ROBERT GILES

MISSION POINT PRESS

Allison Krause

Jeffrey Miller

Sandra Scheuer

William Schroeder

*For Allison, Jeffrey, Sandra
and William — slain by American soldiers*

*And the journalists who reported
the truth of an American tragedy*

Table of Contents

Ohio National Guard troops, dressed for combat, moved unimpeded on the Kent State campus on May 4, 1970. (Kent State University News Service)

A banner displayed the theme of the seventh annual commemoration of the Kent State shootings. On the stage were Dean Kahler, who was shot by a Guardsman on May 4, 1970, and permanently paralyzed below the waist, and others including anti-war activists William Kunstler and Ron Kovic. (Kent State University News Service)

Foreword by Alex S. Jones

This is not a book about the events of May 4, 1970, at Kent State University. That day ended with four students shot dead and nine others with bullet wounds. And from that violence was created an iconic moment of tragedy. This is a book about the relentless effort to learn the truth about what happened that day, and then the heroic determination to tell that truth unvarnished. It is a story of journalism at its most human, and at its best.

Journalism is never the repository of perfect truth. It has been called "history on horseback," and — in this case — at a frenzied gallop. It can be sloppy and reckless. It can also be done with high principle and courage, with the result — ultimately, if not immediately — of revealing the truth. And truth always matters.

The *Akron Beacon Journal*, in 1970, was the local paper of Kent State, which was in a town about 20 minutes drive from downtown Akron. The *Beacon Journal* was what might be called a mid-sized daily paper, but with outsized pride and ambition and a staff committed to its owner's dictum: "Get the truth and print it." The paper's managing editor — and the driving force behind the journalism that followed — was Bob Giles, who is the author of *When Truth Mattered*. He has created an account both vivid and with unsparing candor — including inevitable errors.

The story told in *When Truth Mattered* is one with heroes and, if not villains, revelations of terribly bad judgment and then a massive effort to avoid responsibility for that bad judgment. It is, in a sense, an old story of plenty of blame to go around, and — in this case — a relentless effort to dig out the truth. That doesn't always happen, of course, which makes this showcase of brave journalism all the more worth celebrating.

After half a century, what has changed since 1970 is not journalism. The principles remain in the hearts and minds of editors and reporters and photographers as strongly as they did then. What has changed is the powerful institutional foundation that supported those principles.

The *Akron Beacon Journal* was owned by Knight Newspapers, perhaps the best newspaper chain in the nation. This superstructure of journalistic strength supported the *Beacon Journal's* dogged and costly effort to unearth the whole story and then tell it in the face of threats and denunciations. The power to withstand that pressure came from the economic muscle that newspapers had 50 years ago. That is no longer the case, mainly because of digital technology.

The thing that has changed is not that truth mattered more in 1970. It is that the major vehicle for telling such truth — the nation's newspapers — have been economically hobbled and the institutions that own them weakened. Would today's *Beacon Journal* be able to mount the investigation today that it did in 1970? I fear it would not, and that is as tragic as the events of 1970 themselves. In today's world, the truth, alas, might not be forced into the sunlight.

On May 4, 1970, the *Beacon Journal's* battle to tell the truth began almost immediately after the shots were fired by National Guardsmen into a mass of Kent State students. It was immediately known that there had been deaths, but the initial report was that the deaths were of Guardsmen, based on a misunderstanding by a United Press International reporter. That wrong information was circulated instantly throughout the nation by other newspapers. The *Beacon Journal's* reporter on the scene said it was students who had been killed. The issue was fraught, as one version of events had the students firing on the Guardsmen. But the editors went with their own reporter's version of truth. They stood virtually alone, and risked ridicule if not contempt. But they were correct.

Again and again, the *Beacon Journal's* account proved that, while the students had been defiant and angry, the bad judgment mostly rested with a stubborn governor eager to bolster his chances in a close election. And they exposed a commander of the National Guard unit, whose bull-headedness almost caused more deaths. The paper told the story of a gutsy geology professor who, after the shots were fired, literally stood between the Guardsmen and the students declaring that they would advance "over my dead body."

In the aftermath, when finger-pointing and phony explanations were rife, the *Beacon Journal* again and again told the story of what actually happened with fairness and an absence of bile and deep reporting. When, months later, the paper editorialized that no Guardsman should be indicted for what happened, the advocates for the student victims, who had previously saluted the paper's coverage, vented their wrath

Ultimately, the paper's staff — and it was a team effort from top to bottom — was recognized with a Pulitzer Prize, journalism's highest honor.

The lessons of the *Beacon Journal's* coverage of Kent State are many, but the one most important lesson is that in our complex and always-flawed democracy, journalism is essential to learning the truth. The inspiring thing about this book is that it tells the story of a journalistic mission fulfilled, with challenges overcome and standards upheld. That is — even 50 years later — a cause for hope.

Alex S. Jones is an American journalist who was director of the Shorenstein Center on Media, Politics and Public Policy at Harvard's Kennedy School from July 2000 until June 2015. As a New York Times *reporter, he won the 1987 Pulitzer Prize for his coverage of the breakup of the Bingham family, owner of the Louisville newspapers.*

Students gather on the Commons at noon on May 4; they watch National Guardsmen form lines near the burned-out ROTC building. (Howard Ruffner)

Prologue

Monday, May 4, 1970. It is nearly noon. Kent State University students, many openly defiant, gather on the Commons, a large grassy space at the crossroads of the campus. The ROTC building nearby is a burned-out skeleton, destroyed Saturday night. The protesters — many long-haired hippies — number about 300. Curious onlookers bring the crowd to about 1,500.

Ohio's governor has declared this protest — against the bombings in Cambodia — illegal under the state's Riot Act. So National Guardsmen are forming ranks. Their job: to stop the protest. The Guardsmen carry M-1 rifles. Locked and loaded. Gas masks fit snug against their faces. Steel combat helmets sit on their heads. Young Americans dressed for war.

The protesters are raucous. They ring the Victory Bell — a relic donated by the Erie Railroad in 1950, its clang usually heard after a win by the Golden Flashes football team. "Kill the pigs!" they yell at the Guard. "Stick the pigs!"

The rally is about to start. A Guard jeep moves slowly along the lines of demonstrators. A Kent State policeman, flanked by two Guard riflemen, shouts through a bullhorn: The rally is illegal. You must disperse.

The students defy the warnings with taunts; relentless, the bell clangs on.

Shoulder-to-shoulder, rifles upright and fixed with bayonets, the Guard begins a slow march up the hill toward the demonstrators gathered by the bell. Some Guardsmen fire teargas grenades. They land with a pop and a hiss, like air rushing from punctured tires.

The students scatter up the hill. A few pick up canisters and throw them back at the Guard. One soldier grabs a canister and hurls it in return. The volley of teargas envelops the Commons in smoke. The din grows. The noise and commotion seem to underscore mounting tensions. Anger presses in on both sides, unrelenting. The Guardsmen, more nervous now, are outnumbered; the students, angry but undeterred, are outgunned. More teargas fills the air; there is so much smoke that it looks like a battleground.

The advancing Guardsmen, guns in front, bayonets gleaming, push the students over the Commons and down Blanket Hill into a parking lot on the other side of Taylor and Prentice halls and against an athletic field fence. There, for 10 minutes, the protesters and the Guard exchange rocks and teargas. The lines now seem drawn. Guardsmen committed to their mission. Students resenting soldiers trespassing on their campus.

And then, seemingly, a lull. The Guardsmen reverse themselves and head back up Blanket Hill toward the umbrella-shaped Pagoda, a square bench made of 4-by-4 wooden beams shaded by a concrete umbrella. Some students follow; their taunts continue. Perhaps, though, a retreat?

It is not to be. At 12:24 p.m., the Guardsmen nearest the Pagoda stop and turn. Their rifles are now pointed in various directions but primarily at the crowd. One crouches, points a pistol. They pull their triggers. At least 61 times.

Shouts of disbelief, screams of anguish. Cries. Pandemonium.

The bell falls silent. The grieving begins.

This John Filo photograph quickly became the iconic image of the Kent State tragedy. (John Filo)

Today, the Victory Bell is typically silent on a quiet Commons.
(Robert Giles)

CHAPTER ONE

A Return ... And a Necessary Reminder

On a Friday morning in early May 2018, I began a quest to understand anew the meaning of truth in journalism. The trip had the feeling of a pilgrimage. My destination was Kent State University, a sprawling state school northeast of Akron, Ohio.

For months, I had turned over in my mind some still-vivid details of an American tragedy on that campus. Kent State. May 4, 1970. Bullets fired by soldiers of the Ohio National Guard, killing and wounding students during a campus demonstration against the Vietnam War and, more specifically that day, against the bombing of Cambodia and the unwelcome presence of soldiers on the Kent State campus. A dark moment in an unpopular war.

The Kent State story has been with me for nearly 50 years. It is embedded in my memory. I talk about it often. Audiences large and small have been captivated with my retelling. My newspaper, the *Akron Beacon Journal,* reported this tragedy as it unfolded. We got it right.

The newspaper's account was forged in the timeless fires of deadlines. Details remain sharp. Over drinks or after dinner, the stories flow easily from my memory. Friends have urged me to write. They remind me that most of my newsroom colleagues — the critical observers, fact-gatherers and truth-tellers — are gone.

"You are one of the few survivors who can tell this important story," they say. "You must do it." They press for details about critical decisions made under the pressure of deadlines. They are deeply fascinated in how the newspaper created a singular, truthful account that remains unchallenged over nearly a half century.

A soft rain was falling. My wife, Nancy, and I hunted for a place to park on campus. The scene before us was an eerie reminder of how much had changed — and how much had not changed. It evoked the freshness of a typical spring afternoon on an American college campus. It seemed so ordinary. We walked into the student center and immediately sensed the somber mood of the hundreds gathered that weekend to commemorate 48 years since May 4, 1970.

As the afternoon rolled toward the evening's candlelight vigil, we traced steps and time, climbing the gentle slope called the Commons. We lingered where the antiwar rally began. I quietly rapped my knuckles on the Victory Bell. I imagined how its deep "clang" drew protesters to gather close on that fatal day. I stood under the concrete pagoda where one can imagine the guardsmen's vista as they turned and shot at the gathering of students. I ran my finger around the furred fringe of the hole in a metal sculpture left by an M-1 bullet. A granite bench set in a woody glen near the journalism building offered a moment for reflection on how such a peaceful setting could become a killing ground.

I stood solemnly among the memorial posts in a parking lot next to Prentice Hall, a student dormitory. At the urging of relatives of the four students killed, the university constructed individual permanent markers in 1999 where each of the dead students fell. Six posts frame each space. They are waist high, octagonal in shape, with soft lights that glow from within. On this weekend, flowers and other remembrances had been placed against them.

The posts seem oddly out of place among student vehicles, yet appropriate reminders of young lives wasted. With a surge, I felt a fresh connection. These are stark statements that people died in this place. A nearby Visitors Center — on the first floor of Taylor Hall, which houses the journalism school — offers a commemoration space that emphasizes this reality of ordinary life versus extraordinary tragedy. Compelling exhibits of life and death are carefully, poignantly, displayed on the walls.

These posts are symbolic reminders of death and violence on an American college campus. They evoke a sense of sorrow and anger. Kent State seems like such an ordinary place, a college without much distinction, until you try to reckon with its meaning as a battlefield of the Vietnam War. Many at the 48th Commemoration would linger where the shots had been fired to read the words on a new plaque marking it a National Historical site.

My own objectives during this visit were clear. I wanted more than solemn participation in an annual remembrance. I wanted a deeper understanding of the killings. I wanted to examine them in a journalistic context. I wanted to add a fresh voice to the story of how my newspaper, the *Akron Beacon Journal*, gave the public a truthful narrative of the tragedy and the days, weeks and months that followed. With the 50th commemoration looming, I knew there would be a hunger for understanding why truth mattered.

We mingled with survivors and anti-war activists. Among those we encountered, many mentioned the *Beacon Journal's* important role, especially in the days and weeks after May 4. Tom Grace, a survivor who took a bullet through his left ankle, seemed genuinely pleased when I admired his book, *Kent State: Death and Dissent in the Long Sixties*. It was the best account of May 4 that I had read. At dinner, Donald MacKenzie quietly described how a guardsman's bullet had entered his neck and exited through his cheek. It was a rare disclosure because, over the years, he had protected himself and held his memories close.

Our visit provided greater clarity about how the dead and injured at Kent State fit into a larger tableau of victims of violence. They are remembered as a singular tragedy during a decade when the nation was deeply divided by the killing and chaos of the Vietnam War. Kent State helped define a generation. By August 1970 — 11 years after U.S. armed forces became engaged in Southeast Asia — about 53,000 members of America's armed forces had perished.

During a single year, from August 1969 to August 1970, 9,084 protests on college campuses across the country became statements of rebellious students acting out opposition to the draft and the war raging in Vietnam. On many campuses, classrooms were shut and voices silenced. Kent State was the lone campus where students lay dead.

Countless arrests, month after month, turned college students into rebels as a new counterculture of opposition to Vietnam took hold. This young generation responded with angry alarm to the stark, disturbing contrast between what they believed and the official, falsely optimistic pronouncements from Washington and Saigon.

And as 1969 turned into 1970, mournful ceremonies marked the arrival home of coffins bearing the bodies of service men and women from the war's combat zones. Military archives show 11,780 killed in 1969 and 6,173 in 1970.

Americans were accustomed to supporting wars as acts of patriotism. Increasingly, the critical news coverage from Vietnam was confusing. Stories of mounting casualties and failed jungle engagements with the Vietcong were not welcome news, and not what the country was accustomed to reading and hearing.

Americans prided themselves in the belief that their nation had never lost a war. And yet, the growing reality that the country was failing in its mission to protect South Vietnam and stop the Communist takeover of Southeast Asia seemed to herald defeat.

The students were defenseless. Still, even against the advancing soldiers, they believed they were safe to speak out on their own campus. They were exercising three of the basic freedoms protected by the First Amendment to the Constitution of the United States: freedom of speech, the right to peaceably assemble, and the right to petition the government for redress of grievances.

As we returned to Traverse City on May 5, 2018, Nancy and I talked about our strong impressions of the Commemoration. We had been introduced to an unforgettable community of survivors and sympathizers. We found strength in their quiet determination for a lasting tribute.

The experience of being among them reinforced my desire to tell the story of journalism under fire at Kent State and the *Beacon Journal's* critical role in cementing the reality of what happened on May 4, 1970.

The truthfulness of our coverage gave the tragedy an authentic meaning that has endured for nearly 50 years. We did not anticipate a tragic outcome, but when our staff was unexpectedly confronted with such a story, we were prepared to discover and write the truth, and we did.

The *Beacon Journal* was not alone. Other news organizations gave the public accounts that were notable for their truthfulness and clarity. After May 5, however, journalistic attention by others to the Kent State story was brief and sporadic. A notable exception was the special report by a team of journalists from Knight Newspapers that was published three weeks after the shootings. It was a remarkable example of explanatory journalism.

In the days immediately following May 4, 1970, investigative reports by the *Akron Beacon Journal* produced evidence of incompetent military leadership, reckless and intemperate behavior by student protesters, attempts to falsely place the blame on so-called but unidentified "snipers" and a vicious mindset of hatred toward students. The deeply troubling voice of a popular leader turned demagogue was that of the governor of Ohio, James A. Rhodes, while he was on campus that weekend.

The governor was the loudest detractor of student behavior. He stepped into a momentary vacuum of leadership, assuming authority while condemning students as "brownshirts" and worse in a bitter outburst. Across the country, the anger and sentiment were mixed. "How could this happen?" vs. "Too bad they did not kill more of them!"

The *Beacon Journal's* initial newspaper stories created a narrative that has shaped public understanding to this time. Broadcast accounts, articles, books, *The Report of The President's Commission on Campus Unrest,* and, more recently, a brief episode on Ken Burns' 2017 television special, *Vietnam,* did not alter or modify the truthful account produced by the *Beacon Journal* news staff.

Our efforts extended far beyond the chaos of 13 seconds of that terrible day. The depth of the impact was measured in many ways: iconic photographs, haunting music, rallying cries of confusion, sadness, resistance and lingering resentment. We tried to capture each dimension and write about it as compellingly and as truthfully as we could.

That is the point of this story. This is a story of journalism in 1970 and the pursuit of truth, about how the staff of the *Akron Beacon Journal* gave the public the most accurate available version of the truth. They did it under the pressure of deadline. They did it in the face of powerful opposition from the military, the Nixon administration, the state of Ohio and the university itself, as well as strong currents of negative public attitudes.

My purpose here is to place the reader inside the *Akron Beacon Journal* newsroom. You will meet reporters, editors, photographers and artists who discarded irrelevance and rumor and created instead a solid, singular, truthful narrative.

This story explains how they developed a deep understanding of a culture of protest that was emerging on the Kent State campus, even before it was fully manifested in the spring of 1970. That knowledge enabled them to prepare for whatever might happen that portentous weekend.

Most of the names of our staffers are not widely known. Some went on to notable careers at the *Beacon Journal* and other news organizations. But for many, Kent State became the singular journalistic experience and defining time in their professional lives. On May 4, 1970, and in the months following, these men and women were the public's eyes and ears.

In this memoir, you will learn about these 15 men and women who shared the Pulitzer Prize for local news reporting awarded to the *Beacon Journal* staff in 1971. Many are deceased now. Part of my purpose is to honor them, to salute their courage, their energy and their persistence in braving intimidation. (The contributions of several others also made huge differences day after day, even though they were not identified for the special Pulitzer recognition.)

1970 was a time in America when truth mattered. The public expected journalists to pursue the truth and was inclined to trust them to find out what happened and report it in local newspapers and broadcast outlets.

To be sure, there was town/gown stress in Kent, Ohio. Some townspeople still harbor and nourish resentment, even hatred, in their own memories of anti-war protests. Some continue to harbor grudges against the *Beacon Journal*. Some dismiss the story as it was initially reported. Those denials remain painfully alive after nearly 50 years.

Aside from honoring these colleagues, though, why else write a book that focuses on how a local newspaper covered a national tragedy nearly 50 years ago? Why is that important today? Why should we recall and think seriously about a time when journalism was done differently; when there were no internet, cable TV and social media to shape stories or fan points of view? Are lessons to be found today in what journalism was in the late 1960s, and, specifically, in 1970?

This story can help readers recognize what has been lost in our national dialogue as we start the third decade of the 21st century. We are living in a period marred by attacks on press independence and disbelief in press freedom. Truth as a mission and mandate is under political assault. We no longer live in a time when a journalist can report a factual account and reasonably expect it to be accepted by the public as fair, balanced and as honestly complete as possible.

The politically based attacks on our nation's precious freedoms of press and expression have been amplified by an elected leader, his political allies and followers. They mimic the chants of "fake news" and cheer on a president who, with a sweep of his open hand toward journalists at a press briefing, dismisses them as "the enemy of the people." Doubt and cynicism have become hallmarks of public discourse. This tragic turn of events leaves us to wonder from where will come the encouragement and support of our essential press?

Most journalists today hold passionately to the values of their craft, just as they or their predecessors did in May 1970. They still believe that accuracy and fairness matter. They earnestly strive to exercise those values. They cherish the privilege of practicing the craft of news gathering and storytelling in a manner that is right and true.

Over time, shoe leather reporting, good sources and deep knowledge of the subject at hand build trust — trust between reporters and their sources, trust with readers in knowing that a story has been exhaustively reported, carefully edited and focused on the truth.

Thankfully, that trust continues today. Yet, the threat remains.

In preparing to tell this story, I searched my own memory and notes, re-read pages from old newspapers and read many of the books published since May 4, 1970. I delved into special May 4 collections at the libraries of Kent State University, Yale University and Columbia University. The literary canon against which I evaluated our initial coverage is important and influential. Many of the books tell the story in extensive and painful detail. But, as Jerry M. Lewis and Thomas R. Hensley concluded in their report for the Ohio Council for the Social Studies Review, published in 1998, *The Report of The President's Commission on Campus Unrest* is the "best single source for understanding the events of May 4."

Essential contributions came from a few living staff members whose sharp memories of their roles added to a fuller account.

When Truth Mattered is intended to reinforce the belief that journalism serves a public good when it is anchored in the best available version of the truth. Kent State and the dedication of a staff of hometown journalists reminds us why getting to the truth is hard work.

When Truth Mattered also provides the reader with a guide to what constitutes truthful reporting — the extensive levels of work required to bring truth to light. By knowing what these fundamental components are, you will be able to better judge whether the news media you are digesting today can be believed or not.

That is, after all, the job facing all of us during these precarious and vulnerable times.

Executive Editor Ben Maidenburg, a gruff, demanding leader, was in Israel on May 4, 1970. (Akron Beacon Journal)

CHAPTER TWO

April 28: Transition

As I tossed my keys on my desk in the *Akron Beacon Journal* newsroom this Tuesday morning, April 28, 1970, the importance of the next two weeks loomed. Ben Maidenburg, my boss, had made a decision that left me energized: He would join Akron-area business leaders on a junket to Israel. He wouldn't return until the second week of May.

I was to be in charge of the newsroom.

Maidenburg was the paper's executive editor. I was the managing editor — the second in command. Today was his last day before leaving town.

Maidenburg was a gruff man whose feisty personality cast him as a dominant presence in the *Beacon Journal* newsroom. He and I were connected by mutual respect and shared journalistic values. But we were very different in style.

Maidenburg was especially devoted to *his* boss, John Shively Knight — better known as JSK, and the top editor at the paper. Maidenburg ran a newsroom that reflected the best of Jack Knight.

Knight and his brother Jim had built and shaped the highly respected company known as Knight Newspapers. In 1970, the Knight group, headquartered in Akron since its inception, included the *Miami Herald, Detroit Free Press, Philadelphia Inquirer* and *Charlotte Observer.*

Knight's famous directive — "Get the truth and print it" — had set a pattern of editorial conduct and professional standards in

Knight newsrooms that called for intelligence, sensitivity and guts. Knight spared neither himself nor his newspapers in preserving one of the lifelines of democracy: informing the public on what its government is doing.

While the corporate center of Knight Newspapers was slowly shifting to Miami in 1970, we felt fortunate that JSK's office remained in the corner of the *Beacon Journal* newsroom where he worked about nine months every year. It was a presence that was regarded with awe and not a small sense of apprehension.

Knight named Ben Maidenburg executive editor in 1948. Maidenburg hired me 10 years later. During my 17 years at the paper, both men had an extraordinary influence on me.

My first visit to the *Beacon Journal* was in May 1958. I had a master's degree in journalism that had helped me get a desirable assignment as a soldier at Ft. Monroe, Va. My two years of active-duty service in the U.S. Army was coming to an end that August, and I was ready to set my teeth into a working life that had beckoned me since I was 12. I dreamed of working for *The Plain Dealer* of Cleveland, my hometown paper, hoping eventually to cover the Cleveland Indians. I was ready and confident, but my timing was bad. The recession of 1958, known as the Eisenhower Recession, was slowing newsroom hiring. *The Plain Dealer* told me the best it could offer was a six-month position as a beginning reporter.

Back at Ft. Monroe, where I was posted as a writer in the Public Information Office, my new barracks mate, Johnny Apple, encouraged me to stifle discouragement and try the *Akron Beacon Journal*. Johnny would go on to a distinguished career with *The New York Times*. He came from the family that owned Acme stores, Akron's largest chain of grocery markets. Years earlier, during an internship at the paper, he had met and impressed Knight and Maidenburg. Johnny offered to help me get an interview.

So, on a Saturday morning I walked into the newsroom a few minutes before my 10 a.m. appointment and waited for Maidenburg. He was an imposing man, about 6-foot-4, who sat in a swivel chair and chewed on a cigar while he talked. I was nervous, but he seemed at ease as we chatted about my Army experience. Then he turned to my interest in working for the *Beacon Journal.*

He told me there was an opening for a reporter to cover high school sports and he wanted me to talk with the sports editor, Loren Tibbals. Maidenburg rose from his desk to his full height and summoned Tibbals by yelling for him over his glass office partition. Presently, a large man wearing a rumpled t-shirt shambled in and slumped in a chair across from me. My first thought was: "This man looks like a slob and I do not want to work for him. Maybe sloppy is how he thinks, too." Maidenburg began to tell "Tib," as he was known in the newsroom, about me and his suggestion that I might fill the opening on his sports staff. Maidenburg turned to me for a sign of approval. I blurted out the single thought that unexpectedly gripped me at that moment. "I don't think I want to cover sports, Ben. I want to be a general news reporter."

Maidenburg registered a startled look and dismissed Tibbals. Knowing of his reputation for outbursts of anger, I was expecting an explosion of surprise over my unexpected rejection of his offer. Instead, he turned back to me. He adjusted his glasses. He leaned forward and looked hard at me. He said there was an opening on the state desk for a reporter to cover nearby towns. I said I would be happy to take that position. In late August 1958, I began my newspaper life on a suburban beat covering school boards and local governments in towns with names like Stow, Tallmadge and Mogadore, communities with growing pains just east of Akron.

Maidenburg was an awesome figure in the eyes of a young and impressionable reporter. He was a stickler for accuracy, and his impatience with seeming stupidities would quickly boil into action. I still remember the sound of his long stride as he crossed the newsroom, clutching a copy of an offending story I had written. I could feel him coming. The power of his voice guaranteed that his message would not be missed. At that moment, the work of the newspaper stopped. You could hear a pin drop. Everyone watched him loudly scold me for misspelling the name of a local municipal court judge, C.B. McRae. The memory still stings.

Maidenburg seemed to take a keen interest in my work. In 1959, during my first summer at the paper, with most of the senior reporters on holiday, he arranged for me to accompany Jack Knight to interview Richard M. Nixon. It was my first big break, the rookie reporter getting to ride with the powerful editor to meet the vice president.

Nixon had recently returned from his famous "Kitchen Debate" with Soviet President Nikita Khrushchev. He was coming to Akron as Knight's guest to attend the annual Soap Box Derby. My assignment was to ride along in Knight's limo 38 miles to the Cleveland Airport and listen carefully as the two men talked on the way back to Akron. From JSK there was one admonition: Take no notes.

As we returned to Knight's imposing house in West Akron, I bid Nixon goodbye, then ran to the nearest street corner and sat on the curb to scribble in my notebook what I could remember from their conversation. Then I drove quickly back to the office, trying to compose in my mind a news-analysis story that captured Nixon's thoughts on his confrontation with the Soviet leader. As I sat at my typewriter preparing to write my story, several of my colleagues huddled around me, asking what Nixon was like. I threw off a quick reply, "He's kind of a regular guy, I guess." My story was on top of Page 1 the next day. But the city desk, unforgivingly, had edited the lede — the story's first sentence — to read, "Vice President Richard Nixon is a regular guy." I was teased about that in the newsroom for years, and I promised myself that if I ever became a city editor, I would never make a major change in a reporter's lede without first discussing it.

After two years of reporting on suburban towns, I was moved to the city desk where I covered the labor beat and then city hall. In 1963, I was assigned to the editorial page.

In the fall of 1964, I told Maidenburg I planned to apply for a Nieman Fellowship, which would allow me to study at Harvard University for a year. It was a lofty ambition with a decidedly uncertain outcome. I held my breath when I asked if he would please write a letter of recommendation. "I'll think about it," he dismissively replied. A few days later, he came by my desk with this admonition: "I'll write that damn letter on one condition. If you get the fellowship, you have to promise not to get uppity while you are at Harvard."

The future seemed full of exciting new promise. In August 1965, as we prepared to move to Cambridge for the Nieman year, Maidenburg pulled me aside and, in a paternal way, offered some advice. "If you ever want to run this newspaper, you have to get off the editorial page and work on one of the editing desks."

I tucked away his cautious recommendation. Then, midway through the fall term, I sent a note telling him I wanted to try the path he was suggesting. I understood I would begin as one of the assistant city editors. Unexpectedly, a few weeks before leaving Cambridge to return to Akron, the city editor moved to another paper and Maidenburg gave me his job.

Surprisingly, given his suspicions about liberal Harvard, Maidenburg was a faithful correspondent while I filled my life with learning and a renewed passion for journalism. He sent me a number of memos, updating me on staff changes and comings and goings at the paper. His notes helped me anticipate what I would find when I returned to the newsroom to begin learning how to be a city editor. He seemed to regard me as a confidant.

It was a scary time for me. I had not edited a piece of news copy since my college newspaper days. Now I was expected to oversee the local news report and direct a local news staff of 80 reporters and assistant editors.

His final note before my return was dated May 18, 1966. He wrote that he was putting me back on the payroll with "an increase of 25 clams to start." He described how he had arrived at the figure: $24.33 for being a Harvard man, 67 cents for being City Editor."

Life in charge of the newsroom had its own tempo. One of Maidenburg's rituals was to call the city editor into his office late in the afternoon to discuss that day's issue of the *Beacon Journal*. The meeting was by invitation: He would peer over the glass divider of his office and shout my name. He would motion me to sit next to his desk. Then, without a pause for pleasantries, he would grill me about how a local story was handled or a staff situation had been resolved, or not. Often the message evolved into his disapproving take on my leadership style. His discourse on what I needed to do eventually wound its way around to what I now remember as the moment-of-wisdom-about-being-an-editor: "Bob," he would say, crossing one long leg over the other and staring at his unlit cigar, "you've got to learn to be a son of a bitch."

Thinking back on what was often an uncomfortable introduction to being an editor, I now understand Maidenburg as a mentor in the best sense of the word. He shared his knowledge and his experiences, and he challenged me to find my own answers. They weren't often the answers he would have chosen, and this became a source of continuing friction between us. I wondered: How can I do what he wants me to do and still be myself? The answer to that challenge, I think, reinforced my basic instinct that there are other ways to run a newsroom than by being a son of a bitch. Maidenburg and his pronouncements on being an effective editor drove me to think hard about the work of a directing editor. It eventually inspired me to write a textbook, *Newsroom Management,* in 1987.

In 1963, Maidenburg became publisher while continuing as executive editor. He took his civic role seriously. The apparent conflict between serving on various community boards, as publishers often do, and running a newspaper caused ethical concerns in the newsroom. He made no apologies for the two distinctly different roles. His gruff style could soothe, defuse or inspire action. He understood the power of his position at the helm of a trusted local newspaper. He treated it with respect. When he saw leadership gaps in the community, he stepped in where he thought he could help. He was the keeper of many secrets from the variety of board meetings he attended, but he always protected the newsroom against being scooped on an important developing story in Akron.

By 1970, as Kent State seethed with antiwar fervor, Maidenburg was surprisingly indifferent to the growing tension. This seemed to be an attitude shift, given his admirable sensitivity to free expression. His views about the war in Vietnam and the spreading opposition to it were shaped in part by his experience in World War II. He believed going to war was an act of patriotism. He had served as a captain in a troop carrier squadron on the island of New Guinea in the Pacific, where he contracted malaria. It was a malady that dogged him for years.

Occasionally, he would grumble about "those radical students acting up" on college campuses, as they protested the draft and held anti-war rallies. In those moments, I understood that following orders was real to him. That belief helped define his relationship with Jack Knight and formed his attitudes about many issues that circulated through and shaped the *Beacon Journal* newsroom.

It was now about 4 p.m. April 28. Maidenburg was about to depart for his trip to Israel. Just as he headed out the door, he pulled me aside and gave me instructions on how to reach him in an emergency.

Then, with a rare, warm smile, he added, "You are in charge. Don't screw it up."

I promised him I wouldn't.

President Nixon stood at a map, script in hand, as he announced that American troops had attacked a Communist complex in Cambodia. (The Associated Press)

CHAPTER THREE

April 30: Cambodia

As 9 p.m. approached on Thursday, April 30, 1970, Bob Stopher, the *Beacon Journal's* editorial page editor, settled into the comfortable swivel chair behind the large desk in Jack Knight's spacious oak-paneled office. Knight's office occupied a strategic corner of the newsroom. JSK insisted on a tidy workspace, and his secretary, Elizabeth Sammeth, made sure no papers cluttered the desk when he strode through the newsroom promptly at 9 each morning.

Stopher, 62, was from an academic family. His brother and sister were college professors, and Stopher Hall, a men's dormitory on the Kent State University campus, was named for his father, Emmett, the university registrar for many years. Stopher was a long-time member of the Kent State board of trustees, having been appointed in 1955. The experience armed him with a deep understanding of education and enabled him to write thoughtful opinion pieces about local school issues and the state's university system. He also was deeply knowledgeable about the war in Southeast Asia and wrote many of the paper's daily editorials opposing the American presence there. Known for his precise use of English, Stopher could often be seen at the copy desk holding the day's first edition and gently instructing a wayward editor on correct usage. A common slip-up that Stopher found especially nettlesome was a copy editor's failure to know the difference between "that" and "which."

Knight's color television was perched on a large stand in the corner of his office. The transmission of television images in color had only become commercially available in the early 1960s. In the beginning, the high cost limited the number of American households that could afford a color set. NBC was the leader, beginning in 1965 to broadcast its prime-time schedule in color. CBS and ABC soon followed.

Stopher was there to watch Nixon deliver a speech to the nation — one that would prove infamous for its implications both at home and abroad.

He fiddled with the tuning dial until he found WKYC, Channel 3, the NBC affiliate in nearby Cleveland. He had left open the door to the office and, as Nixon began his remarks, I drifted in along with a few copy editors.

The newspaper closely covered the Vietnam War and, with Maidenburg's absence in Israel, I wanted to be in the newsroom that evening to be certain our coverage of this major speech for the next afternoon's editions went smoothly.

Stopher nodded "hello" and observed that Nixon was about to speak to the country from the Oval Office.

It was the same space where, during his administration, President Lyndon Johnson had given Americans false assurances about the progress of the war in Vietnam.

We watched as the president arrived and prepared to read his script. He was dressed in a dark-gray suit and blue tie. In Nixonian fashion, he hunched forward at the presidential desk, fixing a hard look at his audience on the other end of the television camera. His face was framed by the dark whiskery shadow that did him no favors wherever he appeared. Two microphones were placed to his left.

Next to his desk, resting on an easel, was a large map of Southeast Asia. To help a viewing nation understand the geographical context of his speech, he rose from his leather chair, speech text in his left hand, and gestured to critical crossing points on the Cambodia-South Vietnam border. Svay Rieng Province, about 8,800 miles from Kent State University, forms an international border with Vietnam where the invasion began.

Nixon reminded viewers of his announcement 10 days earlier that an additional 150,000 Americans would be withdrawn from Vietnam, "despite our concern over increased enemy activity in Laos, in Cambodia and in South Vietnam."

Nixon continued to provide background. He expressed particular alarm over new activities that North Vietnam had initiated within Cambodia. He characterized Cambodia's size and neutrality as a small country "of 7 million people (that) has been a neutral nation since the Geneva agreement of 1954." He justified U.S. actions by emphasizing that the United States had "scrupulously respected the neutrality of the Cambodian people."

The president said the government of Cambodia "has sent out a call" to the United States and other nations for assistance in eliminating sanctuaries on the Cambodian-Vietnam border that were serving as bases for attacks on Cambodian, South Vietnamese and American troops along "600 miles of frontier."

Nixon detailed the options before him — do nothing, arm Cambodia's army, or have U.S. and South Vietnam forces launch strikes targeting North Vietnamese strongholds. He had selected the third option, he said.

In anticipation of reaction to his aggressive decision to strike within Cambodia, Nixon insisted that the campaign was not an invasion of Cambodia. "The areas in which these attacks will be launched are completely occupied and controlled by North Vietnamese forces. Our purpose is not to occupy the areas. Once enemy forces are driven out ... and once their military supplies are destroyed, we will withdraw."

The president spoke again of his announced promise to end the war and win a just peace. In his closing passage, he said, "It is not our power but our will and character that is being tested tonight. The question all Americans must ask and answer tonight is this: Does the richest and strongest nation in the history of the world have the character to meet a direct challenge by a group which rejects every effort to win a just peace, ignores our warning, tramples on solemn agreements, violates the neutrality of an unarmed people and uses our prisoners as hostages?

"I realize that in this war there are honest and deep differences in this country about whether we should have become involved, that there are differences as to how the war should have been conducted. But the decision I announce tonight transcends those differences."

A day earlier, on April 29, the secret infiltration of Cambodia had begun. A joint operation of the U.S. Army's 1st Air Cav Division and the 11th Armored Cavalry Regiment, along with troops from the South Vietnamese 1st ARVN Armored Cavalry Regiment and the 3rd ARVN Airborne Brigade had entered Kampong Cham Province of Cambodia. Eighty-four North Vietnamese soldiers were killed in the initial phase of the Cambodian incursion.

As we watched Nixon, this small group of journalists silently recognized that television had delivered to a global audience the news of more violent action by our government — news that was certain to ignite strong reactions. Inherent in that message was the realization that breaking news was now the province of television, no longer the daily newspaper.

Stopher scribbled notes on folded sheets of white copy paper. As Nixon wrapped up his 15-minute talk, Stopher walked briskly to his own desk in a small, glass cubicle at another end of the newsroom. He turned on his IBM Selectric typewriter, removed his dark-rimmed glasses, rubbed his eyes and began to write. He had a quick mind and the words flowed easily, framing an editorial that began with a conclusion:

> President Nixon's decision to send thousands of American combat troops into Cambodia ... is, in our opinion, a serious mistake.

> It escalates the fighting and will inevitably increase American combat deaths and casualties.

He explained that the possible effects and repercussions arising from the action would constitute far more than a calculated risk. "It could produce a disaster."

Stopher recalled that Vietnam had become President Johnson's folly and, as a final thought, wrote, "It could be Nixon's folly now."

He pulled the copy from the typewriter and scribbled this headline: "Nixon Risks Making An Unpopular War Intolerable."

He then walked across the newsroom to the news desk and placed his editorial in a brass and leather cartridge and shoved it into a pneumatic tube where a blast of compressed air shot it off to the composing room to be set in type for Friday's paper. He bid me goodnight and quickly left.

A short while later, I drove home to catch a few hours' sleep. I was usually in the office by 6:30 a.m. to oversee production of the first edition, which went to press at 11 a.m.

But I wanted to be at work a bit early on that Friday, May 1. I had an uncomfortable sense that there might be a strong reaction at Kent State University to the Nixon announcement. The campus was a smoldering center of protest against the Vietnam War. A disturbance at Kent State would send a signal that other protests were likely on campuses across the country.

Editor John S. Knight anticipated U.S. failure in Vietnam and wrote persuasively about it for 16 years. (Akron Beacon Journal)

CHAPTER FOUR

May 1: The Notebook

The powerful influence of John S. Knight was a driving force in focusing the *Beacon Journal* news staff's commitment to the Kent State story. The newspaper's editorial page reflected Knight's long-held views in opposition to the Vietnam War. His directive, "Get the truth and print it," was ingrained in the newsroom culture.

JSK had inherited the newspaper in 1933 on the death of his father, C.L. Knight.

Knight had a clear-eyed view of the expanding conflict in Vietnam going back to 1954, when he anticipated the fall of the French at Dien Bien Phu and the end of its colonial empire in Indochina. In his column for Sunday, Feb. 21, 1954, he had written in the *Beacon Journal*:

> It is almost certain that at some stage France will pull out of Indochina. Are we prepared to cope with such a contingency? The plain answer seems to be no.

Over the next 16 years, in a Sunday commentary called the "Editor's Notebook," JSK effectively laid out the case against U.S. military involvement in Indochina. Stating his views with vigor through five presidential administrations, his reasoned judgment about the folly of the war came close to being a calling. It earned him regard among fellow editors and leaders in the government.

In 1968, Knight, at age 74, won the Pulitzer Prize for "distinguished editorial writing." It was considered by many to be a lifetime award for his perceptive and forceful commentary on Vietnam.

On Sundays, the *Beacon Journal* packaged the "Editor's Note-book" in a section called "News and Views," along with commentary, opinions and letters from readers.

JSK always had plenty on his mind when he sat down each week on Thursday to write his Notebook. He dressed like a banker, and the set of his jaw was firm. During the warm months, he wore a Panama-type straw hat. His bearing was erect in spite of his chronically sore back. He would give a nod and tight smile to Sammeth. His office door would be open. He would take off his suit jacket, sit at his Royal manual typewriter and begin to write.

He always brought to the task several days of intense reading of newspapers and journals of commentary. He would keep a loose-leaf folder with clips and pages ripped from various publications containing both liberal and conservative thought. Along the way he would pick up additional insights in telephone conversations with some of the best sources a journalist could have. Although he stated his views with characteristic bluntness, fairness and truth-telling were the bedrock of the man and how he practiced his craft.

JSK had expressed firm, forthright and often unpopular opinions on every important public issue for more than a quarter of a century. Yet, in the current sense during a turbulent time, he was not a controversial figure. One reason for this, certainly, is that he carefully weighed and balanced the factors that shaped great issues. Rarely was a position taken in the "Notebook" entirely satisfactory to partisans of either side.

It was almost impossible to place him in the political spectrum in accordance with any of the usual litmus tests. His ability to grasp meaning and sift out important details and concentrate on the task at hand amazed those of us who worked for him.

I revered the man and admired his ability to express his views with plain-written elegance. At times he seemed stern. His manner of letting you know when he took issue with something in the paper was to send along a tear sheet with two or three well-chosen words of criticism scribbled in red copy pencil. If he handed you the page, he didn't wait for a response. He knew, correctly, that his sharp comment would occupy your mind and emotions for the next while. JSK's occasional lessons on matters of accuracy, balance and truth-telling were paramount in helping me grow as an editor.

Doing the "Notebook" every Thursday was not a simple task, he once acknowledged. "I am a bleeder, so it doesn't come easy."

Promptly at noon on most Thursdays, Sammeth would come through the newsroom carrying a silver service tray covered by a polished silver dome. Serving JSK lunch in an elegant manner was part of the ritual. For years we were left to wonder what he was having week after week, because it arrived with such a regal presentation. Finally, one of us was bold to ask Sammeth what she brought him every Thursday. She smiled and said, "A hot dog from the Western across the street."

At 3 p.m., a draft of the "Notebook" was usually ready for editing. JSK would carry it — neatly typed on three sheets of copy paper — from his office and hand it to Stopher. They would chat for a moment as he explained what the "Notebook" was trying to get at. Then he would turn quickly and march back to his office. Rarely would Stopher or Jim Jackson, his longtime editorial page sidekick, find anything to challenge or question. JSK wrote with clarity, in spite of his claim that "it doesn't come easy."

This week, though, the routine would be slightly different. Knight, always eager for his commentary to be on top of the news, had delayed until Friday, May 1, to write his "Notebook" for Sunday, May 3.

So, he went to work, pounding away on the typewriter, honing his message. Having absorbed the import of Nixon's announcement and distilled that into a concept for a three-page commentary, he worked quickly. He soon dropped off the latest piece with Stopher, who then did the editing.

Stopher wrote a headline that read: "Cambodia Attack Is A Grave Risk."

Knight wrote,

> The President has acted boldly, but in our opinion, unwisely. He has not been deterred by the political risks, and that is a mark of courage. What further tragedies will be visited upon our nation must await the onrush of developments yet unknown.

JSK reviewed the origins of U.S. involvement in Southeast Asia, which, he wrote, had begun in 1946 under President Harry Truman. He traced the growing depth of our commitment over the years to the casualties under LBJ that by 1970 had reached 48,736 dead.

For the "Notebook" on May 3, 1970, Jack Knight's attention then shifted to Cambodia, "the land of the white parasol."

He wrote:

> The military reasons given by the President have an appealing ring to those who still believe that in escalation lies the fruit of victory.
>
> Despite all reassurances, the Nixon policy can only widen the war. It is a desperate gamble taken in the belief that the war may be ended more quickly by cutting the Communist supply line through Cambodia.
>
> Ultimately, Southeast Asia will be lost to the West no matter what course we pursue. If this be true, and I am convinced that it is, why should we sacrifice countless more American lives in an area of the world where we do not belong?"

It was a profound conclusion to a vexing circumstance that would explode in tragedy the following day.

CHAPTER FIVE

May 1: Fueling the Protests

As I walked into the newsroom on Friday morning, I was met by Eddie Schoenleb, the associate news editor. He was waiting for me with a cup of black coffee in one hand and a clutch of wire stories in the other.

Schoenleb was a wiry man with high energy and a broad smile. He had engineered the news desk's daily output of wire stories for many years. An associate remembered him as one of the best news editors to draw a page at the *Beacon Journal*. But his career had been constrained by a reputation for indecision. That instinct was on full display as I reached for the stories he held in his hand. His usual dilemma was that the *Beacon Journal* was an afternoon newspaper. It strove to cover the previous night's breaking news with stories that would still seem fresh at dinner time the next day. The appeal of each day's front page rested with Schoenleb's ability to mix the news with solid, thoughtful analysis.

He hurriedly explained that the wire service stories were focused on the Nixon speech. He couldn't decide among them and handed the stack to me. As I scanned through the stories, I easily recognized the best candidate for Page 1 was a news analysis written by James McCartney of the Knight Newspapers Washington bureau.

McCartney was a veteran correspondent who had recently returned from a reporting assignment in Indochina. The *Beacon Journal*, being part of the Knight Newspapers organization, made effective use of stories from its Washington bureau.

On Friday, lunchtime readers in downtown Akron found an early edition of the *Beacon Journal* with McCartney's forceful analysis spread over six columns across the top of the front page. Under the heading, "Nixon Follows LBJ Pattern In Move To Escalate War," McCartney's piece began:

Suddenly Richard Nixon has thrown it all up for grabs in Southeast Asia.

For the first time since he became President 15 months ago, he has departed almost overnight on a brand new policy for the Vietnam War.

Suddenly he has ordered U.S. ground combat troops — several thousands of them, according to White House sources — into Cambodia. Despite official denials, he has chosen to escalate the war.

He has come to this immense and complex decision — a fundamental change in U.S. policy — within the last 10 days.

He told the nation about it Thursday night in a nationally televised speech, but he never once used the phrase "ground U.S. combat troops" to make everything perfectly clear.

He referred to it only as a "combined American and South Vietnamese operation," adding "This is not an invasion of Cambodia."

But U.S. troops in strength have already crossed a border they have not violated for five years.

And White House sources — along with the President himself — had difficulty explaining exactly why it should be done now when it hasn't been done before.

The official explanation is that Communist forces have been "pushing out" of base areas in Cambodia ... and increasing the "threat" to U.S. troops...

No convincing evidence was given that the threat from the Communists is any greater now than it was a few weeks ago.

The truth, apparently — a truth that to some extent

*Three shirtless U.S. soldiers advanced in the Fishhook region of
Cambodia on May 4, 1970 — the same day as the Kent State
shootings. (The Associated Press)*

shined through in the President's speech — is that the
administration decided it had a unique opportunity to
punish the Communists...

Yet there is little in the history of the war to suggest
that the Communists are likely to respond to this kind of
approach.

Nixon has apparently returned, at least in part, to the
Lyndon Johnson formula that involves talking about
peace while waging aggressive war.

McCartney, 45, had wrapped up his piece on Thursday evening
soon after the President's speech. It was telegraphed to the news
desks of 31 newspapers that subscribed to the Knight Newspapers
wire service. It was published the following morning on the front

pages of many of those papers, reflecting the judgment of editors looking for a fresh angle that would add context to The Associated Press coverage that most newspaper and broadcast outlets would use.

The analysis was typical for McCartney, who was one of the first journalists to focus on the meaning of President Dwight Eisenhower's farewell address in 1961 in which Ike famously warned of a military industrial complex.

Nuclear weapons policy and the Vietnam War were two topics about which McCartney had great command and about which he wrote extensively. On that spring evening in 1970, after several trips to Vietnam, McCartney was prepared to quickly write a lucid, thoughtful assessment that conveyed the meaning of the Nixon speech. His was an approach that enabled his editors to label it as "news analysis."

When he died in 2011, his old bureau chief, Robert Boyd, reflected on his "curiosity, skepticism and persistence" that helped make "our small bureau one of the best in Washington." For journalists like McCartney, the pursuit of facts and truth were primary elements that drove their work and armed them with the ability to write authoritative analyses for newspapers like the *Beacon Journal*.

Next to the McCartney analysis, Schoenleb packaged two columns of "Cambodia Reaction" taken from wire dispatches that ran down the left side of Page 1. It led with an AP story from Tokyo that summarized criticism from China and North Vietnam. Below that, a short item from the *New York Times* News Service carried a headline, "Condemned by Soviets."

The "Reaction" story included brief quotes "For" and "Against" Nixon's new Cambodia policy. Among the supporters were names familiar to newspaper readers of the day, including Sen. Barry Goldwater (R-Ariz.), Sen. Hugh Scott (R-Pa.) and AFL-CIO president George Meany. The opponents included Sen. J.W. Fulbright (D-Ark.), Hubert H. Humphrey, who Nixon defeated two years earlier in the 1968 presidential election, Sen. Bob Dole (R-Kan.),

Edmund S. Muskie (D-Maine), and Sen. George McGovern (D-S.D.).

At the bottom of "Cambodia Reaction" was an AP map showing where U.S. and South Vietnamese troops had attacked.

On Page 2, reaction to the speech continued with an AP story from Saigon reporting that "More than 25,000 American and South Vietnamese troops pushed deeper into two areas of Cambodia today but for the most part encountered only light resistance."

Other stories reported growing student protests. The campus newspaper at Princeton called for a nationwide student strike. Students at Hobart College in Geneva, N.Y., had firebombed an ROTC building. Police used teargas and made arrests at Stanford after students threw rocks and broke windows. And about 800 anti-war protesters from the University of Cincinnati marched and blocked traffic at Fifth and Walnut, a major downtown intersection.

Page 2 also included highlights of the Nixon speech and a local feature by columnist Mickey Porter, who interviewed local residents on what they thought.

The May 1, 1970, edition of the *Beacon Journal* filled 64 pages with news, commentary, sports, features and advertising. That day's edition was typical of the newspaper's commitment to informing its readers about Vietnam as the story of their times.

What they could not possibly have imagined was how Nixon's Cambodia decision would set aflame anti-war passions just 12 miles from the newsroom. It would fuel an unexpected tragedy that erupted in 13 seconds of gunfire on the campus the following Monday. The mystery of those 13 seconds and their meaning would occupy the *Beacon Journal* staff for the weeks and months ahead. And it would change the newsroom forever.

On Friday evening, May 1, demonstrators, unhappy about being kicked out of their favorite downtown bars along Water Street, rampaged, throwing rocks and bottles. (Akron Beacon Journal)

CHAPTER SIX

May 2: An Active Campus

On Saturday, May 2, I arose early. Our aging brown bungalow overlooking the Cuyahoga River Valley in West Akron was just beginning to fill with spring light. Nancy and our three children were still asleep.

I had turned fitfully during the night. I was on edge. It felt like a sneeze before a cold. I feared that widespread trouble was looming on the nearby campus. Warning signs flickered in the brief demonstration against the Cambodia incursion on Friday afternoon followed by a drunken ruckus that evening in downtown Kent.

I dressed and started our green Volvo station wagon on its familiar path to downtown Akron. At 6 a.m., there was little traffic along the four-mile route to the newspaper. My mind focused on how the staff and I needed to lay out a plan for covering whatever unrest might play out that weekend.

Also playing on my emotions was an apprehension that nagged at the reporters and editors who had watched and dutifully tracked signs of discontent on the Kent State campus since 1968. It was a tension fueled by protests against the Vietnam War. Was it now coming to a boil? Would the spark be President Nixon's bold speech on Thursday night announcing he had ordered U.S. troops to invade Cambodia?

As I walked in, the newsroom was alive with activity and anticipation. I felt prickles of anxiety. It was not just the huge looming story at hand. It was the weight of the reality of what faced me. I was in charge. The proverbial buck would stop with me.

The bustle was not typical. On a normal Saturday, the newsroom is sparsely populated. Major projects for the big Sunday edition are well in hand, awaiting the arrival of the news and copy desk crews to handle breaking news from the wire services or local stories developed on Saturday. Layout of pages fronting the news and sports sections would be sketched by a makeup editor who drew lines and scribbled instructions on white sheets of copy paper showing where stories and photos would be placed. Weekdays, the *Beacon Journal* was an afternoon paper. Live pages for the Saturday paper were closed by 8 a.m. and sent to the composing room to be made ready for the giant presses located in the basement.

The newsroom was abuzz. A group of reporters huddled around Pat Englehart, the state editor. They talked about the implications of the Friday night disturbance in downtown Kent. Beer bottles had been thrown through tavern windows. They wondered about the meaning of a small rally on the campus Commons Friday afternoon where a copy of the U.S. Constitution had been buried. Englehart tried to low-key expectations. Groups of students had been demonstrating all spring. "We always covered the demonstrations, but nothing ever happened," he recalled.

"It was just a small group of students. Usually the same ones every time." He thought there was nothing in this pattern of protest to suggest that Friday's events would dramatically escalate.

Until 1960, Kent State was little more than a school of 7,500 students. It fit easily into the conservative, small-town, neighborly ways of the town of Kent. It was a genial place where people greeted one another by name. In the 1960s, under the leadership of President George Bowman, the physical campus exploded with growth. Massive state and federal grants helped turn Kent State into a sprawling complex of 19,000 students who lived, studied and played in 97 buildings.

The town, no longer secure in its old habits, tried to cope with the university's demand for housing and services. Akron suburbanites moving to Kent and its rural surroundings felt no ties to the university. Old-line residents found the new campus culture abrasive. Not only were there many more students than before, some of them looked strikingly different. Townsfolk felt uncomfortable with the long hair, jeans and love beads, a new freedom of language and behavior. By 1965, town/gown relations had become, at best, uneasy.

Despite its mushrooming enrollment, the campus remained at peace until the fall of 1968, long after many American universities were boiling over with demonstrations against the Vietnam War and the draft.

That November, the police department of Oakland, Calif. — then locked in a bitter battle with the Black Panther Party — came to Kent State to recruit. About 150 members of the Kent State Students for a Democratic Society (SDS) and about 100 members of the Black United Students staged a sit-in in the lobby of the student activities center. According to the *Kent Stater*, the student newspaper, when the protesters left the building, they walked to the president's residence and were heckled by other students who sang "The Star Spangled Banner" and chanted "We Love America."

The university reacted sharply, taking pictures of the demonstrators and threatening to charge them with disorderly conduct. About half of the school's 600 black students walked off campus in protest. After three days, Kent State president Robert I. White said there was "insufficient evidence" to bring charges, and the students returned.

Then, in April 1969, SDS pressed for a set of demands, including abolition of ROTC — the Reserved Officers Training Corps. SDS leaders scuffled with campus police and later occupied the Music and Speech Building. Fifty-eight students were arrested. SDS was banned from the campus and four of its leaders were sentenced to six months for assault and battery.

The bitter aftertaste of these two protests was evident on the Kent State campus in the spring of 1970. Those experiences had convinced the administration that a firm response was the key to preventing further trouble. They watched closely for any resurgence of SDS-type radicalism.

The university was socially liberal in many ways. It allowed beer on campus, and men were free to visit women in their dorm rooms. On political issues, such as the Vietnam War, it attempted to take a neutral stance. Many campus activists rejected this as either short-sighted or cowardly.

Because of its proximity to the *Beacon Journal*, 12 miles, we considered the university a local story. When life on the campus was calm, the university was covered using a staff reporter, the newspaper's education writer and a campus stringer, usually a student in the journalism school. The sports department staffed the home and away games of the school's Golden Flashes.

When there was trouble, we formed a task force drawn from the city and state desks to handle the breaking story and follow-ups.

Beacon Journal editors decided in the early moments of the 1968 confrontation over the Oakland police recruiters that it was the newspaper's responsibility to set forth the facts and feelings in such detail and dimension that the public would have a clear understanding of what was at stake.

The reporters used their insights — and notebooks packed with details, information, names of sources and phone numbers — to craft a series of swift and accurate post-demonstration stories that plumbed the attitudes and temperament of the protesters and university officials, and that explained the issues and underlying factors.

Thus, as students gathered Friday in front of the Victory Bell on the campus Commons to bury a copy of the U.S. Constitution, there was little the *Beacon Journal* had not told its readers about the mood at Kent State.

On Saturday, reporters and editors gathered to plan coverage of the campus demonstration scheduled for that evening. A young copy boy interrupted them as he tossed a stack of papers on Englehart's desk. The group eagerly grabbed copies and read coverage of the series of student actions against the war.

Accounts of burying the Constitution were at the end of a three-column story in the middle of Page 1 under the headline:

On Friday afternoon, students at the Victory Bell stated President Nixon killed the Constitution, and "we are going to bury it." (Kent State University News Service)

"'Down With Nixon,' Scream 500 Rioting Kent Students." The story, by reporters Jeff Sallot and Sanford Levenson, quoted Kent State graduate student Steven Sharoff: "Nixon killed the Constitution last night by entering an undeclared war in Cambodia. It's dead and we are going to bury it." Another graduate student, Jim Geary, told the reporters that he had burned his Army discharge papers. "After hearing Nixon's Cambodian policy, I'm ashamed to say I was a soldier."

The story described the student "rampage" through downtown Kent Friday evening, smashing windows, blocking traffic and throwing bricks and bottles. A window above the Portage National Bank had been broken by a lawn spreader that a demonstrator took from a nearby hardware store. The action moved along Water

Street, where many popular bars were located. All 24 members of the Kent Police and 65 Portage County sheriff's officers used tear-gas to disperse the rioters. By 3 a.m., the disturbance ended and the students retreated to the Kent State campus.

The paper printed names and addresses of seven students and seven non-students who were arrested and held in the Portage County jail on disorderly conduct charges to await a Monday appearance in Kent Municipal Court.

The story also noted that late Friday, Black United Students had called an "emergency" demonstration to present demands to the university administration for "more black programs." No black students were at the Friday disturbance, the story said.

Elsewhere in the Saturday paper, readers learned that Nixon would meet with "miffed" congressmen for a "face-to-face dialogue" about the use of U.S. ground troops in Cambodia.

Student protests on 30 campuses across the country were described in a separate story.

The major news item on Page 1 by staff writer Don Fermoyle told of 800 dissident members of the Akron-area Teamster Local 24 who had voted to end a 31-day strike in the face of opposition from their international union.

Reporter James Herzog, in a Page 3 sidebar, described his tense experience riding with the first convoy of trucks to leave the Consolidated Freightways terminal in the rural town of Richfield a few miles north of Akron.

Thirty-seven semi-trailer trucks and 80 armed members of the Ohio National Guard riding shotgun headed in a convoy for the nearby Ohio Turnpike. A jeep carrying Guard Capt. Ron Snyder led the convoy. "We rolled by a bar — a favorite spot for truckers," wrote Herzog. "In front, about 30 Guardsmen were poised with bayonets fixed as they stood between 25 angry Teamster over-the-road drivers and the convoy."

Unwittingly, Herzog's story introduced readers to Snyder and others in the National Guard unit who would play a central role in the looming campus tragedy.

The group meeting at the state desk with Englehart discussed what might happen next in our news cycle and how they might cover it. They offered a wide range of opinions.

Englehart impatiently took charge. He was 45, a driven man with an unruly mustache and an unlit stub of a De Nobili cigar perpetually clinched in his mouth. His fiery vocabulary would burst forth when he became angry at staffers who tried to slip sloppy stories by him. He spared no wrath, often denouncing the errant staffer as a "fool." He was well suited for his role as state editor and took responsibility for mentoring young reporters and managing a host of part-time correspondents. They covered dozens of small communities spread across three counties — all part of the *Beacon Journal's* circulation area.

He lived in Mogadore, a small village on the southeastern edge of Summit County, eight miles from Akron. He was proud of the little town and easily shrugged off jokes about it that came his way from around the newsroom. Mogadore is an Arabic word for "beautiful," he would remind the punsters trying to needle him. I covered Mogadore in my early days on the paper and recall that my first Page 1 byline as a rookie reporter carried the headline, "Moon over Mogadore."

For more than a year, Englehart had developed a passionate interest in the emerging culture of protest at Kent State. He kept the paper on top of the coverage of that unrest, including the 1968 protests against the police recruiters. A year later, demands for change by SDS was a big story because many of the participants were from out of town. Their presence fueled anger and fear among the townsfolk — a mood that carried over to May 1970. Englehart drove his staff to stay focused on these stories.

John Olesky, a young member of the state desk staff, recalled years later that under Englehart's influence, "Stories poured onto the *BJ* front pages, day after day. Photos and notes piled up into cardboard boxes that Pat used for his files and eventually threatened to fill up the *BJ's* third-floor warehousing area. Pat was relentless, which made the *BJ* unstoppable in its coverage of growing campus unrest. No tip was too insignificant for Pat to explore — or assign a reporter to dig into. If the result didn't satisfy him, he'd tear a little hide and get a deeper and more meaningful story." To bolster his roster of journalists who could be thrust into the Kent State story, he lined up a cadre of reporters hungry as he was, Herzog, Sallot and Ray Redmond to name a few. And he was the zealot driving the chariot.

Saturday noon approached and the situation facing Englehart and his team looked like this: Furious downtown merchants and many townspeople had inspected the damage from the Friday night rampage. The *Beacon Journal* knew that Kent Mayor LeRoy Satrom had declared a state of emergency. He announced a curfew beginning at dusk and lasting until dawn Sunday. The journalists also knew that Satrom had called Columbus, the state capital, and asked the Ohio adjutant general for help. The quick solution to establish a presence in Kent was to release the first battalion, the 145th Infantry of the Ohio National Guard, from the truckers strike on Ohio's major highways. The Guardsmen, weary from a week of riding shotgun with the strikers as they drove back and forth across major Ohio highways, now packed up and moved eight miles from their temporary post at the Akron Rubber Bowl to establish a new bivouac on the edge of the Kent State campus.

By mid-afternoon, word reached the newsroom of a campus rally planned for Saturday night. Targeted for destruction was the World War II-era ROTC building, but the *Beacon Journal* staffers did not know this. Kent State student military activities were housed in the wooden barracks-like structures, built in 1947. They even smelled old.

Englehart sent Sallot and Redmond to observe the demonstration and file a report for the later Sunday editions on May 3. Bob Schumacher, a young rewrite man on the state desk, was on hand to take dictation from the two reporters in the field and write a running story of the night's developments. He was 27 and one among several staffers who came from West Virginia. Sallot, 22, was a journalism student at Kent who worked as a campus stringer

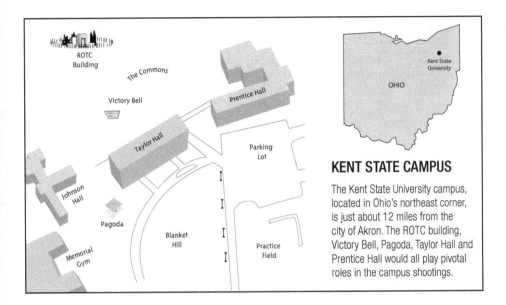

KENT STATE CAMPUS

The Kent State University campus, located in Ohio's northeast corner, is just about 12 miles from the city of Akron. The ROTC building, Victory Bell, Pagoda, Taylor Hall and Prentice Hall would all play pivotal roles in the campus shootings.

for the newspaper. He wore dark-rimmed glasses and a full head of hair that fell over his ears and touched his shirt collar. He possessed a deep base of sources among student leaders and faculty. Redmond, 52, was a longtime reporter in the *Beacon Journal's* Portage County bureau. Both would play critical roles in shaping the newspaper's authoritative accounts in the coming days and weeks.

As the sun set that Saturday, Sallot and Redmond arrived on campus and checked with sources to determine how the demonstration might play out. It would not be a quiet night, they were told.

The *Akron Beacon Journal* Newsroom - 1970

The newsroom of the *Beacon Journal* was organized like most newsrooms of the day, with a line of top editors directing the major news-gathering functions—City Desk, State Desk, News Desk/Copy Desk, Photo and Arts-Graphics. The Editorial Page was distinctly separate from the news-gathering desks, a distinction that remains common in newspapers today. The Sports Desk, Sunday Department, and Feature Department were not involved in the Kent State coverage.

JOHN S. KNIGHT
President and Editor

Rare among newspaper owners; successful business man and enlightened editor, opposed to the Vietnam War since 1954.

BEN MAIDENBURG
Executive Editor & Publisher

Demanding boss and dominant presence in the newsroom. Was in Israel on May 4, 1970.

BOB STOPHER
Editorial Page Editor

Deep understanding of education, the state's university system and, also, the war in Southeast Asia.

BOB GILES
Managing Editor

Directed the newspaper's coverage of the shootings, with Maidenburg's departing message firmly in mind: "You are in charge. Don't screw it up."

AL FITZPATRICK
News Editor

Indispensable in getting the paper out each day when the focus was on Kent State. An avuncular figure widely respected in the newsroom.

PAT ENGLEHART
State Editor

Knew more than anyone about Kent State. Driven to "own" the story and keep his staff on top of it. A gruff taskmaster and effective mentor.

RON CLARK
City Editor

Set up a makeshift city desk on the campus. Still learning how to be a city editor. Kent State was his baptism of fire.

Assistant State Editors

Harry Liggett
John Olesky

Reporters

Kathy Lilly
Jeff Sallot
Ray Redmond
Bob Page
Sandy Levenson
Bob Schumacher
Robert Batz

Washington Bureau

Dave Hess
Bill Vance

PHOTOS, GRAPHICS

Photographers

Julius Greenfield
Don Roese
Paul Tople

Artists

Chuck Ayers
Art Krummel

Reporters

Helen Carringer
Joe Rice
John Dunphy
Tim Smith
Abe Zaidan
Mickey Porter
John De Groot
Lacy McCrary
Jim Herzog
Bill Hershey
Terry Oblander

NEWS DESK

News Desk Editors

Eddie Schoenleb
Hal Fry
Tom Moore

Editorial Writers

Tom Horner
Jim Jackson

The *Akron Beacon Journal* Newsroom
Key Reporters, Editors, Artist, Photographers on May 4, 1970

REPORTERS

JEFF SALLOT
Beacon Journal's key reporter
on campus the day of the
shooting.

KATHY LILLY
Budding young talent who
handled critical interviews on
campus after the shootings.

HELEN CARRINGER
An authority on education.
Had extensive sources at
Kent State.

LACY MCCRARY
Columbus Bureau chief whose
persistent questioning
nettled Governor Rhodes.

RAY REDMOND
Veteran reporter with vast list of
sources in Portage County.

NEWS DESK EDITOR

HAL FRY
Gifted editor of news copy
who became the editing
authority on Kent State.

JIM HERZOG
Peace Corps veteran who
understood the anti-war
generation.

ARTIST, PHOTOGRAPHERS

BOB PAGE
Went to the Ravenna hospital
to get names of victims.

CHUCK AYERS
Talented artist who sketched
May 4 scenes from memory.

ABE ZAIDAN
Veteran political reporter with
deep base of sources in Ohio
and Washington.

DON ROESE
Photographer whose image
dominated Page 1, May 5.

DAVE HESS
Beacon Journal Washington
reporter who covered
Scranton Commission.

PAUL TOPLE
Student photographer's work
proved crucial to coverage.

Components of a Newsroom

Those unfamiliar with newsroom structure might find the compartments of a newsroom confusing. Below are quick definitions of the *Beacon Journal* news desks that were involved in the Kent State coverage.

State Desk was directed by the state editor and two assistant state editors. Its reporters covered cities and towns in five counties surrounding the city of Akron that comprised the newspaper's circulation area.

City Desk was directed by the city editor and four assistant city editors. Coverage was organized around beats such as city hall, politics, education, courts, labor, police, special projects and general news. The Columbus bureau and the *Beacon Journal's* Washington correspondent reported to the city desk.

News Desk, directed by the news editor, oversaw the selection of wire news stories, and the design and production of pages in the main news section. That section included Kent State content produced by the State Desk, City Desk and other *Beacon Journal* news departments.

Copy Desk, led by the copy desk chief, assigned stories to copy editors who gave them a final read, made corrections and wrote headlines.

Photo Desk, directed by the photo editor, served all departments of the newspaper.

Art Desk touched up photos and provided sketches and illustrations for all departments of the *Beacon Journal*.

Editorial Page was led by the editorial page editor. It was independent of all news desks and reported directly to the editor of the newspaper. Four editorial writers wrote daily editorials expressing the newspaper's point of view, selected and edited letters to the editor, and chose syndicated opinion columns.

Other news desks in the *Beacon Journal* newsroom of 1970 did not participate in the Kent State coverage. They were Features, Business News, Sports and Sunday.

Remains of the ROTC building, scorched during a demonstration
Saturday evening, May 2. (Kent State University News Service)

CHAPTER SEVEN

May 3: Sunday Paper

"KSU Rioters Put Torch To ROTC Building."

The headline stretched across eight columns on the front page of Sunday's *Beacon Journal*. That large type size confirmed the town's worst fears: The student demonstrations had only worsened overnight.

The *Beacon Journal* was a heavyweight newspaper on this Sunday, running 271 pages. The news sections were flush with display advertisements from O'Neil's and Polsky's, the city's two major department stores. Fashionable layouts sought to attract buyers for spring and summer apparel. Ads from other merchants helped expand the news and feature sections inside the paper. Classified advertising, a major revenue source for the *Beacon Journal,* filled 28 pages. The *Beacon Journal's* circulation that Sunday was 174,000.

The first edition of the Sunday paper had an early copy close at 8 p.m. Saturday. It carried a Page 1 story confirming that Kent State was in a "state of emergency." The story reported that National Guardsmen were on standby alert to supervise the curfew.

But that story was moved to Page 4 for the second edition as Sallot, Redmond and Schumacher combined for the late-breaking account of rioting students who set fire to the Kent State ROTC building early on Saturday evening.

The story carried all their bylines. Only the most knowing readers would recognize why Schumacher's name was the final one among the three. It meant that he had written the story in the newsroom after the details were dictated over the telephone by Sallot and Redmond, the reporters on the scene. Those details gave readers a graphic picture of how the demonstration targeted the old wooden structure, as well as the efforts of law enforcement and National Guardsmen to establish control at the fire scene.

> The ROTC building was set on fire by an unruly crowd of approximately 600 anti-war demonstrators.
>
> Kent firemen fought the blaze while under the protection of Portage County sheriff's deputies.
>
> About 400 National Guardsmen were dispatched 11 miles from the Akron Rubber Bowl, where they had been bivouacked during the trucker strike, to the Kent State campus. Two busloads of Ohio Highway Patrolmen were sent from the neighboring city of Ravenna, which serves as the seat of government for Portage County.
>
> Flames shot from the roof of the wooden ROTC building after it was set afire for the second time. Firemen had extinguished an earlier, smaller blaze after a brief struggle with demonstrators who seized a hose and turned it on the firemen before control was regained.
>
> Firemen reported one pumper out of service after fire hoses were cut.

The story described how cans of paint had been used to deface buildings with slogans, including "pigs off campus."

Police forced the students away from the burning building. The demonstrators then "started marching on the home of the university president Robert White, located at the opposite end of the Commons from the ROTC building." At the time, White was attending an education conference in Iowa, although his absence was not widely known among the protesters. He flew home Sunday morning, but Ohio Gov. James Rhodes had arrived by helicopter and had taken charge of the university by then.

The story said the blaze from the flames could be seen 75 feet in the air. It quoted a university estimate that the structure was a total loss. Its contents, valued at $50,000, included 1,000 rounds of .22 caliber ammunition, believed to have exploded during the fire.

By 9:30 p.m., National Guard Adjutant Gen. Sylvester Del Corso had arrived and went to the Kent City Police Department to take command of the Guardsmen. In anticipation of what might happen on Monday, Del Corso ordered Guardsmen to shoot any rioter who cut fire hoses.

Sallot and Redmond wrapped up their story by observing that the city of Kent as well as the campus "was completely isolated as police and National Guardsmen set up roadblocks on all highways leading to the city."

Dispatches from the Knight Newspaper's Washington bureau added to the convulsive feeling conveyed by the newspaper's front page that Sunday.

Robert Boyd, the Washington bureau chief, had been invited to North Vietnam to observe the war from the enemy's perspective. At the time, it was rare for American correspondents to obtain credentials to travel there. From Vo Vinh, North Vietnam, Boyd reported that "American planes are bombing North Vietnam, although a halt in U.S. bombing had been announced 18 months ago." (The paper included a note that Boyd's dispatch "has been censored by the North Vietnamese.")

"I watched for 50 minutes," he wrote, "as American planes dropped their bombs in an area about 18 miles north of the Demilitarized Zone." Boyd quoted North Vietnamese officials as saying that the bombs hit the village of Son Thuh.

"Pillars of flame and smoke rose hundreds of feet into the air over the low hills about 12 miles from my vantage point in this little village 10 miles south of the provincial capital of Dong Hoi."

At 42, Boyd was young for a Washington bureau chief, a post he would hold for 20 years. During that time, the bureau grew from a staff of seven to more than 50.

A colleague once described him as "the antithesis of the sort of ego-driven Washington bureau chief who stepped all over his reporters …. He was the best editor I ever had." The *Washington Post* reporter David Broder described Boyd as one of the most honest and fair reporters in Washington. "He's totally independent," Broder said. "I have no idea what his politics may be, and I've known him for 30 years."

Two years later, Boyd and a Knight Washington bureau colleague, Clark Hoyt, would win the Pulitzer Prize for National Reporting "for their disclosure of U.S. Senator Thomas Eagleton's history of psychiatric therapy, resulting in Eagleton's withdrawal as the Democratic vice presidential nominee in 1972."

Boyd was a writing bureau chief. He went to North Vietnam because he loved being where the story was.

Dave Boerner, assistant news editor, had skillfully packaged stories about Nixon, Vietnam and Kent State in an eye-catching display. Placed next to Boyd's first-person report on the bombing of the North Vietnam village was a story by McCartney, his Washington bureau mate, quoting a Pentagon spokesman confirming Boyd's eyewitness account. The spokesman, Jerry Friedheim, offered what McCartney called a "vague explanation," saying that the raid by U.S. bombers was "an instance of protective reaction."

McCartney was not satisfied with this vagary. He explained that the phrase described a military policy that had been followed since the U.S. bombing of North Vietnam was halted by President Johnson in November 1968. "The idea," he wrote, "is that U.S. commanders may protect U.S. forces by bombing or strafing if they believe the forces are threatened in any way. Commanders on the scene are given wide discretion in deciding when to strike."

Another page-one piece on this Sunday, also by McCartney, characterized Nixon's actions as that of a "new Richard Nixon."

> That, in all probability, is the most important aspect of the story behind the decision to send U.S. ground combat troops into Cambodia — the most momentous decision of the Nixon presidency.

> But, it's only part of the story, a story that has unfolded gradually here (in Washington) over the last 10 days.

Other important parts involve a desperate and secret U.S. effort to preserve the neutrality of Cambodia and a quiet, back-stage struggle between the military and many diplomats.

And yet another part is still to unfold. The U.S. plans soon to make a new diplomatic move to try to break open the Paris peace talks.

Most intriguing, in many ways, are gradual changes in the way Richard Nixon is approaching his job as president. The newest Nixon is a tough, hardline Nixon — impatient at being President of the U.S. and finding so many problems so subtle and complex. He is disgusted — and frustrated — at the thought that the world's most powerful nation might be considered a paper tiger.

McCartney concluded with the observation that "U.S. political history for almost 20 years now has been studded with stories about 'new' Nixons — a tribute to the man's complex character. Throughout his career he has been accused of switching from gut fighter to the role of statesman."

It was an unsettling collection of Page 1 stories on this Sunday … unrest at home, unrest in the White House, unrest abroad.

With more student demonstrations planned for Monday, the question in the newsroom Sunday night was, "What's coming next?"

Gov. James A. Rhodes tours the campus during his visit to Kent on Sunday, May 3. (Kent State University News Service)

CHAPTER EIGHT

May 4: The Morning

Confusion best describes the scene in the *Beacon Journal* newsroom when I arrived shortly after 7 on Monday morning, May 4.

The state desk was empty. Englehart had called me at home late Sunday night to tell me that he had a good plan to cover the anti-war rally scheduled for noon on the Kent State campus. He said he would be in the office by 10 and would go over the details then.

Evidence of the confusion was on the news desk where the associate news editor, Eddie Schoenleb, was trying to lay out a front page that covered what had happened at Kent State on Sunday and could be quickly made over if the threat of an anti-war protest materialized that resulted in a confrontation between students and troops from the Ohio National Guard.

Sunday had started quietly. Students were intrigued by the presence of armed Guardsmen in their midst. As the warm, spring day wore on, a relaxed mood emerged. Some soldiers played Frisbee with the students. And in one memorable encounter, Allison Krause, soon to be a victim, put a flower in the rifle barrel of a soldier and said, "Flowers are better than bullets."

The quiet would not hold. Gov. Rhodes held a news conference strongly criticizing the Saturday night riots and the burning of the ROTC building.

Later that evening, demonstrators gathered again on the Commons, some to view the remains of the ROTC building. As their numbers grew, campus police and the Ohio Highway Patrol urgently called for an immediate curfew. In turn, the crowd was given five minutes to disperse. It didn't, and the Guardsmen launched teargas.

The students then split into two groups — one headed toward President White's house, the other to Prentice Gate, a well-known campus gateway. Students were driven from White's house by teargas. At the gate, though, more violence ensued. Eventually, more people were injured, including some from Guardsmen bayonets. Many arrests were made.

By 11:30 p.m. or so, the campus was again quiet.

Our Monday story failed to capture the friendly flavor of the early-Sunday mingling of students and soldiers. The newspaper did report the demonstration that reportedly drew 1,000 and led to the Guardsmen firing teargas to disperse the crowd.

When I walked up, a couple of the editors on the copy desk rim were arguing with Schoenleb over the placement of a story about Rhodes. They were trying to persuade him that Rhodes' comments during a press conference Sunday afternoon were strident, inappropriate and unnecessarily vicious. They thought our story underplayed the significance of the governor's comments.

Rhodes' arrival at Kent State on Sunday morning created an awkward moment. The governor was a candidate for the U.S. Senate in the Republican primary election that was just two days away — on Tuesday, May 5. His opponent was Robert Taft Jr., from Cincinnati, who had served six years in Congress. He was a member of one of Ohio's and the nation's most respected political families. The contrast between the two men was notable. Rhodes was a coal miner's son and Taft a patrician.

The race was close. Taft was said to be ahead, but the polls indicated that Rhodes was closing the gap. The two men engaged in a series of heated debates in Akron and Cleveland during the final days before the primary vote. According to press reports, Taft focused aggressively on his opponent's credibility as governor, loyalty to the Republican party and honesty as a candidate. He deplored what he called the governor's "hucksterism."

The *Beacon Journal* had endorsed Rhodes in late April. The editorial said that while Taft "is well qualified, we endorse Governor James A. Rhodes because he has set an example of dynamic leadership and because, to him, Ohio and Ohioans always come first...."

Earlier in the week, Rhodes had been critical of dissident anti-war groups at Ohio State University and Case Western Reserve University in Cleveland. The Associated Press quoted him as urging federal authorities to "press charges against rioting students involved in the destruction of property."

Disagreement appeared everywhere. Critics of the governor claimed that he was using the campus disturbances as a "campaign tool" for his race against Taft. On Sunday, May 3, the Kent State Student Senate passed a resolution condemning Rhodes for coming to the university on the eve of the primary election and for using their campus as a platform to rail against student demonstrators. Twenty-three members of the Kent State faculty issued their own statement condemning the violence.

As Rhodes continued to spout divisive opinions about anti-war activities on campuses across Ohio, I wondered how deeply these convictions ran. Was the tough line genuine or was it a tactic to appeal to Ohio's conservative voters who were offended by college kids opposed both to the draft and the Vietnam War?

I recalled meeting the governor in 1963 to interview him for a piece for *The Reporter*, an influential, liberal magazine cofounded years earlier by Max Ascoli and James Reston of *The New York Times*. Rhodes was a tall, slightly stooped man of 60, with a tendency toward pedestrian speech. He had a reputation as "a salesman" and expressed an unrestrained enthusiasm for creating jobs and balancing the budget. We met in the large, lavishly furnished living room of the governor's mansion in Columbus, the state capital.

Rhodes, a former state auditor, had won the 1962 election by 555,000 votes. He immediately set out to introduce an era of austerity in Ohio. By early 1963, the belt-tightening was showing signs of crippling state services, including a heavy-handed attempt to cut payroll in the mental health system.

In my magazine story, "*Austerity in Ohio*," I noted that his budget cutting was cheered by a generous press and a citizenry that seems to be in a mood for "economy."

He selected 88 private-management experts, whom Ohio newspapers dubbed the "Little Hoover Commission." It was a big, bold approach. The governor instructed them to reduce duplication and improve efficiency. Eventually, the public and the press began to catch on, seeing the governor as embellishing his austerity program with statistical tricks to make things seem better or worse than they really were.

Rhodes was not happy with my story, and I left my interview in the governor's mansion with an impression of a man who was not to be trusted.

Turning back to the disagreement on the news desk, I said I wanted to know more about the governor's comments the day before and asked Schoenleb for a proof of the Rhodes story. As he handed me the galley, he said quietly "You know, Ben Maidenburg and the governor are good friends."

"Tough shit," I snapped. "Ben's not here."

My frustration with Schoenleb was deep-seated. His indecisiveness typically played out this way: I often walked into the composing room to check on how we were planning to play a significant story the wire services were moving. Typically, Schoenleb would pull a folded copy of the story out of his rear pocket and hand it to me. After some discussion about its news value, he would scribble headline instructions on the top of the copy and hand it to one of the typesetters.

These familiar episodes of uncertainty demonstrated that when Schoenleb often was unsure where a story belonged in the paper, he would tuck a copy in his pocket while he thought about it. Eventually, he would check with me or others for a decision.

Schoenleb was a bright man with a quick wit and was well-liked in the newsroom. His news judgment was sound, overall. He met deadlines and almost always picked the right stories for Page 1. But the truth was, he was scared of Ben Maidenburg and lived in fear of his wrath.

Years earlier, in June 1950, newsroom legend had it that The Associated Press sent a story across the wire late on Saturday night reporting that North Korean troops had invaded South Korea. Schoenleb was alone on the news desk and was unable to reach Maidenburg to check with him on how to play the story. In a moment of uncertainty, Schoenleb put the story about the start of the Korean conflict under a two-column headline on Page 2. There was hell to pay in the newsroom on Monday morning, and apparently he never got over it. The story became a mark of infamy on him.

I scanned the story he handed me, looking for Rhodes' comments. They were well down in the copy, buried under a description of how, on the Kent State campus, "more than 1,000 anti-war demonstrators had clashed with Guardsmen and police Sunday night before they were driven back with bayonets and teargas."

Nine people were reported injured in the rioting, including three Guardsmen, the story said. More than 100 were arrested, mostly for curfew violations.

The story said the governor had arrived at Kent State from Cleveland on Sunday morning to survey damage from the previous two nights' rioting. Our story quoted him: "The fear being inflicted upon the citizens of this community and upon the university is worse than the Nazi brownshirts and the communist element, and also the night-riders and vigilantes."

The story made no mention of the interpretation drawn from the governor's remarks by National Guard officers that Rhodes meant to ban all rallies — no assembly of students, peaceful or otherwise would be allowed on campus on Monday.

My voice rose as I looked at Schoenleb and said, "The governor calling the kids brownshirts is pretty strong stuff and quite threatening, Eddie! Can't we pull it up toward the top of the story?"

"This is what we have been arguing about," he continued, waving his hand toward the copy editors clustered nearby, "but I thought we should be a little cautious. His comments are on the Page 2 jump. We locked that page up early, so there is no way to pull it back."

"I think it was a bad call, Eddie," I said, turning to go back to my office.

A while later, I got a copy of a text of the prepared remarks Rhodes delivered at the press conference. It came from the Kent State radio-TV information staff. It was clear to me that our story had not fully captured the governor's meaning:

"We have seen here at the city of Kent, especially, probably the most vicious form of campus-oriented violence yet perpetrated by dissident groups and their allies in the State of Ohio."

The governor laid out a course of action. "I want to assure you," he said, "that we're going to employ every force of law that we have under our authority not only to get to the bottom of the situation here at Kent — on the campus — in the city." He told of asking for the cooperation of the district attorney and the federal government because, in burning the ROTC building, the students had destroyed federal property.

"The same group we're dealing with here today ... they have only one thing in mind and that is to destroy higher education in Ohio."

Rhodes said of the Saturday night fire at the ROTC building, "We have seen all forms of violence — the worst."

He said he would ask the Ohio General Assembly to make it a felony for any person to "throw a rock, brick or stone at law enforcement." Anyone convicted of such a crime would be automatically dismissed from their state university without a hearing and banned from entering any other public school.

He concluded by demonizing student protesters as "worse than the brownshirts and the communist element and also the 'night-riders' and the vigilantes. They're the worst kind of people we harbor in America. And I want to say that they're not going to take over the campus."

A short while later, Englehart came in and beckoned me over to the state desk. He looked weary. He had worked through several long days of intense activity directing his reporters to stay on the story. At the top of his list the morning of May 4 was preparing for and anticipating Monday's unpredictable events. He told me that he had deployed Sallot and photographer Don Roese to campus to report on whether there would be a rally.

"What do you think is going to happen today?" I asked.

He shrugged. "There's all kinds of rumors flying around. A lot depends on the Guard. They have orders to break up the rally. Rhodes was pretty firm about that. Not sure they know what they are going to do."

"No clue?" I asked.

On Monday morning, Sallot was exhausted from covering the Saturday and Sunday night events. When he and Englehart talked again about 8 a.m., they agreed that Sallot should get over to the campus as soon as possible to get a sense of what was going on. As an afternoon newspaper, the imperative in the newsroom was the need to keep our copy fresh for later editions.

It was demanding, given that our deadlines would hit just after the rally was scheduled to begin … at noon.

Among those gathered on the Commons before the clash with National Guardsmen were Jeffrey Miller (darkened center) and Mary Ann Vecchio (darkened right). Photographer Howard Ruffner highlighted the two in this version of the photograph — also shown on page xiv – for his book about the shootings, Moments of Truth. *Vecchio would meet Miller in a fateful photograph just minutes later. (Howard Ruffner)*

CHAPTER NINE

May 4: Noon

As noon approached, students were again defiantly gathering on the Commons, the large grassy space at the crossroads of the campus. It stretched from the Kent State Union and the burned-out ROTC building up a hill to Taylor Hall, the journalism school building. Among the growing number were students, teachers, an estimated 300 protesters and curious onlookers. The kids vastly outnumbered the faculty.

The growing assembly was a signal that the rally on the Commons was going to go ahead, despite Rhodes' orders to the National Guard to use whatever force necessary to break up the protest.

Rhodes' mandate was confusing to some but gave authorities little room for flexibility. When someone asked him for a definition of a protest, he replied, "Two students walking together."

The first edition of the *Beacon Journal* was known as the 7-star. On Monday, the presses began to roll at 11 a.m. In the mailroom, papers in stacks of 25 were tied in bundles with lengths of twine and tossed onto the backs of trucks to be delivered to the far reaches of the newspaper's circulation area.

The top headline on Page 1 read: "Anti-war Rioting Rips KSU for Third Night." The story began, "A beefed up force of 800 National Guardsmen stood ready today following a third consecutive night of rioting at Kent State University."

The story described an "abortive attempt" by Guardsmen around 9 p.m. on Sunday to scatter demonstrators with teargas volleys, followed by a reading of the Ohio Riot Act. The Guardsman reading

Before noon, a Jeep drove slowly toward demonstrators as Kent State policeman Harold Rice read the Ohio Riot Act through a bullhorn. (Akron Beacon Journal)

the act was drowned by the jeering crowd. Later, around 11 p.m., another teargas volley succeeded in driving the protesters back toward campus.

During Sunday, "self-styled protest leaders" sought "open negotiations" with Mayor Satrom and university president White. Neither man would agree to such a meeting, the story said.

Little change was planned for the next edition, the 2-star. A few minutes before 12:30, the news desk sent word to the composing room that the presses could start on time, 1 p.m.

For Sallot, May 4 was a special day. It was the last day of classes under the journalism school's quarterly system. He was weary after a grueling weekend of covering unrest for the *Beacon Journal*. He slept in and cut his 9 a.m. class. By 11 a.m., he was on campus to begin a day of reporting as a *Beacon Journal* staffer. His first stop was the university news bureau to check in with Jim Bruss, the director. He asked Bruss whether the rally would be allowed to proceed. Bruss brushed him off, insisting he couldn't speak for the National Guard and suggested that he ask the Guard commanders.

Sallot hiked over toward the hill and a small group of uniformed men on the edge of the Commons. He found the National Guard brass huddled near the burned-out ROTC building. City police, university police and an officer from the Ohio Highway Patrol mingled with the military officers as they talked.

He didn't see anyone from the university administration. This was a clear sign to him that the administration was no longer in the communications loop. His was a critical observation: Rhodes had exerted his authority, and his instructions to ban the rally would be carried out.

Armed with this confirming insight, Sallot thought he might pick up some intelligence at the nearby Student Union. He ran into a few people he had seen at the Saturday night ROTC fire and the Sunday night demonstration. They said they were determined that the noon rally on the Commons would take place as advertised.

Sallot walked into the Student Union and shoved coins into a pay phone. Englehart came on the line and asked for an update. As Sallot related the student leaders' intentions, he told Englehart that he thought the rally would proceed peacefully. It would be out in the open, exposed by a bright sun shining on the broad expanse of the Commons, he reasoned. The previous nights' demonstrations had been shrouded by the dark. Daylight would make a difference.

Englehart gave him an update on how the newspaper planned to cover the rally. Two photographers, Roese, 32, and Paul Tople, 21, also were on campus. Roese was a veteran member of the photo staff and Tople, like Sallot, was a Kent State student who worked part-time on weekends for the *Beacon Journal*.

The Guard moved up the Commons, firing teargas grenades as it attempted to disperse demonstrators. (Kent State University News Service)

Tople had covered the Saturday and Sunday night unrest. He captured images of the burning ROTC building, which were published in the early editions on Monday, May 4. His assignment Sunday was to photograph the governor as he held a news conference and then toured the ROTC area. The photos showed the governor in the Kent city fire station, pounding his fist on a table as he fired off his irrational criticism of the student protesters.

On Monday morning, Tople returned to his role as a student. As he walked into the Taylor Hall office of the *Chestnut Burr*, the yearbook, he heard the Victory Bell on the Commons as it began to ring.

What now? Tople went back outside and was drawn toward

Alan Canfora waves a black flag at Guardsmen kneeling in firing positions near the athletic field fence. (John Filo)

a cluster of students watching protesters vigorously clanging the bell. Commotion followed as a line of Guardsmen approached and began to fire teargas grenades. A stinging cloud of gas reached him, burning his eyes and making it hard to focus his camera. He went back inside Taylor Hall and found a back balcony for another view.

From there, Tople could see protesters in the parking lot next to Prentice Hall dormitory. He saw them "throwing things at the Guardsmen" as the troops formed a picket line to pursue a group of demonstrators. Tople could hear obscenities being yelled at the Guardsmen: "Kill the pigs." "Stick the pigs."

Tople's eye was drawn to one student waving a black flag at the Guard in a taunting motion. When he snapped the shutter, he captured an image of the protester, Alan Canfora, about 50 yards from the troops huddled against a fence separating Blanket Hill from an athletic practice field. In Tople's photo, Canfora is alone on the field, holding his flag aloft in his right hand. Photographers from other news organizations captured similar images of Canfora and his black flag. The pictures later became critical pieces of evidence in addressing the claim that the soldiers' lives were in danger. The images expressed protest but showed that the students were not pressing the Guard in a threatening way, as its officers claimed.

As 12:15 p.m. approached, Sallot calculated his deadline. It would be tight. He needed to make sure he could find a phone. He reminded himself that Englehart's nerves would be on fire if he didn't hear regularly from his people in the field. He knew Englehart would have his eye on the wall clock in the newsroom, making the same calculation as its minute hand crept toward deadline.

Sallot got to Taylor Hall before the Guard moved out and began to chase people. He knew the location by heart. Taylor Hall would offer the best vantage point overlooking the Commons. Time and a connection with Englehart were vital but so was satisfying his journalistic compulsion to observe. Taylor Hall would be his place to watch the action from a reporter's perspective.

There were telephones in the J-school office. He raced down the corridor. The office was on the first floor as he came in from the Commons. He paused and then opened the door into the office of Dr. Murvin Perry, director of the J-School. He blurted a "hello" to Margaret Brown, Perry's secretary.

He spotted a phone on a desk in front of a large picture window overlooking the Commons. It was a standard black dial phone that was part of the campus Centrex system. Sallot asked Brown if he could use it. She nodded yes. "Can you keep the line open for me?" Again she nodded yes. It required Brown to stand by while Sallot talked.

Sallot reported his location to Englehart. He said it afforded him a direct view of the developing confrontation. He also gave him the unbelievably good news that he also had an open telephone line. "Good," Englehart said, "make damn sure you keep the line open."

Sallot started his running account by saying that it looked like the rally was going to start. He described a Guard Jeep pulling out to the center of the Commons and slowly moving along the lines of demonstrators. It carried two riflemen, a driver and a Kent State policeman shouting through a bullhorn that the rally was illegal under the Ohio Riot Act.

The students actively ignored the warnings. The noise and their number grew. A majority of the Guard began to march from one edge of the Commons toward the demonstrators gathering on the hill by the Victory Bell. Sallot described the Guardsmen carrying M-1 rifles with bayonets, wearing gas masks and steel combat helmets. He said some of the Guardsmen were armed with grenade launchers. These weapons first appeared in the Vietnam War. Its 14.5-inch barrel was fitted to a rifle stock that was held at the shoulder. It could fire six rounds per minutes and carried the nickname among American soldiers of the "Bloop" gun.

Sallot was looking at a potentially combustible tableau. Tension was mounting as he fixed his eyes on the scene below. The Guardsmen were clearly outnumbered. The students were entirely outgunned.

The Guard began firing teargas canisters as it moved across the Commons and on up the hill. The crowd of students split into two. The teargas grenades arced through the air as they were fired from the M-79 launchers, leaving a trail of smoke that soon enveloped the scene. The sound from the grenades was a "pop" and then a hiss. A few students picked up canisters and threw them back at the Guard. Smoke from the gas grenades created a weird and frighteningly smoky tableau that was dramatically captured in photographs. The teargas became basically ineffective because a 14 mph spring breeze blew most of it away from the demonstrators and back toward the burned-out ROTC building. It looked like a battleground.

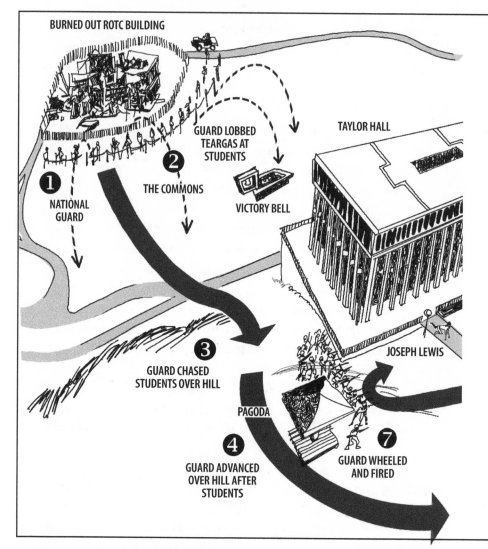

THE KENT STATE SHOOTINGS; TRAGEDY IN 24 MINUTES

This detailed graphic, based on the work of artist Dick Mayer of the *Detroit Free Press*, shows the development of the action on the Kent State campus on May 4, 1970. Just after noon, troops of the Ohio National Guard began their sweep at the ruins of the ROTC building (**1** and **2**) and moved out to disperse students gathered on the Commons. The Guardsmen pursued the demonstrators past the Victory Bell, then up and over Blanket Hill (**3**) and around the Pagoda (**4**), pushing demonstrators before them. The Guardsmen found themselves trapped at an athletic

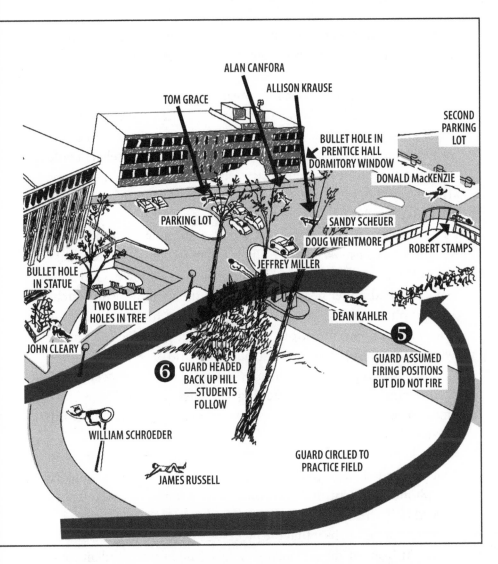

fence where they paused and assumed firing positions (**5**) but did not fire. The Guardsmen then moved back up the front slope of (**6**) Blanket Hill. When they reached the Pagoda (**7**), they turned and fired. It was 12:24 p.m. The bodies of the victims — four dead and nine wounded — can be seen scattered across the campus, 20 yards to 250 yards from the firing line. Observers later noted some problems with the accuracy of the graphic's information, which was based on early FBI reports. Specifically, Tom Grace, William Schroeder and Alan Canfora are significantly out of position.

Sallot's hands were sweating as he held the phone. He looked down at the scene unfolding before him and described it to Englehart in Akron.

"They're firing a hell of a lot of teargas," he said.

Sallot searched for words to capture the chaos he was witnessing. He said he saw one Guardsman pick up a canister tossed by a protester and throw it back toward the students. Englehart could hear the tumult of the demonstration from his end of the phone. The angry shouts from the knots of demonstrators created a din that enveloped the Commons.

As unpleasant and scary as it was, the stinging gas did little to scatter the protesters. Taylor Hall's ventilation system started sucking in the teargas. Sallot would later recall: "Ms. Brown, God bless her, crouched under her desk away from the window," still clutching the phone and its critical connection from him to the *Beacon Journal* newsroom in Akron. This selfless act provided the link by which truth found its way to the outside world.

Tension was palpable in the newsroom. Several of us were gathered around the state desk listening to Englehart shouting instructions to Sallot; the stub of his cigar moved up and down in the corner of his mouth as he talked.

He kept firing questions at his young reporter. Sallot insisted that he needed to go back outside. Englehart forbid him to leave the phone. Sallot turned to Brown, who assured him she would indeed hold the open line for him.

Sallot told Englehart that the protesters were keeping "a safe distance" in front of the advancing Guard. The crowd, students and soldiers, swarmed past Taylor Hall. He could see the Guard split and go around Taylor Hall from both ends. Students and the Guard units moved beyond Sallot's line of sight from the J-School office window. He briefly continued his running account for Englehart and then said he needed to go back outside to catch up with the flow of the action. He handed the phone back to Brown and ran to a Taylor Hall exit near the veranda.

Guardsmen turned near the Pagoda and faced protesters before opening fire. (Howard Ruffner)

From there he could see the Guardsmen headed back up Blanket Hill toward the Pagoda, which stood at the crest of the hill.

Another brief lull in the commotion gave Sallot the idea that the Guard had completed its mission. Maybe the rally was over. He guessed that most people would begin to wander off to lunch or afternoon classes.

He had to alert his editor that the Guard seemed to be standing down and moving back toward its bivouac area near the ROTC building. He headed back to reclaim the telephone in Taylor Hall.

He had reached the veranda at the front of the building when he heard gunfire. In an eyewitness account for the *Beacon Journal*, he wrote, "Some people say there was a single shot followed by a volley. It seemed like just one volley to me."

As the Guardsmen fired, students scattered for cover behind cars in the Prentice parking lot. (Kent State University News Service)

Sallot looked to his left and saw that the Guardsmen next to the Pagoda had turned and fired. Rifles seemed pointed in several directions, and he could see that he was in an exposed position. "Some people thought these shots were blanks being fired. I knew this was live fire when I saw a clump of dirt near me puff up where a shot hit the ground." He dove for safety, moving out of the arc of fire.

Sallot saw that he was just a few yards away from a student who was shot in the back. (This was Bill Schroeder.)

He scrambled back into Taylor Hall. It was a few minutes past 12:30 p.m. He ran down two flights of stairs from the veranda to the J-School office. Brown, trembling, handed him the phone with its open line to Englehart.

Sallot breathlessly shouted into the phone, "The Guard fired! They fired! They fired right in front of me. Some people were hit. One guy looks dead. He was hit in the head." (This was Jeffrey Miller.)

Englehart yelled all of this to the newsroom.

Minutes later, a bell on The Associated Press wire machine began to sound its "ding, ding, ding, ding, ding" announcing that a news FLASH was moving. "Shots fired at Kent State." The AP story offered no other details.

"Where is Sallot?!" I shouted.

"He is checking the rally!" replied Englehart.

The newsroom exploded into action. People moved. Instructions were given. Questions demanded answers, fast. Suggested ledes and headlines ideas were tossed out. News trickled in at first.

I ordered the news desk to hold the press start for the home edition. It was a moment that came close to fulfilling an editor's dream of shouting, "Stop the Presses!!"

We had an eyewitness to tragedy. I was now certain there were casualties, maybe dead students. We needed every hand we could get.

Al Fitzpatrick, the news editor, had the day off. I found him at home. Within an hour he was in the office, taking charge of the news desk. Tom Moore, deputy news editor and one of the old-timers on the news desk, worked with the production department and urgently negotiated a press start as late as possible. We needed to increase the press run for the day's last edition, a street-sale edition that carried stock prices from the market's close.

Voices rose in the newsroom, but the decision makers were calm. We were trained for this —functioning effectively and swiftly on deadline. A big story. It had to be told with precision.

Ben Maidenburg and Jack Knight were not in the newsroom, but I knew what they would demand. Truth and accuracy. Fundamental elements to a news story. Maidenburg had pounded that message into our "thick skulls" from the first day on the job. Don't rush news into print until you are certain you have the best

Teenager Mary Ann Vecchio (kneeling) and others surround the body of Kent State University student Jeffrey Miller, who was among those killed. (John Filo)

available version of the truth. Then go with it. Better be right than sorry. A breaking tragedy like this, where our young reporter was trying to count bodies, demanded caution. Facts. We needed facts. Names. Details. Numbers.

Unlike an assassination or a war or a mass murder in a far-off city, this story was ours. On a warm spring day here in Ohio. In a college town next door. Instinctively, what kicked in was our training, our experience and our deep knowledge of the history of campus unrest at Kent State. Now, were we ready?

Guardsmen shot at kids, Sallot told Englehart. Bodies down. No names. Confusion. The campus seemed to explode in pandemonium.

Students provided comfort and aid to one of the wounded, John Cleary. (Howard Ruffner)

Minutes after the horrific sound of rifle volleys, then screams for help, a reporter from United Press International began to dictate from a phone in the National Guard command post near the University Center on the other side of the Commons.

Wire service journalists are always on deadline. This reporter saw that the action was moving away from him. He was tethered to the Guard's land line, but from that spot, he was able to listen to the National Guard radio over a Portage County sheriff's department frequency. He heard one officer call out for ambulances, "We've got two dead up here."

The UPI journalist assumed this meant two dead Guardsmen. And that is what he filed. His competitive heart beat fast. His first priority on a big, breaking story demanded this: Don't let the AP be first.

Students gently loaded a shooting victim on a university ambulance. (Akron Beacon Journal)

His dispatch went to the UPI news bureau in Cleveland. The reporter was instructed to get over to the other side of the building to find out what else had happened. He hung up the phone in the guard command post minutes before the Ohio Bell phone system collapsed because of the flood of calls coming into the campus from parents, family and friends worried about their loved ones.

Carl Miller, assistant managing editor in the UPI Columbus bureau, later said he telephoned the university news service after receiving reports from the Cleveland bureau and other news media that two Guardsmen were killed.

Miller said he asked the university news service, "We have

reports from your office that two Guardsmen were killed. Is that correct?'

Miller said the reply was, "Yes, there were two Guardsmen killed."

Within minutes, the wire service moved a bulletin attributing the report to Joe Durbin, managing editor of University News and Information.

AP's bulletin said the dead were four students. Englehart clutched the UPI bulletin as he asked Sallot several times if he was absolutely certain there were no Guardsmen down, just students. Sallot said he thought so. At that moment the thought crossed his mind, "If I am wrong, this might be the end of my newspaper career."

Beacon Journal editors were scrambling to put together as compete a story as possible, and the production manager was yelling that he needed start the presses.

Tension was at the breaking point as we faced a critical choice: Go with the UPI story from an experienced reporter that two Guardsmen were among the dead. Or trust Jeff Sallot, our own reporter on the scene, who was telling us he thought the four dead were students.

Englehart turned to me. "What should we do?"

"Let's go with Jeff," I ordered, almost without hesitation.

The desk swung into action. Across the newsroom someone shouted, "What if we're wrong?!"

"Jeff saw the Guard shoot at the students. We have to trust him."

The press room called the news desk to warn them. "You've got 15 minutes. We roll the presses at 1:15!"

More fresh details from Sallot about casualties he had seen gave us enough for the edition on deadline. Observed. Reported. Out to the world.

For what seemed an eternity, competing versions of reality were alive in the outside world. Sallot's report that four Kent State students were shot and killed by Ohio National Guardsmen was being distributed on The Associated Press wire. And the UPI story about two Guardsmen and two students being killed in an anti-war demonstration was being quickly edited on news desks in small newspapers and radio stations around Ohio.

Station managers interrupted scheduled programming to broadcast bulletins with the erroneous report. Someone on the *Beacon Journal* state desk yelled across the newsroom that radio stations were going with the UPI story.

I knew that if this error wasn't soon corrected, many Ohioans and listeners across the country would come to believe as true earlier rumors that snipers were on the campus and radicals were to blame for this serious trouble.

A printer in the *Beacon Journal* composing room hastily inserted three grafs of fresh lead type in the metal page form. Minutes later, the pressroom foreman pressed a big green "start" button, and the gigantic press cylinders began to turn.

Four Protesters Shot In New KSU Outburst.

KENT — Four persons were shot shortly after noon today behind Taylor Hall on the Kent State University campus. Identities were not immediately known and there was no indication of who did the shooting.

The shootings came as about 50 National Guardsmen attempted to disperse about 500 demonstrators who had gathered on the campus in front of Taylor Hall.

Beacon Journal photographer Don Roese reported some of the students had guns.

Our first story reported only what we knew. Four fatalities, two men and two women. Sallot's sure-footed observation that the shots came from the National Guard was confirmed too late for the edition on the presses now rumbling at the other end of the *Beacon Journal* building. We had surmised the shots came from the National Guard, but we were not certain. Reports of an armed student being apprehended by police signaled caution about immediately identifying the source of the shooting. We decided to wait for confirmation. We had to get it right.

The importance of Sallot's ability to secure an open phone line soon became apparent. We learned later that afternoon how critical it was. He had the only working phone line out of Kent State. Keeping it open to our newsroom was essential; no one on campus but the *Beacon Journal* reporter would be able to call out, no one would be able to call in. A terrible tragedy was erupting just beyond Margaret Brown's office window. She was Sallot's steadfast ally in keeping the phone line open for him and his urgent and truthful minute-by-minute reports from campus.

All Sallot knew in those early moments was that one student had been shot and killed. He needed to get back outside. As he handed Brown the phone, she was crying and unable to talk. Through her tears, she nodded assurance that she would keep the phone line open.

As Sallot left Taylor Hall, he noted that the Guard had already moved on. It felt safe enough to go out to assess human damage and count bodies. He didn't get a full count. By this time the body of Allison Krause and other victims had been taken in cars to Robinson Memorial Hospital in neighboring Ravenna.

Once more back to the phone, he gave Englehart his incomplete count. Englehart wanted to know why the Guard fired. Sallot didn't know. (That's still an open question.) He said he had to run out and talk to more witnesses.

Englehart said, "Don't you dare! You are a fucking witness. Stay here on the line."

Sallot continued to describe what he had seen. Two apparent deaths. Jeffrey Miller had half his head blown away and Bill Schroder had a big hole in the center of his back and wasn't moving.

Englehart read back the account to make sure he had understood completely what Sallot had told him. Sallot remembers his own distress. By this time he was "badly shaken and wasn't thinking very clearly."

Englehart told Sallot that his account had made the edition. Other reporters were now beginning to arrive on campus. Sallot said later, "I seem to have collapsed. I have only fleeting recollections of the rest of the afternoon. I could see a large group of students staging a defiant sit-down on the slope of the hill, facing off with the Guard commanders. I recall my geology professor, Glenn Frank, pleading with the students to disperse because the Guard might fire again."

In truth, Sallot continued to do his job even as the trauma of what he was seeing took hold. Others told him they saw him on the hill, taking notes and watching the Guard and then going back into Taylor Hall where he found Brown still guarding the open line for him.

By this time, some of the J-School faculty crowded into the director's office to see what was happening. Murv Perry suggested that Sallot use a second line to call his parents and tell them he was OK. Sallot cautiously pushed the second button on the phone, but there was no dial tone on that line. It was the first sign that the phone system on the Kent State campus had shut down.

At that moment, Sallot held in his hand a phone receiver with the only connection to the outside world. It would give the *Beacon Journal* an exclusive conduit from a campus in turmoil to a newsroom scrambling to publish an account of the biggest, most tragic local story in the *Beacon Journal*'s long history.

Photographer Roese showed up and got on the phone with Englehart to tell him he had film and would rush back to the office in Akron. Englehart began to question him about what he had seen. Fear entered the picture. Roese said he did not want to be quoted. Sallot realized he might be quoted, too. He was afraid that if his name appeared in the paper as a witness, he might face retaliation. Englehart scratched his head in disbelief but assured Sallot he wouldn't use his name. He would be cited as an "anonymous newspaperman."

After conferring with the production and circulation departments, Fitzpatrick, the news editor, bargained successfully for extra time for the 1-star, the large home-delivery edition for residential neighborhoods in Akron. As the 1-star went to press, Fitzpatrick, Englehart and the news desk were pressing to put together a more complete story based on reports from campus by Sallot and Roese and from Robinson Memorial Hospital in Ravenna. Reporter Bob Page had been sent there by Englehart and was in the emergency room as the dead and wounded started to arrive. He was able to confirm Sallot's eyewitness report and record the names of the dead students and most of the wounded.

The presses for the 1-star edition began to roll at 2 p.m. The top line in large, black type read:

4 Dead, 11 Wounded

In New KSU Trouble

The story, running nearly a full column, began:

KENT — Four persons — two boys and two girls — were shot to death and 11 wounded today as National Guardsmen fired into a crowd on the Kent State University campus.

Gunshots rang out about 12:30 p.m., half an hour after Guardsmen fired teargas into a crowd of 500 on the commons behind the university administration offices. Demonstrators hurled rocks and empty teargas grenades back as they scattered.

Police are holding a man who said he used a gun he was carrying when he was attacked by demonstrators. The man reportedly had press credentials and carried a camera.

A newspaperman, an eyewitness to the shooting, said the gunshots rang out after one student hurled a rock as Guardsmen were turning away after clearing the Commons.

"One section of the Guard turned around and fired and then all the Guardsmen turned and fired," he said.

According to the witness, some of the Guardsmen were firing in the air while others were firing straight ahead.

Guardsmen and police immediately cordoned off all buildings on the campus, permitting no one to enter or leave.

The final edition of May 4 went to press at 4:30 p.m. and carried a two-line banner headline in bold, all-caps type:

4 DEAD, 11 WOUNDED AS GUARD

FIRES INTO RIOTERS AT KSU

KENT — Four persons were killed and at least 11 others wounded as National Guardsmen fired into a group of rock-throwing protesters at Kent State University today.

Three of the dead were tentatively identified as:

William Schroeder, Jeffrey Miller and Allison Krause.

The fourth was an unidentified girl.

Injured were:

Dean Mahler. Thomas Grace, Joe Lewis, John Cleary, Alan Canford, Robert Stamp, Dennis Brackenridge, Doug Wrentmore, and Bill Herschler. Two of the nine are National Guardsmen.

Six of those taken to Robinson Memorial Hospital suffered gunshot wounds. Three were in critical condition. Two of those taken to the hospital were identified as Guardsmen suffering from shock. One of the Guardsmen was released this afternoon.

As more details flooded the news desks that afternoon, we learned the name of the fourth fatality: Sandy Scheuer.

We also noted with great regret that we had misspelled the names of two students, both wounded: Dean Kahler as "Mahler," and Alan Canfora as "Canford."

(Minutes after photographers snapped Canfora waving his black flag, a bullet from a National Guard rifle struck him in the right wrist. He fell, but the images of him and his flag remain fixed in the public mind as a symbol of protest, not threat.)

Our story excluded the names of two wounded victims, Donald MacKenzie and James Russell, and added names of two Guardsmen, Dennis Breckenridge and Bill Herschler, as if they were students. Breckenridge had fainted and was carried off by stretcher. Herschler was checked for hypertension and released. We knew we couldn't fix the misspellings and misidentifications until Tuesday's paper. We alerted the news desks to correct the spelling of names with great care.

Telephone communications between Akron and Kent were severed at about 1 p.m. A call to the Ohio Bell Telephone Co. in Kent brought this recorded message: "Due to the martial law in effect in Kent, the telephone company is closed."

Farther down in the story, additional fresh details were inserted:

> The wounded were unconscious and covered with blood. At least one was shot in the leg and two others were shot in the abdomen.

> The shooting broke out after students had rallied on the Commons at the center of the campus in defiance of an order not to assemble.

Details of the late-morning confrontation between the Guard and demonstrators was carried over from earlier stories, leading to this description of the moment shots were fired:

> Apparently without orders, the Guardsmen turned and aimed their M-1 rifles at the charging students and began firing.

> Students in the emergency room at Robinson Memorial who would not give their names said they wanted to get off the Commons to discuss demands.

> They said as they started gathering, the Guardsmen started throwing "pepper" gas at them, and the students started throwing rocks.

> Then, they said, the firing started.

> One non-student with a guru mustache and long hair said:

> "They'll pay for it. It's not radicals, it's the most conservative groups on campus who will bring the university down now."

> One youth said the most conservative groups on campus are out screaming the same as the long-hair kids.

The press run for the last edition was jumped by 20,000. Circulation crews made their normal runs to replenish news racks and street boxes, then dropped bundles for home delivery on residential street corners in upscale neighborhoods of West Akron.

Readers of the final edition on Monday, May 4, got copies of the *Beacon Journal* with as complete a version of the Kent State tragedy as was available anywhere so soon after the tragedy.

We breathed collective sighs of relief that we had made the correct call by trusting our young reporter and his observation that the four dead were all students. We learned later that the *Ravenna Record-Courier,* our competition in the Kent area, published the UPI story with the erroneous headline across Page 1. It stated that two Guardsmen and a student were dead. The error was discovered as the press run ended. The *Record-Courier* corrected the error for a later edition.

Other newspapers around Ohio also went with the false UPI report of two Guardsmen killed. Among them were the *Cleveland Press, Alliance Review, Circleville Herald, Mansfield News, Ashland Times-Gazette* and *The Lorain Journal.* The UPI byline on at least one of these stories was that of Robert Corbett. These northern Ohio newspapers covered communities that were home to many KSU students, where reports of National Guardsmen being killed was an additional shock.

It was not only an error but part of the tragedy.

In our newsroom, we turned to preparing the *Beacon Journal* for Tuesday, May 5. It loomed as a monumental task: telling a huge, tragic story with details whose meaning we were just beginning to grasp. Its details and unexpected twists would unfold gradually over days, weeks, months, years. Some parts of the story are still a mystery nearly 50 years later.

One thing is crystal clear: On May 4, 1970, truth mattered, and it still does.

The three editions of the Akron Beacon Journal on May 4, 1970, show the progression of the coverage and the growing importance of the breaking news. The "two-star edition," upper left, went to press at about 1 p.m. The "one-star edition," lower left, printed at about 2 p.m., and the "final edition" printed at about 4:30 p.m.

61 Bullets

The Guardsmen's M-1 rifles, with fixed bayonets, carried bullets on May 4. (Kent State University News Service)

Following the tragic events of May 4, evidence would show that a cluster of shots were aimed in the direction of the Prentice Hall parking lot. The bullets struck bodies as close as 60 feet and as far as 750 feet from the Guard's impromptu firing line.

During the investigation for *The President's Commission on Campus Unrest,* 28 soldiers acknowledged firing from Blanket Hill. Of these, 25 fired 55 shots from rifles, two fired five shots from .45 caliber pistols, and one fired a single blast from a shotgun.

Later, in defending their actions, some Guardsmen spoke of being afraid, of feeling surrounded. Some had been struck by stones and rocks. During the investigations following the shootings, the FBI, the National Guard, and Kent Police gathered rocks from the killing field. By one count, the rock collection weighed 175 pounds and numbered about 340.

The Guardsmen had many other options to carry out their mission. There were other ways for a military unit to break up the rally that day. Instead, these 28 soldiers chose to point and shoot their weapons at students.

Bullets from an M-1 rifle are lethal. The weapon is designed to kill an enemy on the battlefield. Fired into students scattered across a campus hillside and dormitory parking lot, the effect is no different.

Four of the bullets followed fatal trajectories, taking life from Allison Krause, Jeffrey Miller, Sandra Scheuer, and Bill Schroeder. Eleven bullets wounded nine students: Alan Canfora, Thomas Grace, Robby Stamps, Doug Wrentmore, Donald MacKenzie, Jim Russell, John Cleary, Joseph Lewis ... and Dean Kahler, who was permanently paralyzed below the waist.

What happens when bullets enter the human body? They rip through skin. Then through a layer of fatty tissue. Then muscle. Sometimes they shatter bones before reaching inner organs. In all cases, bleeding results, and the body is seized by trauma. In some cases, the heart stops beating.

A single bullet exploded in Jeff Miller's mouth. He died instantly. Jeff was 265 feet from the Guardsman whose bullet killed him.

A single bullet went through Allison Krause's upper left arm, tore open the left side of her chest, then fragmented, causing massive, fatal, internal trauma. Allison was 343 feet from the Guardsman whose bullet killed her.

A single bullet ripped into William Schroeder's left chest at the seventh rib, piercing his left lung. Bullet and bone fragments flew from the top of his left shoulder. He survived for almost an hour before dying in surgery at Robinson Memorial Hospital in nearby Ravenna. Bill was 382 feet from the Guardsman whose bullet killed him.

A single bullet severed Sandra Scheuer's jugular vein. She bled to death. Sandy was 390 feet from the Guardsman whose bullet killed her.

It was official violence. Weapons were fired, lives were taken, with malice as the intent. The killings later were officially defended as sanctioned acts by soldiers of the Ohio National Guard who believed they were following orders to break up an illegal rally against the war. This explanation does not dilute the reality of dead students scattered across a dormitory parking lot or of the wounded whose bodies and emotions would never fully mend.

An ambulance carried a student victim up the Commons, past Taylor Hall, to Robinson Memorial Hospital. (Kent State University News Service)

CHAPTER TEN

May 4: Counting the Victims

As the shock of the tragedy gripped us and the reality of fast-approaching press deadlines loomed, we asked ourselves other crucial questions: Who were these victims of National Guard bullets? Names? Hometowns? Details on bullet wounds? Fatal injuries? We needed information, fast.

Englehart's eyes scanned the newsroom. The reporter desks were empty. He knew he had sent every available reporter scrambling toward Kent with instructions to take orders from Ron Clark and his temporary city desk. "Interview as many Guardsmen as you can. Get to the students before they are all off campus," he shouted after them as they hustled toward the parking deck.

Englehart spotted a young reporter at a desk near the sports department. "Page, get over here!" he yelled. Bob Page was 24, with a high forehead and a pleasant demeanor. He was a Kent State graduate and had been on the *Beacon Journal* only two years.

As Page approached the state desk, Englehart stood and got close to his face, continuing to chomp on his evil-smelling cigar. "There's been a shooting at Kent State. The goddamn Guard shot some students. There are victims, maybe dozens. I think they are being taken to Robinson Memorial in Ravenna. Get over there as fast as you can! Get the names. Stay there until I tell you to leave."

Page grabbed a notebook and jumped into his 1969 VW Beetle. He headed east on I-76 toward the hospital, 19 miles away. Along the way, he passed Kent and wondered what he might see if he briefly detoured to the campus. His car radio was belching the news that "upwards of 50" had been shot at Kent State. Students and Guardsmen were both among the victims, the radio reports said. He checked his watch and decided to stick to his orders: Get to the hospital and grab names of the victims.

Page was in a state of disbelief as his VW chugged along the highway. From his student days, he was familiar with the pattern of escalating points of view on the Kent State campus. It seemed that everyone had sharp opinions over the proliferation of a war being fought halfway around the globe. There was not much middle ground. Even against that backdrop, he couldn't imagine such violence there.

He recalled his own experience just three years earlier. He was among the new graduates of Kent State hired by the *Beacon Journal,* only to be called for a physical exam by his draft board in Ashtabula, Ohio. He worried then that he would be on his way to Vietnam. This fear was on the mind of every draft-eligible young man. To his great relief, dangerously high blood pressure levels meant a medical deferment. He remembered offering God credit for the intervention. Military doctors mandated frequent blood pressure readings. Page complied. The readings returned to normal, but he never was called to report for active duty.

Page covered the 19 miles in 30 minutes. He arrived at Robinson Memorial Hospital on Ravenna's north side, six miles from the Kent State campus. It was an old two-story brick building owned by Portage County and named for a former judge, George F. Robinson, and his wife, Mary. It was built in 1920, but by the time of the Kent State shootings, it had been expanded to a 48-bed hospital.

Page quickly noted that the building was locked down. No one was being allowed in. He saw the door to the Emergency Room was being guarded by two elderly security officers. They weren't letting anyone in the building either.

A group of about 40 distraught students had assembled in the parking lot. They were noisily demanding updates on the conditions of friends who had been wounded. No one was telling them anything. Tempers were fueled by anger, panic and fear.

Page approached one of the milling students and introduced himself. She told him her name was Rosemary Canfora. "Everybody calls me 'Chic.'" She was in hysterics over the wounding of her brother, Alan Canfora. She was trying to get into the hospital to learn more about his condition. Page tried to calm her. He told her his first beat on the *Beacon Journal* was covering news in the city of Barberton just southwest of Akron, where he knew her dad as a longtime city councilman.

Page saw Chic turn in frustration toward one of the pudgy guards at the ER door. "Pig," she spat. The guard's face grew crimson. He struggled to yank his billy club out of a holster on his belt. It took a bit of doing, Page noticed. The guard had a bulging waistline that made it a difficult to free the weapon. The harder he tugged, the redder his face grew.

With the club finally in hand, the guard waded into the group of students and walloped Chic across the upper back while shouting, "No one calls me a 'pig' and gets away with it!"

A mini brawl broke out, and the second security guard pushed into the scrum to rescue his partner.

OK, what do I do? Page thought to himself in the midst of the roiling upset. "Is this going to turn into something I need to cover? No, Pat told me to get the names and the story is inside the hospital." He stayed the course.

The confrontation had drawn the two guards away from the entrance to the building, giving Page his moment to hurry though the unsecured door. He was not familiar with the hospital, but his first impression was that it was dreary and decrepit. It had linoleum-like tiles on the floor of the emergency area and along the corridors.

Page moved cautiously down the hallway, peering into treatment rooms. Through one door, he saw that sheets had been draped over two bodies lying on gurneys.

A nurse walked by and asked who he was. Page identified himself as a reporter from the *Beacon Journal*. She told him to follow her. Reflecting later on her unexpected invitation, he concluded that she was familiar with the paper's coverage of Kent State. That may have prompted her to trust him. The nurse led him to another room where he watched a doctor pull a covering over a girl's face. Nearby, he saw another sheet-draped body. There are at least four dead, Page told himself.

M-1 bullets had killed students Jeff Miller, Allison Krause and Bill Schroeder. Sandy Scheuer was alive when she fell to the Prentice Hall parking lot pavement. The single bullet severed her jugular vein. A futile attempt at mouth-to-mouth resuscitation was made. She bled to death.

The sight of bodies lying under those sheets startled the reporter. He knew they were dead students. Victims of bullets from National Guard rifles. He fought the urge to look away.

Page asked the doctor how many were being treated. The doctor confirmed four were dead and 11 more had various wounds, some quite serious. "Are there any Guardsmen among those being treated?" Page asked. "There is no one wearing a uniform," the doctor replied. "I can't tell you any more."

Page rushed away in search of a pay phone. "Thank God I remembered Englehart's command to never leave the office without a pocket full of dimes," he recounted later. He found a pay phone and shoved dimes in the slot. He got through to Englehart in the newsroom and told him what he had seen. The editor told him he thought additional victims might have been taken to other hospitals. To cover that possibility, he had assigned reporters to call every hospital in a 50-mile radius of Kent. This collective effort did not yield any names. But it was enough to convince Englehart there were no shooting victims at any other hospital. All had been rushed to Ravenna by ambulance or in the cars or trucks of friends or strangers.

Page could see that the initial story was being contained. He organized an inventory in his head. There were not "dozens" who had been shot. Nor "more than 50," he thought to himself. No

"Guardsmen down," as some news outlets were broadcasting, just students.

Englehart instructed Page to give him the number of the pay phone. "Hang up," the editor said. "I'll call you right back."

Englehart called. Page answered. He told Englehart the open line probably would be secure because the telephone was on a wall in an area where there did not seem to be many people. Englehart told him to let the receiver dangle from its cord so the line would stay open to the *Beacon Journal* newsroom. Page gently let the receiver go. It bounced like a yo-yo on its chord as it settled against the wall. He went off to gather more information.

An hour had passed. It was nearing 3 p.m. and Page knew the deadline for the final edition was near. He encountered a middle-aged couple looking visibly shaken and supporting one another as a hospital attendant led them down a corridor. He approached them and introduced himself. The man accepted his greeting and said he was Donald Wrentmore. Page asked if he had a son or daughter who had been shot? "Yes," replied Wrentmore. Their son, Doug, had been wounded and was now in surgery. "Could I interview him when he's able to talk?" There was no response from the couple. They continued on, hurrying toward a waiting room near the surgical suite, where their son's knee was being repaired.

Sensing a need to help Page at the hospital, an editor instructed Tim Smith, a city desk reporter, to drive to Ravenna. He was cautioned to avoid the main roads, where law enforcement officials had set up blockades. Just south of Kent, Smith encountered a group of men armed with shotguns. He described his mission and the urgency of getting to the hospital. If he couldn't get to his assignment at the hospital, he ran the risk of getting fired, he explained. He was allowed to move on.

At the final crossroads near Ravenna, he encountered a vigilante wielding a pitchfork. In his most respectful and deferential manner, Smith again explained he was going to the hospital in Ravenna, not the campus in Kent, and was permitted to pass.

By the time he reached the hospital to team up with Page, the main door had reopened and reporters from newspapers, wire services, and broadcast outlets were flooding in. They were clearly unfamiliar with Robinson Memorial. Their necks craned in search of bodies or someone who might have information. They noisily pressed into a conference room near the ER that had been designated as "press headquarters."

About 3:30 p.m., the local congressman, J. William Stanton, appeared and announced that he was acting as a spokesman for the hospital. He would be giving official updates. He announced that four students had been killed, two male and two female, and 11 others were being treated for a variety of injuries. That matched Page's toll. He and Smith discussed what they knew and how they might confirm the names.

Stanton, 46, was a Republican who had been the representative from Ohio's 11th District since 1965. His strong anti-Communist views were compatible with the conservative nature of the electorate that sent him to Congress. He said another update was scheduled for 6:30 p.m. Next of kin had to be notified first. That was a problem for the *Beacon Journal*; 6:30 was well after the final edition went to press. Editors were demanding identities. Page and Smith conferred on how they were going to get names of the victims by 4 p.m., in time for the last edition of May 4.

Smith noticed that Stanton was holding at his right side an 8½-by-11-inch sheet of paper with typewritten names on it.

Smith stepped in. He knew the congressman from the politics beat. He and Page decided Smith would distract Stanton with conversation while Page stood off to the side. The plan was to see if he could read the list of names. Page could ... and started at the top, copying names and hometowns of the victims.

At some point, they did a tag-team. Page picked up the conversation with the congressman and Smith copied names from the bottom up. They checked their lists periodically and kept occupying the talkative politician until they had all 15 names — four dead and 11 wounded, including two Guardsmen. The Guardsmen, it turned out, had been released after being treated.

It was nearly 4 p.m. when Page sprinted to the phone. The receiver still hung against the wall and the line was still open to the state desk. Page gave Englehart the names for the final edition. "Hot damn," the editor exclaimed. "Good work."

The press conference, scheduled for 6:30, was delayed until 7:15 p.m. Stanton now gave copies of the information sheet with the names of the victims to the mass of reporters crowded in the hastily arranged press center. By then, the *Beacon Journal*, through the enterprise of Bob Page and Tim Smith, was the first and only newspaper on May 4 to have reliably published the list of victims in its complete story of the killings on the Kent State campus.

The Wrentmores were brought into the press conference. They gave a brief report on their son. They told the reporters that Doug had been walking with his girlfriend across campus when the shots were fired, and he fell, in a tragic blink, with a bullet through his knee cap.

The press had been instructed that the Wrentmores had agreed to allow representatives of two news outlets — one print, one electronic — interview their son. The reporters sprang to their feet shouting, "Me! Me! Me!" Undeterred, the couple walked toward Page. "This man will get the first interview."

As Page sat at Doug Wrentmore's bedside, he was struck by how the young man appeared to be the proverbial "all-American boy" — handsome, clean-cut, respectful, studious, focused on his future. At such a moment of protest and dissent, when so many protesters wore headbands and bell-bottom jeans and spoke in language laced with profanity, this young man seemed to Page to be a credit to his family, his school and his country.

With pages of notes tucked carefully in his hand, Page left the hospital about 8:30 p.m. and headed back to the newsroom. He found a tired group of reporters and editors putting together stories for the Tuesday, May 5, editions of the *Beacon Journal*. Page went to his desk to begin writing his first-hand report.

Englehart had called Page's wife, Linda, to assure her Bob was safe but that he wouldn't be home until his piece was finished to the editor's satisfaction. It was well after midnight when the exhausted reporter got home. He was totally drained. His state of disbelief was layered with shock at having seen the human victims of a terrible tragedy. He had a hard time falling asleep that night. He kept recounting his steps through the day.

He knew he had made the correct decision to go through the ER doors while the guards were distracted by the scuffle in the parking lot. He continued to wonder what had happened there. An untold story, he guessed. Most unsettling was thinking about the covered bodies on the emergency room gurneys. Those memories lingered in his mind for many years. The Kent State story was now part of him.

Page's story in the Tuesday edition of the *Beacon Journal* described Doug Wrentmore, a sophomore majoring in psychology, as he lay in a bed in Room 107 at Robinson Memorial Hospital with a compound fracture of the right leg. Wrentmore said he was on the Commons as an observer who believed in protest but not violence.

"There were 500 people between me and the Guard," Wrentmore said. "I heard what sounded like fireworks and turned around and looked. Suddenly, I was on the ground. I ducked and crawled under a car and some kids helped me to safety and brought me" to the hospital.

The generational divide over the war prevailed at that moment of hurt and worry. As Page left Wrentmore's hospital room, his mother turned to Page and told him that she backed Nixon on Cambodia. Even her own son's wounded knee had not changed her mind.

CHAPTER ELEVEN

May 4: Reporting a National Tragedy

Immediately after the shootings, the students were in a daze. Their bold face-off with armed soldiers had unexpectedly turned bloody. Their young minds struggled to grasp the tragic scene. Bodies seemed everywhere on and near the Prentice Hall parking lot. The students felt vulnerable. Panic gripped them; there was an overwhelming sense of disbelief. They yelled at the Guardsmen. Shouts of protest mixed with frantic screams of horror and deep anger.

Controlled chaos prevailed among the Guardsmen. Some soldiers wandered uncertainly among the students. One Guardsman callously pushed the toe of his combat boot under a motionless body and flipped it over. A faculty member, watching the aimless and disorganized movements, recalled later that the Guardsmen looked "scared to death ... a bunch of summertime soldiers." Many of the Guardsmen went back, over Blanket Hill, to their bivouac area at the edge of the Commons. Officers were checking the M-1 rifles of the 28 soldiers believed to have fired their weapons.

The scene was punctuated by the wail of sirens. Emergency vehicles screamed on to the campus to carry off the dead and wounded. Some students linked arms and formed rings to protect the fallen. Fear and panic prevailed.

Students watched and wept in disbelief and bewilderment as the four dead and some of the injured survivors were gently lifted on stretchers and placed in ambulances. They struggled to make sense of the pandemonium that engulfed them.

Brig. Gen. Robert Canterbury, left, the National Guard commander, and Prof. Glenn Frank faced off as Frank begged Canterbury not to advance on students after the shootings. (Akron Beacon Journal)

A large group of students began to cluster on the other side of Blanket Hill, near Johnson Hall, on a grassy place overlooking the Commons. They sat down in protest, to show solidarity with the dead and injured.

Guard officers, seemingly not deterred by the killings, sharply commanded the students to disperse. It was clear that those who stayed or approached the Guard ran the risk of being shot at again.

Out of the utter chaos, a heroic moment of sanity followed. Glenn Frank, a geology professor, his voice straining with emotion, pleaded as tensions rose again and threatened more violence.

Frank was a husky figure, dressed as if he had just stepped out of a classroom. He wore a white shirt and dark suit. His striped tie was held tight to his shirt with a metal clip. He rushed into the midst of shattered young people and shouted out to the Guard commander, his voice carrying the firm tone of authority. Frank emotionally beseeched the commander to order his troops to stand down and the students to disperse.

Brig. Gen. Robert Canterbury, 55, commanded the National Guard force of more than 100 soldiers at Kent State. He had 23 years of military experience, which included several civil disturbances in Ohio. One of the critical photographs, taken at the instant the shots were fired, shows him at the rear of his military unit, wearing a dark suit and tie with a gas mask propped on his head. He knew now he could not tolerate another assembly of students spitting their anger. The general pushed near the professor. He was unmoved by Frank's plea. The general insisted his orders were to maintain law and order. The cost would be clear. He promised that his troops would fire again.

The students bunched together, unmoving, unmovable. Frank assessed the incendiary scene. Students cried. Others seethed with hatred. Fear, panic and anger held sway. The professor was terrified to realize that the volatile mood might erupt into more confrontation. The scene became even more tense as the Guardsmen fanned out and surrounded the densely packed student group.

Maj. Harry Jones of the National Guard approached the group. He sensed the crowd's volatile mood.

Frank shouted, "For God's sake, don't come any closer!"

Jones said, "My orders are to move ahead."

Frank replied, "Over my dead body."

Repeatedly, Frank pleaded for enough time to get the students to leave. Canterbury said, "You've got five minutes."

The crew-cut professor turned back to the students and shouted, "I'm begging you right now. If you don't disperse right now, they're going to move in, and there can only be a slaughter. Jesus Christ, I don't want to be part of this."

A large group of students (shown toward the top of this photo) gathered on the hill following the shootings. Troops were lined up again in front of the burned-out ROTC building. Geology professor Glenn Frank intervened, preventing more violence. (Akron Beacon Journal)

An eerie quiet descended on the group. They looked about for meaning and direction. Finally, Frank's warning began to take hold. Slowly, the students rose. They staggered forward and began their dispirited journey to a safer place. They struggled to realize the truth: dead, wounded. It was the reality of a future they could barely comprehend.

Roese was still on campus and shot an emotional image of Frank and Canterbury in an intense, face-to-face confrontation.

The newspaper's journalists were still making their way to the campus to begin the search for survivors to interview. But the awful facts of Kent State on May 4, 1970, were captured on film by photographers on the scene. An account of Frank's bravery in persuading the students to leave was vividly recalled in stories published later in the week and for months to come.

The scenes of death that Sallot had witnessed seared his emotions and left him with few clear recollections of the rest of that immortal Monday. In spite of this acute stress, he kept working. He interviewed a demonstrator before he left campus and wrote a story for Tuesday's *Beacon Journal*. It captured the emotion and fear that engulfed the campus as the Guard fired its weapons.

Ron Steele, an 18-year-old freshman from Buffalo, recounted for Sallot "the thought that kept pounding in my mind as I saw people falling all around me: 'My God! My God! They're killing us!'"

Steele acknowledged that he was one of the demonstrators who pelted the Guard with stones. "There was no reason for them to fire on students," he insisted. "That's murder."

With Sallot hanging on to the only open line to the Kent State campus, we recognized that communications to our staff could become a problem. Around 2:15 p.m., we got the idea to try for a telephone car, which phone companies owned and used for emergency situations. Ron Clark, the city editor, called Bill Giermann at Ohio Bell. He was able to locate a car. He cautioned that if communications got really bad, the phone company would need to take it back so it could be used by civilian authorities.

It was nearing 3:15 p.m. when Clark arrived in Kent. The faint acrid-smelling traces from the teargas grenades still hung over the campus. He had proper press credentials, so with no difficulty he drove through town, onto the campus and parked behind the administration building. That is where he set up the *Beacon Journal's* temporary city desk.

When he tried to activate the mobile phone to call Englehart, he quickly discovered that the mobile phones worked on a party line basis. At that hour on May 4, several parties were trying to place calls. When he finally got access to the line and dialed into the state desk, Englehart answered. Clark told him he was in place and ready for action. The two editors breathed collective sighs of relief. They excitedly exchanged information and ideas for what needed to be done. Clark pinpointed his location so that reporters could find him.

Contact with reporters on the campus was a challenge that "practically had to be made face-to-face," Clark told me. The city editor tried to stick fairly close to the phone car so he could hear if someone in Akron had been trying to reach him. Occasionally, he left the car and went to where he knew the reporters were.

There was an urgency to their work. Announcements were being blasted throughout the campus that the university had been ordered closed and evacuated. As the afternoon wore on and the campus cleared out, Clark found he was able to place calls without difficulty.

Several hands of authority were involved in the decision to close the campus, which added to the confusion and disruption.

Kent State President White had ordered the campus closed for the rest of the week. Portage County Prosecutor Ronald Kane wanted Kent State shut down indefinitely and attempted to telephone Rhodes of his intent to seek such an injunction. Rhodes delayed in responding, and Kane turned to Albert Caris, the Portage County Common Pleas Court judge. By late afternoon, Caris signed the injunction officially closing Kent State University until further notice.

For everyone, immediate practical concerns collided with escalating emotions and unanswered questions. Did the university have a plan to move thousands of students off campus in a few hours under the chaotic pressure driven by fear and a deep sense of loss? How do you shut down lab experiments? How do you cancel intramural games and varsity sports scheduled for that afternoon? What was to be done with the meals being prepared for evening dinner in food halls across the campus? What cohesive message about the future could be crafted for parents and students?

By 6 p.m., more than 12,000 students had been evacuated. Special buses transported students to every major city in Ohio. One caravan of 18 buses took 1,100 students to the suburban Shaker Rapid Transit terminal east of Cleveland.

With the campus rapidly emptying, it was a challenge for *Beacon Journal* reporters to find witnesses to interview. Many had already fled campus. Others came along clutching suitcases and duffle bags as they hustled to catch the waiting buses. Fear and disbelief were written on every face.

The afternoon of May 4 flowed into evening. My mind was a jumble of thoughts. And apprehensions. What did the moment demand, I asked myself? The pursuit of truth and information. To be sure. Journalistic leadership. Yes, of course. I looked across a newsroom of women and men staring intently at typewriters, talking loudly into telephones cradled against ears, scribbling editing marks on copy paper spread before them. I knew why but I wondered how. Would we be able to do this?

With the *Beacon Journal's* advantage of an early start on the story, we were able to report from many angles. Preparation paid off. And because we had such a deep institutional background from months of reporting on unrest at Kent State, our reporters knew the right people and the right questions to ask. I knew they could brave intimidation from officials seeking to spin the story to justify the Guard's actions and lay blame for the tragedy on the students.

Still, I wondered, was this band of earnest journalists up to the task? Would their passion for seeking the truth enable them to sort facts from false claims about causes and motives? Could they fulfill the mission of helping the public understand this terrible wrong? How could they withstand the impact of the emotionally divisive events — as people, neighbors, parents?

I recognized they had not begun to confront the burden of stress they would bear. Time and tempers, training and ambitions could all have an impact on our efforts that day and in the time that lay ahead. They were used to pulling work shifts that ran well beyond normal quitting time. But their daunting task was to explain the reality of a world that had suddenly changed forever, right before their eyes. That was the story to be told. Added to that was the quick understanding that this was a national — a global — story, with universal impact. And they were the journalists closest to it, with the most knowledge and expertise about it.

There was little time for reflection. The moment was defined by the demand for speed and the pursuit of elusive details to frame the story. Instinct, training and experience, or painful lack of it, drove us. We struggled to get our minds and emotions around a brutal truth: The freedom to speak against the Vietnam War had been shattered by the awful fact that soldiers as agents of the United States government had shot, killed and wounded college students exercising their constitutional rights of speech and assembly.

In newsrooms of the 1960s and 1970s, there was no such things as stress counseling. We were left to grieve in our own private ways. We were human, but in our newsroom at that moment we were, first of all, professional journalists. None of us could possibly have imagined such a stunning turn to the story of ongoing campus demonstrations, which we had faithfully tracked over weeks and months.

Our work, our values, our efforts were challenged from many directions. It was ugly and sad and stunning for each of us.

The work of journalism on the Kent State campus and in the *Beacon Journal* newsroom on the evening of May 4 would implant vivid memories in each of us. For many, it would be their singular journalistic experience, a defining time in our professional lives. For others, nearly 50 years later, it would be a subject too profoundly upsetting to discuss.

At the moment, with the May 4 editions out, our minds and energies shifted to the next day's newspaper. How do we tell the story in real time of a national tragedy about real people — a story that risked overwhelming us?

First, the logistics. Columns added to the Tuesday paper opened eight full pages for stories, commentary, pictures and sketches. We flooded the Kent State campus with reporters and photographers. The list of staff names would total 32 members of the *Beacon Journal* news staff who contributed to the paper's coverage on May 5.

I huddled with the editors in Akron to determine what stories would go on the front page and each of the pages inside the paper designated for Kent State coverage. We quickly realized that with so many reporters still scattered across the campus, we did not know the shape of the pieces that would emerge. Drawing lines now on the page dummies to indicate placement of stories would be futile that early. The task would wait, perhaps until midnight or later.

As darkness fell across the ghost-like campus and a curfew was being enforced in the city of Kent, our crew of journalists began to make their way back to the *Beacon Journal* building. Clark exchanged the seat in the portable news car for his chair at the city desk. He began to write the lede-all, the main story that would be spread across the top of Page 1 on May 5. He needed to write the story late Monday in order to make the very-early deadlines of the May 5 first edition. With his memory of the day's events still fresh, he plunged into the task before him. He knew how vital was his choice of words. He began his story this way:

> KENT – The war whose blood stained the rolling campus at Kent State University Monday is over, but the shock and reaction continue to spread across the nation.
>
> The war brought four student deaths — the first in the U.S. caused by campus anti-war rioting — and produced orders to investigate the four days of violence which led to Monday's tragic climax.
>
> The confrontation was the bloodiest of the student revolution spawned in the mid-1960s by the war in Vietnam. It was not the first time Kent State had seen violence.

Brief snapshots of the four dead students followed and then the story ran on for several columns describing how the Monday shooting had occurred and its aftermath.

The story was workmanlike, and its account of the May 4 tragedy contained the essential details. Still, it lacked the emotional kickers, the compelling descriptives that would bring this horrific event alive in the minds of our readers.

The May 5 edition carried the first of several exclusive stories that would become a hallmark of the *Beacon Journal's* Kent State coverage. The extensive detail in these stories was gathered, mostly, on deadline. They would be stories no other news organization had. They would bring alive the people and ideas, thoughts and emotions that were at the core of factual truth that would make our coverage commendable.

Reporters on the Kent State story found themselves juggling two themes: portraits of loss and sorrow and the journalistic quest for accountability. The so-called "soft" stories were exceedingly hard to report and write. Collecting the raw material for pieces that would define four young American lives, tragically ended — some would say murdered — fell to many of the young journalists on our staff. Most of them were not much older than the victims themselves. In death, the public would first meet Allison Krause, Jeff Miller, Bill Schroeder and Sandy Scheuer in the pages of the *Akron Beacon Journal.*

On the parallel track was the journalistic quest for accountability. This was a noisy crime story. How did this tragedy happen? Who was to blame? Who was responsible for ordering the killing of four innocent young men and women? Was there an order to fire? Was there a conspiracy that could be traced to the Guard leadership? *Beacon Journal* reporters would be out there, on the Kent State campus, in the city of Kent and wherever fresh links to the truth would take them.

They would be asking questions, looking for answers. They would be fact-checking claims. The *Beacon Journal's* grasp of the larger story would rest on the persistent probing by these journalists as they talked with people who might know something. Their deep knowledge of the story prepared them to ask the right questions. Their mission was to put things together. Make connections among people, explain their actions and the terrible acts that had just exploded on the Kent State campus. They sat through hearings and trials and sought to analyze the meaning of what they learned. The editors focused on our command of the story and the paper's commitment to balance and fairness. It was ours and we wanted it to remain so. The reporters brought understanding to the world with their exclusive reports of the bloody story as it unfolded.

Under the surface, the staff carried their private emotions about May 4, but as they went about their work, day after day, grasping for a better understanding of the story, they demonstrated a laser-like focus on the essential unanswered questions.

The editors led by Pat Englehart and me could see where the story was going. We could look ahead toward developments that might open new avenues to critical information and see where that might take our coverage. We were trying to steer an institution as ponderous as a daily newspaper. We were pushing it to be nimble enough to do what we wanted it to do. On Tuesday, May 5, within 24 hours of the eruption of National Guard rifles, we published a full account of the tragedy.

The first piece that revealed fresh, substantial information was placed at the bottom of Page 1. Herzog, 26, found a young guardsman who had been on the firing line. Herzog was a Peace Corps veteran who wore a full dark beard that was rare in our newsroom at the time. His colleagues admired his warmth and capacity for building friendships.

Herzog had waded into a scene of screaming, yelling pandemonium. Soldiers were milling around as officers moved among them, collecting rifles that had been fired. Each Guardsman who had discharged his weapon now stood in fear that fatal bullets would be recovered and matched to his rifle.

We were amazed at Herzog's ability to make a timely and sensible connection with a soldier who could be persuaded, in that tense moment, to talk to a reporter. The soldier shielded his name badge on the front of his uniform, but he began to tell his story. He told Herzog he did not fire at the demonstrators because "I really didn't feel my life was in danger."

Herzog pressed on, asking the Guardsman what he remembered. What did the soldiers say to one another? Did they discuss when they would or would not pull the trigger?

"You don't really talk about that sort of thing in specifics. You react if your life is threatened. There is a lot of disgust among the troops that Rhodes sent us in. It wasn't necessary. It was a waste of time, effort and, as it turned out, lives."

The Guardsman said that after the shooting, the troops went back to the company area near the burned-out ROTC building and "the men who fired were interviewed" by military authorities.

By 6 p.m. on May 4, five hours after the shootings, the Ohio National Guard had begun its effort to shape a version of events putting its officers and armed troops in the best light. How could those 13 seconds be explained and justified?

Canterbury held a news conference on the edge of the Commons. Robert Batz covered it for the *Beacon Journal*. In his story he described the general as speaking slowly and choosing his words carefully as he read from a prepared statement.

Canterbury said the Guardsmen were not ordered to fire on the students but added, "A military man always has the right to fire if he feels his life is in danger."

Asked whether he thought the lives of his troops were being threatened by the demonstrators, the general replied, "Conditions on the hill were extremely violent. I feel they were in danger."

Batz's story explained that Canterbury's prepared statement focused on the events that occurred on the campus before Guardsmen fired at students.

Canterbury concluded his statement with an apology. "We deeply regret that people were shot. We deeply regret that a confrontation took place that provided the potential for violence such as occurred here today."

The general told the journalists that, "A single shot was fired, closely followed by several other shots, these by Guardsmen."

The general was asked if the shot was fired by a student or a Guardsman. "I do not know who fired that (single) shot," he replied.

Canterbury said that shortly before the shooting, he had thought that the crowd had been dispelled. "I gave the order to return to the Commons."

Batz ended his story with Canterbury's claim that "many" of the Guardsmen were injured by stones but acknowledged that "the injuries were minor."

Helen Carringer, 46, had covered education for the *Beacon Journal* since 1966. She was a soft-spoken person widely regarded as an authority on Akron public schools and the two large universities we covered, Kent State and the University of Akron. There was a business-like elegance to her manner. Even as she pursued information about Kent State, she marched through the administration buildings wearing high heels, skirt, blouse and jacket. Over the years on the education beat, Carringer could often be seen huddling with Bob Stopher, the editorial page editor, to discuss issues related to higher education.

On the afternoon of May 4, Carringer stepped up to apply her thorough and careful interviewing skills in a series of phone calls to Akron area parents of Kent State students. She had phone books and her own list of contacts, which she worked for several hours, reaching some 25 parents of Kent State students. Across the board, she encountered similar reactions: sadness, anger, fear and frustration. It was apparent that the deadly actions of the Guardsmen had not changed minds about the duty of the soldiers or the course of the war.

"It isn't right," one parent told her. "I can understand the kids' reaction to the war in Vietnam and Cambodia, but this isn't the way to correct anything."

Others were more vehement in their responses to Helen's calls. The opinions reflected the wide arc of public opinion. She wrote that some wanted the radicals to be thrown out of the university

Reprinted with permission of *The Akron Beacon Journal*

Sketch by Akron Beacon Journal *artist Chuck Ayers shows National Guardsmen standing ready on the campus near the site of the ROTC building, which had burned to the ground Saturday night. Six illustrations that Ayers drew from memory on the afternoon of May 4 can be found in the Addendum.*

and never be allowed into any other institution. These reactions were similar to town/gown attitudes the newspaper had encountered over many months: a state university with a liberal-minded faculty and student body nestled in a conservative-leaning small town. We routinely heard from residents who were sympathetic to the war and offended by the opposition to it on the nearby campus.

Kathy Lilly had another story to tell. Lilly, 23, whose recent work at the paper had revealed an emerging gift for storytelling, described the emotional peril of students hastily departing the campus. She found groups of students gripped by the horror of watching the shooting as they experienced the closeness of the terrible dynamics of violence. A high school student provided an eyewitness account to Lilly, describing how her hands dripped in blood after helping one of the wounded find an ambulance.

"As I ran by, the Guardsmen were smiling," another student said. "One of them pointed a gun at me. 'Why don't you shoot me, too?' I yelled. I told one he was sick, and he wiped the smile off his face," she said.

A bearded Kent State freshman offered a philosophical view: "The best way in the world to radicalize people is to lob pepper gas at them. It was a ridiculous attempt at crowd control."

He blamed Rhodes' visit to the campus on Sunday for touching off more trouble. "This law-and-order bit was purely a political move by Rhodes. I'm almost certain this touched off further trouble."

Chuck Ayers, 22, was a gentle bear of a young man who worked part-time as an artist for the *Beacon Journal*. He was often on campus taking courses to complete his studies as a senior art student at the university.

He was on the campus at noon on May 4 watching the gathering of protesters at the Victory Bell. From his perch along the edges of the Commons, he aimed his camera to capture images he planned to use for a photography class he was taking during the spring semester.

His eye took in the National Guard troops using tear gas and bayonets to drive the protesters from the Commons. He watched the standoff at the football practice field. As the Guard began to move away from the fence and back up Blanket Hill, Chuck thought the confrontation was over. As he neared Taylor Hall, he unexpectedly came upon a dozen Guardsmen facing off with a group of students. A friend in the knot of protesters recognized him and shouted, "Hey, Ayers! What the hell are you doing in there?"

The Guardsmen swung around and pointed their M-1 rifles at Ayers. He wasn't immediately frightened, he said later, but realized he had chosen a deadly location between the Guard and the demonstrators. He rushed inside Taylor Hall just as the Guardsmen turned and fired at the demonstrators.

In 2000, Ayers wrote an account of his experience for the *Beacon Journal's* special news section marking the 30th anniversary of the tragedy. "The first thing I saw when I went back outside was the body of Jeff Miller on the ground, a river of blood flowing from his head." Twenty yards away, "I saw Allison Krause being carried on a stretcher to a waiting ambulance."

Ayers drove to the *Beacon Journal* where reporters and editors interviewed him about what he had seen. Later, an editor asked him to do some eyewitness sketches for the paper. "I remember minute details of most of what I did and saw for about five days around May 4, but much of those five or six hours at the newspaper as I sketched are a blur."

Six of Ayers' illustrations re-creating the turmoil were spread across the front of the local news section on Tuesday, May 5. He completed the drawings within hours of the shooting. His images came from his memory; he had not yet seen any of the scenes captured by the famous photographs that came to define the tragedy.

Ayers drew soldiers standing ready near the burned-out ROTC building, a view of Guardsmen firing teargas grenades, students throwing rocks at the soldiers, students tending to a student who had been shot, Ohio Highway Patrolmen arriving after the shooting and faculty pleading with students to disperse.

Art Krummel was a hybrid in the *Beacon Journal* newsroom. He was an artist for the paper and a sergeant in the 145th Infantry of the Ohio National Guard on duty at Kent State in May 1970. On Saturday, May 2, he had been assigned to guard two roadblocks to keep all traffic out of downtown Kent. He had joined the Guard in 1964 to stay out of the Vietnam War but found that his unit was frequently called to duty for racial disturbances. Just the week before, it was activated to help deal with the Teamsters strike.

On the Kent State campus, Krummel, 26, discovered that Guard members and many students were there for the same reason:

a desire to avoid military service in Vietnam. On Monday, May 4, Art drew an assignment that kept him off campus. He was in charge of a squad sent to protect the sewage treatment plant in case students would attempt to disable it.

It took years for Krummel to talk openly about the Kent State shootings and activities that weekend. Thirty years afterward, in a piece for the *Beacon Journal*, he wrote, "I can't find a way to justify shooting into a group of innocent, unarmed students. But I also know that there were times that weekend when I felt my life or the lives of my friends were in danger."

Ray Redmond was the last *Beacon Journal* reporter on the near-empty campus as darkness fell, bringing with it "an eerie, spooky quiet in this college town of 35,000." Before returning to Akron, Redmond walked through downtown Kent, noting that "riot guns poked out from storefronts on usually bustling Main Street."

Platoons of Ohio Highway Patrolmen, campus police and sheriff's deputies joined the Guardsmen, who were still wearing their olive-drab combat fatigues. The armed law officers were charged with enforcing the dusk-to-dawn curfew. A patrolman cautioned Redmond, "Don't move around town tonight. They will probably shoot anything that moves."

On the editorial page for the May 5 edition, Jim Jackson, associate editorial page editor, wrote a hard-edged opinion addressing the question everyone was asking: Why did it happen?

Jackson's progressive views were often reflected in his editorials for the *Beacon Journal*, including opposition to the Vietnam War. His commentary about the May 4 tragedy, however, was read by many as disapproving of the disruptive actions of the Kent State protesters.

He admitted to a hesitation "to make categorical judgments," but urged the "most searching investigation" to answer a basic question, "Was the shooting justifiable?"

Jackson acknowledged that student protests against the war were nationally widespread on college campuses over the weekend. "But, why did the protesters at Kent choose to dramatize their discontent by going on a window-smashing rampage in the downtown business district? How could a N. Water St. shopkeeper be held responsible for the move into Cambodia?"

Jackson wondered how "twisted minds" could make the ROTC building a logical target for arson, unless "it were a symbol of war."

His editorial also referred to rumors and allegations heard often in the community from supporters of America's presence in Vietnam: "Was the violence at Kent planned or encouraged by career revolutionaries from other cities, perhaps other states?"

What happened at Kent, Jackson observed, was not a spontaneous demonstration of pacific sentiments but a planned confrontation with violence as its goal.

He concluded with thoughts more centered on the victims. "Planned or unplanned, the confrontation has taken a toll which is terrible beyond description or measure: Four young students dead ... other students and Guardsmen injured ... the university community divided ... public opinion inflamed.

"Stunned by all this, we come back to another question, the fundamental question.

"Why did it happen?"

As I reflected on my role as managing editor on May 4 and what misjudgments I may have made, I found myself focusing on a mini tempest that arose over the main news story on Page 1. A number of the reporters in the field had contributed details for the lead story, but the only byline was that of city editor Ron Clark. I didn't recognize it at that moment, but I soon came to understand that authorizing a lone byline was poor judgment on my part. We needed a better device to identify the many reporters who had made essential contributions to the story.

When the world's telephone link to Kent State failed and Pat Englehart had resourcefully found the phone car, Clark was the only senior editor available to send to the campus to direct our coverage. Upon his return to the newsroom at dusk on May 4, he seemed to be the natural choice to write an authoritative lead story for Page 1. I failed to anticipate that the single byline would lead some on the staff to perceive that the city editor was trying to muscle in on the Kent State story. This was not Clark's fault. He was told to write the main story. I had to get this straight.

Clark, 26, was new in his job and had not been involved in the continuing coverage of Kent State through the spring. He was a gentle man, still learning the supervisory skills demanded of a city editor. This was a baptism of fire for him. Oftentimes, he tried to cover his managerial inexperience by putting on a stern face. He struggled to grasp the nuances of team building. A reporter who worked for him on the city desk recalled that when he turned in a story, Clark wouldn't read it. Rather, he would roll a fresh sheet of copy paper in his typewriter and start rewriting it. "It was not an endearing quality," the reporter remembered.

Questions grew and became the basis for chatter in the newsroom about what Clark's role would be going forward. I saw this as a personal challenge to my authority. Maidenburg had transferred a charge to me in his absence. His words echoed in my head, "You are in charge. Don't screw it up." I knew I had to quell the undercurrent about the byline.

To clear the air and keep control of the coverage where it belonged, Al Fitzpatrick, the news editor, and I called a brief meeting in my office that evening. There wasn't room for everyone to sit. We stood there — Englehart, Fitzpatrick, assistant state editors Harry Liggett and John Olesky, and me.

I laid out a plan: Englehart would be in charge of Kent State coverage. Liggett and Olesky would run the day-to-day operation of the state desk. I reminded them that we still had school boards and town councils to cover. Liggett and Olesky would handle that. Liggett asked about Clark, noting that his name was on the big story of that day, May 5. "Ron will continue to run the city desk," I replied. "I just want to be very clear. This story will be with us for a long time, and I don't want any confusion about roles and responsibilities. I want to make certain that those in the field and those on the desk get equal credit for their contributions. Pat is in charge. He will make decisions on how we cover this and who does the reporting. Al and I will contribute ideas. Hell, everyone is welcome to make suggestions for our coverage." With so much critical news gathering ahead of us, knowing that Englehart would be in charge was reassuring to the staff. The mini tempest over a byline and its innate challenge quickly faded.

Liggett was solid, the right choice to lead the state desk. Englehart trusted him. Liggett cared about details. He was determined, if a bit gruff, and a fine journalist. Liggett himself would often check the facts in a story he was editing. He was soft-spoken but firm in giving woe to the young reporter who was careless with facts. He stood for the mandate of truth every bit as much as Englehart did.

Liggett and Olesky were two of the unsung heroes of that time. They, and others, made critical decisions needed to get the paper out every day. Englehart would drive the exceptional story in our midst. Liggett and Olesky would maintain the normal pace of the daily newsroom grind. They never let go of the expectation that the coverage would be complete and fair. They got little of the attention that fell to those who shared in the prizes and the praise for the Kent State story.

As the weeks rolled on, we all knew we couldn't have been successful without them.

CHAPTER TWELVE
The Bullet Hole

As the sound of Ohio National Guard rifles erupted on May 4, a single M-1 bullet spiraled through a metal sculpture a few feet from Taylor Hall. A rust-colored cloud floated to the green grass below. The bullet burrowed into a nearby tree, a northern red oak, knocking off a chunk of bark.

The hole in the sculpture quickly became a source of high interest, fueling emotions and renewed convictions in what became known as the "sniper theory."

The theory was simple: A sniper was among the protesters and fired at the soldiers. Imagined sightings of someone firing from the roof of a classroom building or a dormitory fed the theory. Those who subscribed to the theory were only too willing to accept this notion. Allegations that there was an armed killer among the protesters served only to heighten divisions of opinion that were taking hold in the larger community about who was to blame.

To the untrained eye, the shape of the bullet hole — about the size of a penny — affirmed the sniper theory. Metal from the hole splayed in the direction of the Guardsmen as they fired their rifles. The smaller, smoother edge was on the other side of the sculpture, away from the soldiers. This seemed to clinch the sniper argument: a smooth hole where the bullet entered and ragged edges where it exited on its way toward the soldiers.

Canterbury, the Guard commander, was not willing to say there was definitely a sniper present, but Adj. Gen. Sylvester Del Corso

Beacon Journal *photos of the test shots demonstrated that a bullet hole in a metal sculpture near the shooting scene was not fired by a sniper.*

showed no hesitation. He insisted that a sniper had endangered the Guardsmen.

Del Corso was not at the scene on May 4, but he had a firm opinion. Speaking from his office in Columbus, he told reporters, "A sniper opened fire against the Guardsmen from a nearby rooftop."

In *The Report of The President's Commission on Campus Unrest*, the assertion that Guardsmen were responding to a sniper shooting was attributed to both Canterbury and Del Corso.

On the afternoon of May 4, Mickey Porter, a local columnist for the *Beacon Journal*, interviewed Terry Norman, a Kent State junior and freelance photographer. He told Porter that when he packed his camera bag to go to the campus that morning, he took along his .38 caliber pistol.

Porter, in his story, described Norman's experience:

"He heard what he thought was a shot from the roof of Taylor Hall … Guardsman opened fire into the students, while others fired warning shots over their heads and into car windows in a nearby parking lot…. He saw four students killed and when he stooped to aid a stricken youth, he was surrounded by others who raged, 'Get the pig, get the pig,' thinking Norman was a police photographer.

"Norman pulled out his pistol, waved it and scared them off, then ran into the arms of National Guardsmen. He surrendered his revolver. The gun was immediately examined by a campus policeman, who found that it had not been fired." The photograph that ran with Porter's story shows a policeman taking Norman's gun from him.

Norman remained a controversial figure. He was thought by some to be an undercover FBI agent. Porter, in his story published in the *Beacon Journal* on May 5, 1970, was the only reporter to interview him.

The sniper theory was fueled by National Guard officials and those who wanted to fault the students for causing the shooting. It was sustained by such rumors as contained in a front-page story in the Ravenna *Record-Courier* reporting a search "for a female sniper who is said to have started the shooting at Kent."

The aftermath of May 4 roiled public opinion and comment. Many spoke with certainty about where the blame lay: *This was the result of outsiders. They should have killed more of them.*

Kathy Lilly's daily routine on the *Beacon Journal* state desk started at 7 a.m. She would spend the morning in the time-honored tradition of writing obits. One of the hardest parts of the job, she recalls, was calling the families of young men killed in Vietnam to get the stories of their lives. Honoring lives well-lived into late

The metal sculpture, created of steel plates by artist Don Drumm, was placed on the Kent State campus near the journalism school in 1967. (Akron Beacon Journal)

adulthood was one thing. Writing about deaths in her own generation was difficult.

Lilly described the newspaper's reporting on the Kent State story as "fair, accurate and measured, a real feat considering how high the emotions were on every side. The paper's reporting was testament to the kind of journalism we young reporters were learning on the state desk."

"Not surprising was the the way, on that very first day, we quoted officials saying they were looking for a sniper. We did not report that there was a sniper. The reporting was straightforward, never hysterical."

Englehart was behind this kind of meticulous work. He was a stickler for facts, for getting it right. He insisted that reporters carry a measuring tape. You didn't guess that a fatal collision occurred 20 feet from the intersection; you measured it. This was emblematic of his approach to gathering the facts.

The mystery of the hole in the campus sculpture continued to nag at him. He wanted the paper to do some detective work. He and Lilly talked about how to do that and how the story Lilly would write might shed light on the sniper theory. "Let's test it," he said finally. "Let's find a piece of metal and shoot a bullet through it." Now certain that this would be a path to the truth about the bullet hole, he wanted to move quickly.

The sculpture was the creation of Don Drumm, 35, an artist with degrees from Kent State who was then artist-in-residence at Bowling Green State University. The sculpture stood 15 feet high and was built of half-inch plates of Cor-Ten steel set oddly at different angles. The steel was chosen because its surfaces weathered into a rust-like patina that eliminated the need for painting. It was called Solar Totem #1 and placed on the Kent State campus near Taylor Hall in 1967. From that perspective, it presented a stark silhouette at the top of Blanket Hill.

Drumm thought it would stand for the ages as a tribute to the sun and its place in life. The idea, he said, was that the "sun would shine through this" and as it changes in its movement across the

Over the years, the bullet hole has become a place for expressions of protest and a yearning for peace.
(Akron Beacon Journal)

sky, "different shadows would be thrown from one plate to the other."

Englehart was intensely focused on the sculpture and took charge of organizing the ballistics test. He found someone with an M-1 rifle and .30 caliber ammunition identical to that used by the National Guard. He also scouted out a farmer's field in Suffield Township, near his home in Mogadore, where the test would be done. "This was where Pat lived and where he knew everyone and everything," Lilly remembers.

Englehart also worked with Drumm to find a piece of Cor-Ten steel that matched that of the sculpture.

She interviewed Drumm about preparations for the test, and about the sculpture and his work. He told her the sculpture was created through National Defense Education Act funds. He drew on the labor of 25 industrial arts teachers from 20 states who aided in the welding.

Lilly was careful to point out that her role was passive; to watch as an observer, not as a participant, in the newspaper's test. After her interview with Drumm and the man who would bring the gun and ammunition, and then fire it at the steel plate, Lilly believed she would be able to report the facts of the test dispassionately and with confidence.

Lilly watched the bullet being fired. She saw that the metal splayed out from where the bullet had entered the steel plate, rather than from the exit. The metal splayed back toward the Guard position, showing that it had been fired from the general direction of the soldier's firing position, not from the opposite direction. The hole on the side of the sculpture facing away from the Guardsmen was round and smooth.

Lilly was accustomed to writing stories under Englehart's intense gaze. "He would lean over me as I typed, one foot up on my desk, a gentle dust of cigar ash floating my way. 'Goddammit, Kath, is that the way you want the lede?' 'No,' I would say. And we would talk about the point of the story and the best way to get it across. Gruff? Yes. But most of all, he was inspiring. He cared so much about good reporting. So did his reporters. He made us into a great team."

Englehart did not tell Lilly how to write the bullet-and-sculpture story. He trusted that she could craft the story without his close supervision. The piece was restrained. It described the test, but did not boast about the reality that the *Beacon Journal's* enterprise was responsible for a breakthrough in solving the sniper theory. That was not the newspaper's style.

The story explained that the test "did not show that the shot was fired by a Guardsman, but only that it was fired in the same general direction the Guardsmen had fired when four KSU students were killed and nine wounded last Monday. There had been speculation the hole gave proof that a sniper had fired at the Guardsmen."

The story captured Drumm's feelings. "That bullet hole is a fingerprint of time. It is a powerful reminder of a great tragedy. I don't want anyone to touch that bullet hole. It is a record of a tragic time and to me is a symbol of peace."

Through the years, the bullet hole has become a statement of its own. People are drawn to it because it is a remaining physical confirmation that bullets were fired at students, that freedom of speech and freedom of assembly could be challenged with guns, with live ammunition.

The rest of the evidence has disappeared into the annals of time, replaced by memorial markers and memories. But the hole is real. You can look through it. You can rub you finger around the smooth exit point or feel the frayed metal where the bullet tore through. On certain sunny days, at certain hours, a tiny beam of sunlight will show. Messages around the hole written in chalk are common. Peace signs, or expressions yearning for a better world, are abundant. Feelings still run high during the annual campus commemorations of the tragedy, as visitors and survivors cluster around the sculpture.

Lilly's story ran on Page 10 in the Sunday *Beacon Journal*, May 10. It carried no byline. In the 1970s, bylines were not automatically placed atop every story, unlike today, when the story template comes up on computers with the byline already in place. An editor decided whether the story merited a byline. Lilly recalls, "Part of the thinking was that the paper was involved in this news and that always made us somewhat uncomfortable. There was a desire for omniscience in this particular story" about the bullet hole and the question of a sniper. "Maybe we didn't understand how important it was as we were working on it. It wasn't even on Page 1. Basically, I think it was supposed to represent reporting by the paper, not a particular person."

In days and weeks following, the claim of a sniper faded from the public conversation. The question of who fired the first shot and whether there was a command to fire remain unanswered a half-century afterward. The Ohio Highway Patrol investigated the shooting and found no evidence to support conclusively the presence of sniper fire or shooting from the crowd. In his testimony before *The President's Commission on Campus Unrest*, Del Corso backed away from his strong original statement on May 4 that Guardsmen were responding to a sniper shooting. "We never identified a sniper as such, as defined in the military."

The Guard advances up the Commons in a cloud of smoke from teargas grenades. This image indicates that the Guard was not being pressed by the demonstrators. (Kent State University News Service)

CHAPTER THIRTEEN

Images

Truth links the hard realities connecting news photographs and violence. During the Vietnam War, shooters embedded with combat troops produced photographic evidence of war's violence. Some of those images are iconic, eternally fixed in our memories of what happened on the battlefield and the home front. Truth shaped these visual testimonials. Images that spoke terrible truths occupied a nation's attention and, eventually, influenced the war's end.

Photo images of Vietnam's atrocities haunted the nation's conscience as early as 1963. A photograph by Malcolm Browne of The Associated Press documented the death of a Buddhist monk after he lit himself afire to protest persecution. In 1968, AP's Eddie Adams captured the actual instant a bullet fired by the South Vietnamese national police chief from a few inches away impacted the head of a Viet Cong suspect.

Ron Haeberle was a U.S. Army photographer assigned to Charlie Company, a unit of the 23rd "American" Infantry Division. In March 1968, Charlie Company came upon the grizzly and ominous remains of dead Vietnamese citizens scattered along a ditch. This was the atrocious discovery of the My Lai Massacre. The starkness of the atrocity was revealed in words by Seymour Hersh, a freelance journalist. He broke the shocking story that 504 Vietnamese had been murdered by American soldiers. The Pentagon tried to cover up the horrid massacre, but Hersh's dogged investigation and stubborn persistence won out.

Both *Life* and *Look* magazines reviewed the story and turned it down. Initially, so did major U.S. newspapers. Hersh eventually found a willing publisher in Dispatch News Service (DNS), a news agency founded only the year before. The story finally was published in 30 newspapers in November 1969. Haeberle's shocking photograph of the murdered villagers was first published on the front page of *The Plain Dealer* on Nov. 20, 1969. Together, Hersh's story and Haeberle's photo fueled public outrage over the evidence that Americans at war were capable of such atrocities.

The intensity of these images captured the brutality of war. They offered no illusions. Only the reality of death. In the 1960s and into the 1970s, stark black-and-white photographs linked violence and war. Images of dead soldiers were becoming commonplace. TV footage of dead and wounded men and women from both sides flickered at Americans gathered to watch the evening news.

It was unexpectedly jolting to see pictures of students shot dead at Kent State. In the American mind, portraits of death in far-away jungles were now seen as one with murder on an American college campus. No official effort at coverup or statements of unsupportable rationales could undo the shock of visual truth.

Fifty years on, we have a truthful and iconic portrait of the Kent State story. On May 4, 1970, four young cameramen captured images that helped show America what did, and did not, happen on that day.

John Filo and John Darnell were seniors at Kent State, both 21, just about done being college kids but still living under the shadow of the military draft. Howard Ruffner was a veteran. At 24, he was older, but only a second-year student at Kent State who had served four years in the U.S. Air Force where he learned photography. Each of the three was still trying to figure the connection between journalism and photography, and whether either had a place in their young lives. Filo and Darnell were in the journalism school. Ruffner was a major in broadcast communications.

The veteran professional cameraman on campus that day was Don Roese, 33. He had been on the *Beacon Journal's* photo staff for 13 years. Roese's assignment on May 4 was to photograph the scheduled noon rally. He arrived on campus well before noon. His sense of the impending drama was strong. As the confrontation between soldiers and protesters began to hotly evolve, he snapped a panoramic shot from the top of the Commons near Taylor Hall. It showed several hundred students watching and taunting the line of more than 100 approaching Guardsmen.

Then Roese moved behind the Guardsmen and followed their skirmish line as it pushed the students scrambling up the Commons toward the Victory Bell. As he trailed the action, he was just out of position when the shots were fired. Thirteen critical seconds. A thunderous barrage. Bodies fell. Others ducked or ran. Roese stayed with the story. He snapped a scene from the Taylor Hall veranda seconds after the shooting began as students scattered for cover.

In the chaos that followed, Roese found the office in Taylor Hall with the *Beacon Journal's* open telephone line. His voice was filled with anguish as he told Englehart what he had seen. The editor caught the anxiety in his voice and assured him that his was an important eyewitness account that would help the *Beacon Journal* get to press quickly with an accurate description of events for the paper's final afternoon edition. The photographer knew he had an important story to tell. As he finished, the sounds outside were frightening. He grew cautious and said he didn't want to be quoted. Englehart agreed to identify him as an "anonymous newspaperman."

After he ended his phone call, Roese dashed for his car and rushed back to the *Beacon Journal* photo department to develop his film. Roese had an ironic mentality. Normally cheerful and given to wisecracks, he was shaken by what he had seen. The unbelievable shock of his witness seared his memory and conscious. To this day, he is reluctant to talk about his experience on May 4.

The editors examined the individual frames of his negatives, arguing over which best captured the story of a confrontation exploding into tragic reality. Their choice was a dynamic image of National Guard troops advancing up the gentle slope of the Commons past the Victory Bell and toward Taylor Hall. Clouds of teargas framed the scene and conveyed an unmistakable truth that trouble was at hand. Violence and tragedy were just over the hill.

Roese's photo was published six columns wide. It dominated Page 1 on Tuesday, May 5, under Clark's lead story and the headline, "KSU Shock, Reaction Roll Across Nation."

Roese's image established this truth: The National Guard advance up the Commons did not encounter mass resistance from students and spectators. The heavy use of teargas seemed excessive against unprotected protesters with no way to fend off the stinging impact of the gas clouds. In his photograph, the skirmish line of soldiers appeared to be succeeding in carrying out its orders to force the students to clear the Commons, the site of the planned rally.

Filo had spent a couple of days before May 4 more than 200 miles away in the forests of central Pennsylvania wrapping up his senior photographic portfolio. He carried with him a large format camera to shoot extreme closeups of tiny flora, such as moss and teaberries. The finished project was due before graduation.

The weather was well into spring as he drove his VW Beetle back to Kent State on Sunday evening, May 3. Trees framing Taylor Hall showed early leaf buds. As he arrived on campus, he found a relaxed atmosphere of students playing Frisbee with National Guardsmen. But then he began to pick up unsettling stories of the weekend's unrest. He had a hard time digesting Nixon's rhetoric of expanding the war to shorten it. He was distraught, and his anguished thought was this: What if this was the biggest story of his life and he missed it?

On Monday morning, May 4, Filo reported to the journalism school photo lab in Taylor Hall. He was in charge of mixing chemicals and handing out cameras. He discovered that while he was away, many of his classmates had hustled assignments to shoot additional protests with major publications such as *Life* and *Newsweek*. He was the one without a gig, even though he felt he had the most experience from working summers on a small newspaper in western Pennsylvania. He felt disgruntled as he began his job of distributing cameras to student photographers ready to strike out to record the action.

As midday approached, Filo realized there was only one camera body left, a Nikon. He borrowed a 43-86mm zoom lens from fellow photo student Ruffner, attached it to the camera and stuffed six rolls of Tri-X film in his right front pocket.

It was close to noon, when his lunch hour would begin. He rushed from Taylor Hall and headed out to the anti-war rally. He found the field packed with about 3,000 demonstrators and spectators. Guardsmen were firing teargas grenades from canisters in an effort to spoil the gathering. His first image was of the Guard, spread single file across the Commons, advancing toward the students. He later characterized the expressions on the students' faces as one of, "They're chasing us now. Let's get out of here."

Filo followed a Guard unit down Blanket Hill toward a fence surrounding a practice athletic field. He instinctively watched the action, observing that the soldiers appeared to be confused and unsure what to do and where to turn. Some stood in groups, appearing mystified at how they had made the strategic mistake of allowing themselves to be trapped against a fence.

A single student, Alan Canfora, walked alone onto the field, about 50 yards from the soldiers. He carried a black flag and boldly stood waving it. Eight soldiers came away from the fence, knelt and held their M-1 rifles in a firing position pointed at Canfora. It was a show of intimidation at the young man taunting them with his black flag. At that moment, he was a rebel student, the symbol of resistance. The soldiers did not pull their triggers. But the threat to do so heightened the sense of anger among the protesters.

Filo snapped the shutter. He said later that "I was very happy with myself. I was able to see this picture, to be in position, to have the right lens and compose this photograph of student protest in America against an overwhelming armed force. It was a picture I would call a 'keeper.'" Filo's photo added another important per-

John Filo believes his image of Alan Canfora waving a black flag at crouching Guardsmen "was the best picture I had ever taken." (John Filo)

spective to the visual documentation of the unfolding tragedy. In his frame, Canfora stood by himself on the field. No other students can be seen. No rock throwers are visible.

The image memorialized that terrifying moment. The photo also undercut the insistence of Guard officers that the protesters pressed close and threatened the lives of the soldiers. The photograph serves as another truthful statement that the guardsmen's lives were not in danger. Other photographers were there and shot the same scene. Filo had maneuvered himself into a position with a clear view. He clicked the shutter. His masterful eye caught the best angle of the daring taunt and the flag at its apex.

During a talk at Kent State in 2009, Filo said he thought his picture of Canfora "was the picture I was seeking to symbolize student protest in America. It was the best picture I had ever taken."

The single image of a determined student standing alone in the field with his flag spoke of courage in the face of threatened violence. It would become one of several photographs on May 4 that served to destroy the official lie that students had to die and suffer because an anti-war mob had threatened the Guardsmen's lives. There were students arrayed behind Canfora and his flag, Filo recalled, "but not that many."

Filo tracked the Guard unit as it regrouped and retreated back up Blanket Hill toward the Pagoda. He and others thought the Guard had completed its mission to break up the rally and were moving informally back to their company headquarters near the ashes of the ROTC building. Unexpectedly, the soldiers took firing positions next to the Pagoda. Squinting through the camera view finder, Filo saw the sidewalk, a tree, the metal sculpture in front of the journalism building — and a Guardsman pointing his rifle.

"Oh, OK," Filo thought, "you shoot at me, I'll shoot a picture of you."

As he was about to press the shutter to capture the Guardsman's pose, the image of the gun filling Filo's viewfinder exploded. A rust-colored puff floated from the metal sculpture nearby. A chunk of bark came flying off a tree just a few feet away. The air was suddenly full of noise, and pandemonium seemed to be everywhere. He knew the Guard was shooting live ammunition.

A split second later, Filo staggered and turned. Everyone seemed to be on the ground, but the body of Jeff Miller "was convulsing its last. The amount of blood on the street was like someone tipped over a bucket. It was that much and that quick."

Filo's first frame after the shooting was of Miller lying alone in the street. Filo said he overcame his instinct to flee and said to himself, "I have to stop. I have to get this picture."

As the 61-shot volley from National Guard rifles erupted, Mary Ann Vecchio, a 14-year-old runaway from Florida, was standing near the entrance to the Prentice Hall parking lot. She saw Miller fall, blood pouring from the fatal wound in his mouth.

As Filo moved toward Miller, Vecchio came onto the scene. She ran to his side. She knelt on one knee and raised her arms in shocked disbelief. The fingers of her right hand were stretched as if beseeching for help. Her mouth opened in a scream that we can still hear.

Over the years, as Filo thought of her reaction, he reasoned that because she was young, she reacted that way. She was trying to help, to do something. If she had been older, perhaps she might have just looked at the body. When the teenager realized there was nothing she could do, her frustration drove her to scream.

Filo ran down the hill toward her kneeling pose. He squinted through the eyepiece of his Nikon camera. Instinctively, he pressed the shutter and captured that horrific instant for all time. It was pure anguish, the moment the Vietnam War came home to America.

The frame he snapped became the iconic photograph that spoke the truth of the Kent State tragedy. People describing the image today typically raise their arms in reflective horror as an expression of witness to a war brought home to a college campus on a warm spring day.

Another frame shows a woman leaning over Miller's body, touching him. Filo learned later that she was an art teacher who explained she kept touching Miller because "she just wanted him to know he didn't die alone."

In the public mind, the body of Jeff Miller with life bleeding out of him and the frantic teenager are linked forever as a single, symbolic visual statement of a national tragedy. It evokes overwhelming emotion, an indelible and enduring image of horror, death and helplessness. It speaks to us with a powerful message about the tragic truth of Kent State. It reminds us that on May 4, 1970, the Kent State campus became a battlefield and a place of death. American soldiers shot and killed American college students.

Like Filo, Darnell had spent the weekend before May 4 away

from the Kent State campus, but for a different reason. His father owned *The Boardman News,* a weekly newspaper in a residential community just outside Youngstown, nearly 45 miles east of the Kent State campus. He had grown up with his dad's newspaper, covering local sports since he was young. As a Kent State student, Darnell's routine was to go home every other weekend to write stories for the paper.

When he returned to his campus flat on Sunday evening, May 3, he learned that the university was under martial law and students were not allowed to be out at night. Darnell decided he was more than a student. He remembered that he had taken a press pass from his father's newspaper office and brought it back to school. It was a simple task to alter the identification on the press card to read, "Student photographer, *Boardman News.*"

On Monday morning, Darnell found CBS correspondent Ike Pappas, who had a film crew with him. It was the only television network present at Kent State on May 4. When Darnell learned that Pappas had permission to follow the Guard, he joined the news crew. He was carrying a Nicca-33 camera that was 15 years old at the time.

Darnell was standing behind one of the columns at the front of Taylor Hall when the Guardsmen turned and began to fire. His iconic picture — showing a side view of the Guardsmen, guns erupting — was taken "one or two seconds after the firing began."

In an interview, he told a *Beacon Journal* reporter that "I was about 5 feet from the railing when they turned and started to fire. I did not see a man raise a stick over his head as if to give an order, and I did not hear any sniper."

Darnell took three pictures. He said he stopped shooting film when they stopped firing.

Frozen in time was his third exposure. Three dozen Guardsmen in combat gear, wearing gas masks. Some clustered under the Pagoda, the rest behind it. In front was a sergeant crouched in a firing position, his extended left arm pointing a pistol. Behind him, soldiers aimed rifles straight ahead. Others pointed their weapons at the sky. Still a few others held their rifles in front diagonally near their chests, as if obeying a command of "Parade Rest." These were not organized, trained firing positions. It was a picture of random confusion pending death and chaos. At the rear of the unit was their commander, Canterbury, dressed as a civilian in business suit and tie, gas mask propped on his head, hand raised in an apparent effort to order a cease-fire.

Darnell's initial fear of being shot turned to anxiety. Would the Guard confiscate his film? He rewound two rolls, which he was sure held good images. He stuffed the rolls in his pants and put a fresh roll in his camera. As he feared, a Guardsman approached and demanded his camera. He reached out and thrust it at the soldier. He watched as he opened the camera and pulled out the film inside. He said later that "in my underwear were the two good rolls."

Darnell rushed back to *The Boardman News* to develop the film. He called two prominent magazines, *Life* and *Look. Life* made the better offer. It was one of the photographs *Life* ran as part of a seven-page spread the magazine published in its May 15, 1970, issue.

Darnell's photo conveyed another important truth about May 4 at Kent State. His image framed the determined but disorganized stances of the National Guard soldiers as they fired their weapons. The photo was spread over two full pages in *Life*. The image stretches from the corner of Taylor Hall on the right to a point at least 10 feet in front of where the sergeant pointed his .45 caliber pistol. No single student can be seen in this scene from Darnell's camera. His photo, and others, confirm that the Guardsmen were not being closely pressed by the demonstrators in any way that might endanger their lives.

Meanwhile, Ruffner, who worked for the *Chestnut Burr,* the student yearbook, had been all around the campus taking pictures as the action played out that weekend. The campus was a human pressure cooker building steam, a place where protesters and soldiers alike sought outlets for their frustrations. He had made a photographic record of students burying the Constitution during the

John Darnell captured the instant when the killing shots were fired.
Gen. Canterbury can be seen at the rear of the Guard
unit, wearing a business suit with a gas mask on his head.
(John Darnell)

Friday afternoon rally. He captured the ruckus in downtown Kent that night. He shot scenes of the ROTC building as it burned Saturday evening. He recorded the arrival of the National Guard and, on Sunday, he tracked the governor, James Rhodes, as he made his vicious verbal attack on the demonstrators.

On Monday morning, the Chicago bureau of *Life* magazine called the office of the *Kent Stater* requesting a photographer to shoot the rally scheduled for noon. Ruffner was their man. He knew it was an important assignment. He thought it was a big deal. He didn't want to mess it up. As he started walking toward the Commons, he was carrying two cameras, one with a 200mm lens, the other with a 105mm lens. He was comforted that he had Guard-issued credentials that enabled him to go anywhere on campus.

Moments after the shooting, Ruffner and Darnell came upon a wounded student lying on the grass being tended to by others. The victim was John Cleary, who was only 37 yards from the firing line when the bullet struck him in the upper left chest. He had been standing near the sculpture, an innocent bystander trying to take a picture with his Polaroid camera.

Ruffner and Darnell each captured a dramatic image of that scene. They showed how Cleary lay, head back, mouth open, on a sloping patch of grass close to the Taylor Hall veranda. Ruffner had the better angle and a tighter composition of the three students administering aid as they bent over the wounded young man. His photograph was on the cover of the May 15 issue of *Life*. The magazine paid him $2,000.

Ruffner's photo is part of the visual record of what happened when the Vietnam War came home to America. The fallen Cleary reminded us of scenes from battlefields far away. It was striking in its horrific similarity to the countless photographs of wounded American soldiers that the public saw in their newspapers and on TV.

The five photographs — two by Filo, one each by Roese, Darnell and Ruffner — left Americans with few illusions. Only reality. Imprecise interpretations didn't fit. The camera did not lie. Critics of the protesters' message found no comfort in the facts that these images established. Many found it challenging to study the images and still maintain core convictions that National Guardsmen were justified in shooting students.

The three young photographers — Filo, Darnell and Ruffner — received high journalism honors for their pictures. Each received the George Polk Memorial Award, and Filo also won the Pulitzer Prize. Filo said later he "felt cocky for about two days." Then he received a letter from another Pulitzer Prize-winning photogra-

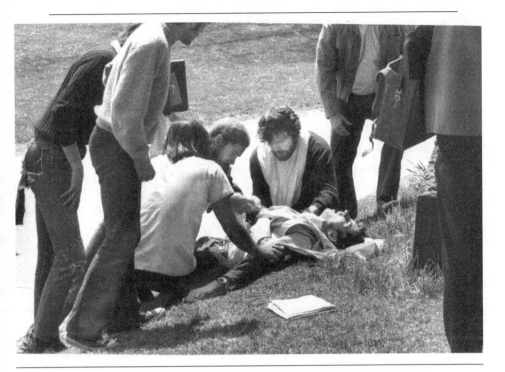

Howard Ruffner's photo of wounded student John Cleary, being tended to by fellow students, was published on the cover of Life magazine. (Howard Ruffner)

pher, Eddie Adams. Under an AP Newsfeatures letterhead, dated May 6, 1971, it read: "Dear John. You have my deepest congratulations. Hold your head up high. Now, let's see what you can do tomorrow. Sincerely, Eddie Adams."

Over the next few days, I developed an unsettling sense about the *Beacon Journal*'s photo coverage. The photo staff produced some good images. But the truth was, we had been beaten by three college students. Over and over, I asked myself why we didn't have more photographers at Kent State on May 4? The answer was always the same: Who knew that this was going to happen?

Others explained to me a reality about the demands of getting great photographs in the midst of such violence. Anticipating where the action will occur is part luck, part planning, part talent. Memorable scenes come and go in the flick of an eye or the click of a camera shutter. Judgment and opportunity at the same instant are essential.

Most unsettling to me was a back story involving Filo. After the shootings, he quickly decided to jump into his Volkswagen and take his rolls of film to the *News Valley Dispatch,* the newspaper in his hometown of New Kensington, Penn., rather than to the *Beacon Journal* with its newsroom just a few miles from the Kent State campus. The explanation for his decision staggered me.

In a routine practice established years ago, photo-journalism students at Kent State would bring their rolls of film from classroom assignments to the *Beacon Journal* photo lab. There, *Beacon Journal* photographers would develop the negatives and store them. When students needed to print the negatives to meet deadlines for class projects, student photographers would get them out of cold storage in our photo lab, print the pictures and return them to the newspaper's negatives archives.

Early in 1970, just weeks before May 4, Filo had come to the *Beacon Journal* photo lab to retrieve negatives to print for a class project. The negatives could not be found. He was upset and thought this was a costly act of carelessness by the newspaper. That mistake shaped his decision, in a fraught moment on the Kent State campus, that he could not entrust his precious rolls of film to the *Akron Beacon Journal.* He pointed his VW Beetle homeward.

As he drove off campus, he said he saw National Guardsmen on telephone poles locking down phone cables. "I couldn't figure out what was going on." He pushed his car toward the Pennsylvania line at 45 mph. It took two hours and 20 minutes to cover the 110 miles to the familiarity of the photo lab at the *Valley News.*

Filo quickly developed the frame with the Mary Ann Vecchio picture, but then the challenge was to find a 10-minute window when he could upload the photo to The Associated Press's photo-wire service. That was the time required to scan a photo with

The image of Jeff Miller as his life bled away and the frantic teenager are linked forever in John Filo's photo as a single, symbolic visual statement of a national tragedy. (John Filo)

1970 analog technology and move it to AP's headquarters in New York. The AP photo editor was puzzled by the request from the *Valley News* to send a picture from the Kent State shootings. "The *Beacon Journal* has all the pictures," the AP said. Soon, however, the AP sent a message that a picture on the *Beacon Journal*'s scanner had jammed and the Filo picture could move on the photo wire in its place.

As the drum on the AP scanner completed its slow revolutions, the end of the transmission was greeted with unexpected silence. Filo wondered if he had screwed up. Finally, the technician in New York who was running the photo network that day broke in and said, "Wow, kid, that's a great picture. Do you have any more?"

When I learned for the first time about a year later of how our photo staff had misplaced the Filo negatives, my anger boiled over. It was a moment to raise hell with Julius Greenfield, the newspaper's longtime photo editor. A small, wiry, talkative man, Greenie stood speechless as I snapped, "Your carelessness and disrespect for the work of students cost this newspaper a great photograph."

CHAPTER FOURTEEN

Probing the Governor's Misdeeds

On Wednesday, May 6, 1970 — just two days after the campus shootings — the results of Ohio's primary election dominated the front page of the *Akron Beacon Journal*. The coverage reflected layers of tension and uncertainty across the state. A major story was the outcome of the race for the Republican nomination for the U.S. Senate: Rep. Bob Taft Jr. had narrowly defeated Gov. James A. Rhodes.

It was a moment of truth for the governor. He had turned to vicious attacks on student protesters in the final days of campaigning. It was a gamble. Taft was a well-regarded congressman from a family with established credentials in the Ohio political firmament. It was Rhodes' language that alarmed commentators. They wondered whether his aggressive, inflammatory remarks during a press conference soon after he arrived at Kent State on May 3 made a difference in the close race. Rhodes had called the protesters "worse than the brownshirts and the communist element, and also the night-riders and vigilantes."

Joe Rice, the *Beacon Journal's* political writer, reported that Taft had a small margin — slightly more than 3,000 votes out of more than 930,000 cast by Republican primary voters. Many people felt that the governor's remarks worsened an already tense situation. Some, including many Kent State students, believed the governor was hoping to tip the balance with his overly zealous promise to use the state's authority to shut down "the radicals." Would his

Ohio Gov. James Rhodes, right, attended a luncheon in Columbus, Ohio, for the Ohio Billion Dollar Club on May 4 ... the same day as the shootings. Rhodes received death threats that day. (The Associated Press)

words and actions give him additional angry conservative votes to win the primary election?

The late returns and close finish between the two candidates left Rice with little opportunity to apply his political writer's skills to an analysis of the meaning of Rhodes' role at the university, his impact on the eventual shootings, and the possible influence on Ohio's primary voters.

At the bottom of Page 1 on May 6 was a story by metropolitan editor John DeGroot. It shed additional light on Rhodes' behavior at Kent State. DeGroot, 32, was a bear of a man, a Hemingway-type character. He had a snarky sense of humor that was often accompanied by a boisterous laugh. He was fond of wearing cowboy boots, jeans and dark aviator sunglasses. He was widely admired in the newsroom for the erudition he brought to his writing and his ability to brighten his copy with well-turned phrases. His writing gave life to events and people.

DeGroot's piece revealed a critical fact about an action the governor refused to take that could have spared lives and pain. Rhodes, in a secret Sunday morning meeting with local officials, had blocked a move to close the university. DeGroot wrote that he had learned of the meeting from Kane, the prosecutor, who told of meeting the governor and two of his aides in the Kent city building.

The editors thought DeGroot's piece was a breakthrough in identifying the governor's stubborn behavior and influence in setting the stage for Monday's tragic killings. We put a copyright tag under his byline, obligating other news organizations that quoted from the story to acknowledge the *Beacon Journal* as the source.

DeGroot described how Kane, 34, explained to Rhodes that he wanted to close the campus "then and there" and would get a court order to do so. The governor vehemently disagreed. It became a standoff between the young prosecutor and the hard-headed governor. DeGroot captured Rhodes' reasoning: "A court order would be playing into the hands of the SDS and the Weathermen," two radical groups.

Two law enforcement officials present at the meeting — Del Corso and Col. Robert Chiaramonte, superintendent of the Ohio Highway Patrol — were unsure and imprecise in their memory of any call by Kane for closing Kent State. When pressed for details, Del Corso shrugged and said, "Well, ask the governor."

Kane insisted he told Rhodes, "As far as I was concerned, we were sitting on a keg of dynamite that could blow any moment. I wanted those kids out of town."

Monday afternoon, after the shooting, Kane made another plea to the governor to authorize closing the campus. Rhodes, calculating the political consequences he now faced, dallied. Kane, fearful that fresh eruptions awaited if the campus remained open, was done with waiting. Instead, he turned to Judge Caris, who promptly issued the order.

The prosecutor told DeGroot, "I'm just sorry that we didn't

go ahead last Sunday and send that court order. Those four kids would be alive today." And the ones that were "wounded would be safe at home." It would have been an inconvenience for thousands in the university community, but no one would have died or suffered from bullet wounds.

On Thursday, May 7, the paper noted the anger expressed by Kane at the governor's unexpected decision to order National Guard troops to leave the Kent State campus. They would be out by noon Friday, May 8. Kane wanted the troops to remain through the weekend. "The situation is still a potentially eruptive and explosive one," he said.

The *Beacon Journal* continued its aggressive digging for details of Rhodes' puzzling actions at Kent State. In the paper's May 8 edition, Lacy McCrary, 36, chief of the newspaper's statehouse bureau in Columbus, wrote about the strong reaction to DeGroot's piece from John McElroy, the governor's chief assistant. McElroy firmly denied that Rhodes turned down a recommendation on May 3 from Kane to close the university. As the interview went on, McElroy's wrath cooled a bit. He acknowledged that he really didn't know, conceding to McCrary that Kane was "in a position to have a better recollection" than he (McElroy) about the decision to shut down Kent State.

McElroy told McCrary that the governor felt the prosecutor was moving too quickly and too broadly on Monday afternoon with his injunction. "Rhodes wanted him to wait an hour to think things through and come up with another proposal, something that would do a little less violence to the ordinary way of doing things." Kane knew what the violence had wrought. For him, enough was enough.

McElroy said the governor believed that if the university were to be closed, the decision should be made by KSU officials and not the county prosecutor. He described Kane as being "a little hotheaded about it." He labeled Kane as "the real pusher up there. We just felt he needed to be slowed down a little. We didn't think there should have been a czar up there running things."

Abe Zaidan had a special love for politics. He had joined the *Beacon Journal* in 1968, along with his sidekick, Dave Hess. Earlier, Zaidan had edited *The Commentator*, a liberal public affairs magazine in Columbus that was celebrated for its civil rights coverage in the 1960s. Zaidan, 38, was self-assured. He evoked confidence in his grasp of Ohio and national politics. He was known for his crisp, authoritative commentary. Many of his pieces were published by *The Washington Post*, for whom he worked as its Ohio correspondent. Hess, an intense man whose talent won him a spot representing the *Beacon Journal* in the Knight Washington bureau, once wrote of Zaidan, "Hardly any of the state's biggest political fish have eluded his net or dodged the sting of his barbed gaff."

Zaidan wore dark-rimmed glasses and smoked a pipe. His Pittsburgh Pirates were a team on the rise in 1970, and he loved to talk about Roberto Clemente and Willie Stargell. On a typical afternoon, he could be found in the newsroom, leaning back in his chair, one hand on the back of his head, the other cradling a telephone receiver as he gabbed with someone from his deep reservoir of political sources. Politicians rarely refused to take a call from Abe.

On Saturday, May 2, Zaidan had been in Cleveland to report on the debate between Rhodes and Taft. It had been televised on WAKR-TV in Akron. By Zaidan's observation, it was Taft's most aggressive showing. The tenor of the joint appearance on the eve of the primary underscored the reality that tempers were rising.

After the primary results narrowly gave the GOP nomination to Taft, Zaidan set out to evaluate Rhodes' political future. He could not run again for governor, having served two terms. As he worked his sources, Zaidan came upon a new angle about Rhodes' actions at Kent State: Soon after the governor's arrival on the campus Sunday morning, Rhodes had assumed control of the confusing situation. As he did so, he began issuing orders, Zaidan learned, without consulting National Guard or university officials.

Zaidan's unidentified source was in the National Guard. He told Zaidan that one of the orders Rhodes gave was to the Guardsmen. They were to break up all campus assemblies — peaceful or otherwise. He pledged that they would remain on the campus 12 months a year, if it were necessary, to shut down the conflict and restore order.

"Our mission," the Guard source claimed, "was to protect lives and property, and not to spend our time chasing kids. But Sunday's meeting was the governor's show. There were no objections by anyone there, no discussion — it wouldn't have done any good. The governor had made up his mind."

Zaidan's source laid bare the extent of Rhodes' anger and intemperate instruction. The truth of that revelation was that it had set the Guard on its mission the next day, wearing combat gear and toting weapons — locked and loaded — that would result in a tragic bloodbath.

In the coming days, Zaidan had more to report on the governor. Taking note of his primary election loss to Taft, Zaidan posed the obvious question: Where does Rhodes go from here? He noted that Rhodes' failure to make a public appearance after his loss was an indication that he was not taking lightly the election day rebuff by his fellow Republicans.

In a separate piece that also ran on Thursday, May 7, Zaidan drew from McElroy the revelation that Kent State had persuaded Rhodes to "think a long time before sending in" state law enforcement including the National Guard. Especially, McElroy added, when "the campus community is not interested in supporting order."

During his nine years as a *Beacon Journal* reporter, McCrary was rarely seen without a broad smile across his face. He was a reliable ally of truth and fairness. His assignment for the Sunday newspaper, May 10, was to track the governor and give him a chance to respond to our exclusive stories earlier in the week.

The truth that McCrary reported in his Sunday column was short and to the point: The governor had gone underground. He had proved to be "invisible."

McCrary's widely read commentary was called "View from

Columbus." He began by recalling that, "For several weeks before last Tuesday's primary election, Governor Rhodes called a press conference almost every other day. The obvious assumption was that he was eager to talk to newsmen .... Then came Monday's tragic shootings at Kent State University. And the next day came the election in which Rhodes was defeated for the GOP nomination for U.S. Senate by Rep. Robert Taft Jr."

McCrary observed that "almost no one has seen or heard from James Allen Rhodes since those two events. The governor has been 'in the weed patch' and totally unavailable to any newsmen." McCrary said he had seen him for five seconds Thursday afternoon, May 7, as he left the executive suite at the statehouse followed by plainclothes Ohio Highway Patrolmen. The damage had been done.

"It is hard to tell if the governor is avoiding reporters because he doesn't want to answer questions about Kent State or about his election defeat.

"The real issue," McCrary wrote, "is the governor's refusal to face the press, and thereby the public of Ohio, to give at least his account" of the Kent State trouble.

During the difficult days before and after May 4, the *Beacon Journal* had published a series of fact-filled observations about Rhodes. Three reporters disclosed comments and actions that tarnished the reputation of the popular two-term governor.

It began the day before May 4 in a hot-headed diatribe against student protesters followed by his impulsive decision to grab control of the university without consulting law enforcement authorities or university officials. That was followed by ignoring a reasonable request to close the campus, both before the shooting and afterward. Finally, he ducked reporters looking for explanations for his actions. Our reporting had revealed the governor's willingness to overlook issues and ignore risks. He was driven by an overwhelming desire to win a primary election and played dramatically to his base of conservative voters. He knew they had little patience for protests against the Vietnam War. He was counting on the power of his anti-protest pronouncements as voters filled in their ballots on Tuesday, May 5.

It was a bet Rhodes lost. At a moment of high public emotion, his actions initiated a series of unintended consequences. *Beacon Journal* reporters Zaidan, DeGroot and McCrary skillfully connected the dots. They gave readers insights into the governor's influential, if irresponsible, behavior and held him to account for actions he wanted quickly to deny.

CHAPTER FIFTEEN

President White Speaks Out

At 2 p.m. on Friday afternoon, May 8, Robert I. White walked to a speaker's podium in the University Auditorium in Cartwright Hall. He turned to face the faculty at a spot less than 1,200 feet from Monday's killing field.

It was an awkward moment for the 61-year-old educator who, seven years earlier, had risen to become Kent State president after a long tenure in the School of Education. White didn't plan to dwell on the May 4 tragedy. The murder of four students was a searing memory. He needed to focus, instead, on steps to reopen the campus and to address his fear that the future of Kent State was in doubt.

Reporter Jeff Sallot thought of White as "a favorite uncle and a bit old school." He was a soft-spoken man with a shock of dark hair showing gray at the temples who was rarely seen in anything other than a business suit and tie. He is remembered by some as Kent State's "last teacher president."

White was well-liked for his laissez-faire style, but that low-key nature may have enabled others to grab control of his university when the lethal chaos and confusion of May 4 loomed.

There was a mystery about his absence as the weekend began to unfold. It was not generally known that late on Friday afternoon White had flown to Iowa for the weekend.

It was a long-planned trip for a brief reunion with his sister and

Kent State president Robert White was a central figure in the tragedy even though he was not on campus until Sunday morning, May 3. (Kent State University News Service)

then a Sunday meeting of the American College Testing Program in Mason City.

Earlier Friday, he had received reports of two peaceful rallies at Kent State. One summarized the student gathering on the Commons to bury a copy of the U.S. Constitution. It was a statement of contempt for Nixon's televised announcement the night before to send troops to Cambodia. The other reported on an assembly of United Black Students to discuss campus protests.

Satisfied that the campus situation was calm, White left town.

During his absence, the president's authority fell victim to a series of decisions that wrested control of the university from the school's administration into the hands of the ambitious Rhodes and the leadership of the Ohio National Guard. The governor was a wily, calculating figure bent on turning his presence at Kent State to political advantage given that the Ohio primary election was just days away.

No one contacted White in Iowa to inform him of the dramatic shifts in the dynamics at the university. The Guard's Saturday-night arrival on the Kent State campus was a surprise.

The university president and the governor had a brief meeting at the airport around noon Sunday; it was a moment when Rhodes was preparing to board his helicopter to return to Columbus and White was arriving back from Iowa.

White learned that control of the campus had been ceded to the National Guard whose troops were poised to carry out Rhodes' mandate to "ban all assemblies, peaceful or otherwise." The brief exchange seemed to confuse rather than clear up lines of authority. White would later testify that he and other university administrators felt "out of the loop" as a showdown over Monday's planned noon rally approached.

Carringer and colleague Sallot were on hand Friday afternoon, May 8, to cover White's remarks for the *Beacon Journal*. Their story described White as he mounted the speaker's platform. He looked every bit a man who had been through hell and had not yet found an exit.

More than 1,000 faculty members rose as one and gave their president a long, standing ovation. They knew he had not been responsible for a series of questionable decisions leading to the murderous gunfire aimed at students. He was not to be blamed. They wanted to share their appreciation for his presence and the evenhanded, rational leadership he represented and for which he had stood for nearly a decade.

His audience also was aware of the deeply expressive statement that was circulated under his name on May 4:

> Everyone without exception is horror struck at the tragedy of the last few hours. Unfortunately, no one is able to say with certainty what the facts of the situation are. There are many unconfirmed reports of gunfire from various sources. We are asking for every possible appropriate investigation which we shall undertake to pursue to the limit. We have closed the university to permit investigation and to provide for the full restitution of the university's program. We need the cooperation of all, especially including the presentation of factual information by anyone who possesses it.

The president had taken additional actions. Few in his audience were aware of his telegram to the parents of the dead students shortly after the shootings:

> THE THOUGHTS OF MRS. WHITE AND I ARE WITH YOU IN YOUR TERRIBLE LOSS. AS PARENTS, WE ARE FILLED WITH HORROR AND SHOCK. WE PRAY FOR SUPPORT TO YOU IN THIS HOUR.

After the long applause faded and the faculty sat once again in the old auditorium, White acknowledged the display of support. "That's the first nice thing in many, many days — and a sign of loyalty to Kent State University."

His remarks were informal. He explained that he was speaking from a series of scribbled notes because there had been no time to prepare a written statement. He began by reaffirming that the campus would remain closed under the injunction because of the "threat of renewed violence."

The president was emphatic that a guarantee of safety was a key condition for opening the campus to its faculty and students. The emergency closure was proving to be expensive to science labs, food storage, employee wages and graduation plans, in addition to its interruption of final exams and the informal ending to the school year.

He lamented the diminished protection when the National Guard troops began to leave the campus. About half of the Guardsmen left on Wednesday, May 6. Another group departed on Thursday, and the final unit on Friday, May 8.

White said: "Everyone who has been asked to study the situation and look at it has advised that it would be unsafe to bring the students back. There are guns. There is the danger of fire. There are publications which have advocated the killing of certain people.

"And there is no one who can say to a parent, 'We can give reasonable assurance for the safety or convenience of your son or daughter.'"

White described the Monday shootings as "moments of shock and horror I never want to live through again. Since then, preservation of the university has been our first goal and it still remains that. We are up against it."

He spoke of an appearance on a national television program where he told his interviewer that what concerned him most about the future of the university was the welfare of the faculty. He said he feared that talented teachers he had worked hard to recruit would be vulnerable to hiring by other universities.

The mood in the large room was somber. The pace of his talk was slow and measured, his tone flat. He did not summon any emotional accents in speaking of the shootings or mourning the dead students. It was a talk about the logistics of reopening the campus and saving the university.

As he moved toward his conclusion, White raised the prospect of a separate investigation of the shootings by the university. "We need our own internal investigation agency. This is a broad assignment," he said, directing the meaning to the faculty. "We must watch other investigations and evaluate them to see if they were adequate or not. And if things were not moving as we think they should, we might wish to undertake whatever investigation we could, recognizing the limitation of not having subpoena power."

The faculty meeting lasted 90 minutes and, as it concluded, White said, "There is a haunting realization that the very existence of the university may be in jeopardy." On that sober note, he ended to more extended applause, and then the faculty filed out of the auditorium.

Since May 4, White had shared his feelings in other forms. In a statement mailed to Kent State parents on May 7, he wrote:

"Dear K.S.U. Parents:

"Nowhere in the world is the shock of the Kent State campus tragedy more fully felt and more deeply regretted than within our university community. Evidence of the horrors of the violence and disorder are clearly visible."

He described the university as "calm" but added, "Before reopening, however, we must and will provide assurances for the safety of those within our charge. We seek normalcy and ask your assistance in reaching that goal."

A few days later, he sent a telegram to President Nixon renewing a plea "for a high-level investigating commission to delve into K.S.U. events to clarify evidence, furnish perspective and do so in a way fully credible publicly."

On May 5, the National Guard gave White permission to hold a press conference on campus where he and Rep. J. William Stanton, whose district included Kent, announced a joint request for a White House investigation. White suggested that he was hoping for something like the Warren Commission that investigated the assassination of President Kennedy in 1963.

As he began talking, White was interrupted by Ben Silver of CBS News who asked him to "hold off for about 30 seconds while

I reload film." It took 18 seconds and then White resumed with his commitment to press Nixon for "the most thorough possible, the highest possible level of an investigation."

He turned next to the reopening of the university and laid out two conditions. "Obviously, there must be assurance of normalcy and safety. A second one, and Gen. Canterbury and I are in agreement on this, we should not attempt to reopen with the National Guard in command of the campus."

A reporter asked White, "Do you think bringing the National Guard troops on to the campus is the proper response to student-inflicted property damage, such as the burning of the ROTC building?"

Noting that he was out of town when the Guard was requested by Kent city officials, the president said, "I am just afraid that had I been here and seen what was happening, I, too, might have requested the National Guard. And I think had you been here you might have."

White supported Kane's expression of regret at the exodus of the Ohio National Guard from campus. The *Beacon Journal* reported that about 400 of the troops departed on Wednesday, May 6, and the rest would be gone by Friday.

Powerful questions to be answered and troubling issues to be addressed were high on White's agenda:

What led to the fatal shootings? How many non-students were imported to the Kent campus? How many guns were held by students during the disturbances? Was there any organized planning in the disturbances?

The president declared that the campus would not be reopened while the National Guard remained in command.

The *Beacon Journal* also reported these major developments:

> A group of university faculty blamed Adj. Gen. Sylvester Del Corso and Gov. Rhodes for the deaths.

> The American Civil Liberties Union demanded Del Corso's resignation and offered free legal services to the families of the victims.

The militant Weathermen passed out leaflets announcing, "The time is right for fighting in the streets."

On June 3, 1970, the university announced plans for commencement, a ceremony White said would be held "in spite of some risk." His caution led the administration to scuttle its original plan for graduation to be held in the new Kent State football stadium.

Carringer arrived early on Saturday, June 13, to secure a seat in the Memorial Gymnasium where 1,250 graduates would be awarded degrees in the university's 57th annual spring commencement. It marked the first opening of the campus since May 4.

Elaborate preparations had been made for maintaining order. The university had 100 campus policemen on duty and had mapped out areas where security was tight.

The gymnasium was filled to its capacity of more than 7,000. Graduates sat in folding metal chairs on the floor. Friends and families were in the bleachers surrounding the basketball court.

The *Beacon Journal* noted on Sunday, June 14, the "exemplary behavior" exhibited "by men and women who listened courteously and alertly to their speakers. The things that should happen at a graduation did happen. Proud parents, husbands and wives snapped pictures of the capped and gowned students and some who chose not to wear traditional gowns. Only one peace symbol appeared on the sea of mortar boards."

Carringer anxiously awaited the beginning of the academic procession at 10:30 a.m. In her hand she held a copy of White's prepared remarks. It had been made available to her on Friday, which allowed her to write her story for Saturday's first edition. As White began his address, she checked his spoken words against those on the prepared text. She planned to phone in any major deviations to be inserted in her story for later editions.

She wrote that the May 4 tragedy "pervaded his remarks for the closing ceremony of the year and the commencement of a new era at the university."

White addressed the class as "unique in American collegiate

history. As a graduating class, you have shared an experience which no other graduating class has had in American history."

He acknowledged that the "terrible memories and scars of the tragedy will rest with the university for a long time."

The president's remarks struck a theme of reconciliation, warning against judging the "millions of distressed college students who hold lofty goals and impeccable integrity" by actions of an "infinitely smaller number of committed burners or out-and-out destroyers."

During the commencement ceremonies, a telephone on the dais rang. It was the White House calling to tell White that Nixon had appointed a blue-ribbon commission to investigate the Kent State disorders and campus unrest generally across the country. The commission would be led by former Pennsylvania Governor William Scranton.

Carringer's commencement story in the Sunday *Beacon Journal* described White's press conference after graduation in which he said the White House announcement "came at a fortuitous time." It offers the possibility of "outlining for Congress and legislatures the complexity of the problems." He added that the report of the president's commission "could deal with the extent of enforcement desirable and necessary to prevent or control such outbreaks of disorder."

Turning to the graduation ceremonies, White expressed pleasure that it was peaceful, a "rewarding conclusion" to a tumultuous time. As a result, White said he saw hope that Caris would soon lift the injunction that had been in place for five weeks. He even ventured an expectation that the judge would release the university from exile by week's end.

The *Beacon Journal's* extensive coverage in the Sunday paper included a first-person reflection by Sallot, the reporter who was now a Kent State graduate. He had witnessed the "bloody moments" seeing classmates, dead and wounded, "bleeding on green grass" near Taylor Hall.

He wrote, "We had all lived through a tragedy, but the fact that we were once again together on our campus with our professors, even for just a few hours, renewed us and gave us strength." As the graduates prepared to march into Memorial Gymnasium, Sallot thought that "the mood was one of joy, as if some terrible weight had been lifted from our shoulders."

White's wish to free the campus came true sooner than he anticipated. Monday morning, June 15, Caris lifted the injunction. The *Beacon Journal's* story explained that students, faculty members and administrators "are required to carry valid identification cards and visitors are permitted on campus only with special passes." Special security measures that had been imposed by university trustees would remain in effect. Even with restrictions, there was a sense of forward movement.

On Monday evening, White was interviewed on a Youngstown television station where he expressed "a little dismay" at the indication from Scranton that the panel would not "try to find out who is guilty at Kent State University." White said the panel's mission was to look into the general underlying causes and make recommendations.

White told his interviewer of his hopes and expectations for the commission: "Spare no one and nothing in assessing the blame."

CHAPTER SIXTEEN

Who to Blame?

During the days following May 4, Beacon Journal reporters and editors were handling a varied and amazing run of important local news: a scandal at the state mental hospital located in Akron, local elections and a statewide primary for both major political parties, a new work stoppage by rubber workers at B.F. Goodrich, and the long-running Teamster strike that brought the Ohio National Guard within a phone call's distance from the Kent State campus.

The compelling charge to fairly and completely tell the story of death and tragedy at Kent State gripped us all. It dominated our thinking, drove our planning and consumed our energies. It was a local story, but its meaning and impact reached into the heart of a nation at war. In many ways, the Kent State story was about a nation at war with itself. Readers around the world stopped to consider the depth of division and disaster that May 4 evoked and symbolized.

Denials of culpability rose from National Guard officers who were still posted on campus and were willing to talk with reporters in their effort to shape the story, place the blame and defer the assignment of fault. Interviews with Guardsmen and surviving students, reactions from the Kent community, comments from state and national figures, details of memorial services for the dead students, and growing anger about the implications of the Vietnam War also got prominent play in the *Beacon Journal*.

Exclusive stories and the bylines identifying the newspaper's reporters energized the staff and helped give the public a full, factual understanding of the terrible events that had stunned and shaken the world the previous Monday.

Fatigue from long days and endless demands of a tragic story gripped all of us. Almost everyone wanted to be in on this fast-moving story. Moments of weariness and lingering shock did not diminish satisfaction of the paper's work and individual staffers. Reporters continued their relentless pursuit of the whole story, seeking clarity in helping the public understand what happened on that fatal day and why. They probed for evidence of the tragic flaws in decisions made, orders carried out. The handprints of panic and confusion were everywhere. The journalists' tasks seemed basic enough, but finding the truth is hard and always complicated.

This is why you want to be a journalist, I thought as I looked over the newsroom at the assembly of earnest, dedicated women and men. I struggled with my own complicated feelings. *You are in command of a huge international story and, so far, you have covered it with enterprise and distinction*, I told myself. I felt some satisfaction. I knew that many hurdles lay between our very best efforts and the truth of why and what. My darkest questions were predictable. What could go wrong?

I worried about two things. Pat Englehart and his troops needed rest. They had been chasing this story with unyielding passion and energy. We had to guard against the burden of stress and sleeplessness that can take a physical and emotional toll, that would leave the staff running on fumes. Fatigue can lead to mistakes and misjudgments. We had to keep the compass on truth, fairness and sustaining trust.

I also fretted that truthful accounts published in the *Beacon Journal* pitted us against powerful people who didn't see Kent State as we did. There were two prominent and distinct views. Our commitment to be fair and balanced, and to give voice to the truth, came face to face with special interests: President Nixon, the governor of Ohio, university officials, National Guard officers, student radicals and angry townsfolk.

This cropped photograph shows Gen. Canterbury, the Guard commander, at the rear of his troops as they fired on the students. He is in the upper right in business attire with a gas mask on his head. (John Darnell)

As journalists, we held to the fundamental virtue of knowing and believing that facts always mattered. Fairness was a bedrock. We laid out the story line in laymen's terms. We were after clarification and trustworthy explanations.

Our moral authority came with truth telling. Some accused the paper of bias. Such a charge had a ring of truth to it. That might have been an accurate charge. We were biased, not leaning right or left but biased toward the people's belief in a free press. The public trusted the information that filled the pages of our newspaper.

The huge public outcry saw reasonable people pointing fingers in all directions, and the *Beacon Journal* dutifully recorded the varied views of those who were convinced of where to place blame.

We measured ourselves against our local competition in the Kent-Ravenna area, the *Record-Courier*. It was owned and published by Robert C. Dix. He was known for his civic contributions, including 32 years of service on the Kent State Board of Trustees. He was a fervent anti-communist and expressed his views in an occasional commentary called "Along the Way."

He wrote a piece on Sunday, May 3, that was published on Page 4 of the *Record-Courier* the day of the shooting.

It began, "The blunt earthiness of Governor Jim Rhodes on his visit to Kent State on Sunday was a salve to a wound. They're trying to destroy higher education in Ohio … and we're not going to let them do it."

On the front page that day, the *Record-Courier* also published a strongly worded editorial.

"Ohio will no longer tolerate its state universities being used as sanctuaries by lawbreaking hooligans who destroy, terrorize and burn and then seek protection in the academic community. That was the major message of Governor James Rhodes, who visited Kent Sunday morning and termed the rioting in Kent as the worst the state has suffered."

We kept an eye on the *Record-Courier*, although it was not a frequent topic in our newsroom.

In the days following the shooting, our reporters spent time running after rumors and debunking some of the nasty stories that were circulating. Sallot remembers that "a lot of people were defending the Guard and saw the *Beacon Journal* as a tool of the anti-war movement." Some rumors were fed by fear and loathing like this one: "The nurses at the hospital found lice on the bodies of the two dead women students." Another rumor insisted that "there really were two dead Guardsmen taken to the hospital, but someone had switched their uniforms for hippie clothing." Sallot had a label for such rumors: "It was insane."

Englehart talked to me about Sallot's big fear that someone would subpoena him as a witness, either for the grand jury or the Scranton Commission. As a journalist, the young reporter did not want to go there. But the FBI proved to be persistent.

With my OK, Englehart and Sallot eventually worked out a deal that the FBI could ask him about anything that he had written for the paper and he would confirm that he wrote it and believed it to be accurate. But the FBI wouldn't get anything more from Sallot about what he did or what he saw.

Meanwhile, Maidenburg had returned early the following week from his trip to Israel. He and I had not talked while he was gone, but his secretary, Shirley Follo, kept him apprised of the essential details of May 4. Upon his return, his towering presence momentarily interrupted the rhythm of the newsroom. He said a few quiet "hellos" and indicated he wanted time to catch up on our coverage. I could see him at his desk going through the newspaper, page by page. Finally, he walked from his office next door and stood in my open door. I looked at him in anticipation. He said, "You did a good job. You were a bit rough on the governor, but you did a good job." Then he turned and retreated to his office.

His comment rang hollow. I desperately wanted a more heartfelt "well done!" I needed him and the staff needed him to acknowledge the skill and dedication with which we had covered this tragedy without him. As I thought more about it, I recognized the probability of his deep regret that he had missed a seminal moment in the life of his newspaper. I detected a touch of envy in this proud man.

Our reporters were closely tracking National Guard officials and state and federal investigators as they initiated an intense search for clues that would explain the shooting by the Guard.

That search was not to serve the need for accountability. Rather, it appeared to be uniformed men of high rank seeking vindications for those under their command. Theirs was a pointed search for facts that placed the blame someplace other than with the Ohio National Guard and its chain of command.

The *Beacon Journal* reported that the bodies of the dead were released to their parents after autopsies. Private grieving did not soften public anger. Nor did it calm the controversies.

Portage County Coroner Robert Sybert said he had not been able to determine "for certain" if bullets came from guns the Guardsmen carried.

The *Beacon Journal* explained that the campus continued to be closed to all but National Guardsmen and individuals with individually issued passes granting permission to be on campus. Students, teachers, all things academic had ground to a halt.

Previous years of patiently building the trust of sources paid off for many on the staff. Carringer interviewed one of her familiar sources on the education beat, Ronald Roskens, vice president for administration at Kent State, who sought to spread the blame widely. "The blood of the four students killed when the National Guard fired on rioters is on the hands of students who espouse violence." He extended the reach of his criticism even further to place shares of the blame with "government leaders, anyone within the university community who encourages violence and parents — in fact, all of us — for our failure to deal responsibly with these serious problems." For some, Roskens was the voice of the university administration.

On Tuesday, May 5, the Kent State faculty wanted to meet to discuss the tragedy. With the campus closed, 600 faculty and teaching assistants met in the Unitarian-Universalist Church in the Akron suburb of Fairlawn. The *Beacon Journal* reported that under the guidance of Dr. Thomas R. Meyer, acting president of the Faculty Senate, they adopted two resolutions strongly condemning the shooting of the four students and the use of violence.

"We hold the Guardsmen, acting under orders and under severe psychological pressure, less responsible than are Governor Rhodes and Adjutant Gen. del Corso, whose inflammatory indoctrination produced those pressures," they wrote. "We deplore the prolonged and unduly provocative military presence on the campus not only because we regard the use of massive military force against unarmed students inappropriate in itself, but because it symbolizes the rule of force in our society and international life."

The resolution also declared that student protests organized against the rule of force are "their prerogative."

The second resolution condemned the use of arson by the students in burning the ROTC building, but acknowledged that this violence could not be seen as separate from the "violence in which the American government is involved in Southeast Asia .... It is chiefly responsible for the frustration and anger which is increasingly apparent among university students."

The paper described Kent State as "quiet" on Tuesday as Guardsmen and state and federal officials combed the campus for evidence from the shooting. The search yielded a single shell casing found in a parking lot near Taylor Hall. An early report indicated it was not from the type of bullet used by Guardsmen, the *Beacon Journal* wrote, initiating another round of rumors about a sniper.

In these early hours following the tragedy, references to a "single shot" rose and waned. Reporter Robert Batz focused on this alleged trigger and the continuing mystery over whether a single shot initiated the lethal barrage of bullets from Guardsmen.

In his story reporting a news conference with Canterbury, Batz wrote that the Guard commander had first mentioned the single-shot explanation during a meeting with reporters on the afternoon of May 4.

When he talked with reporters again on Tuesday, the 5th, they pressed Canterbury on that crucial point. The commander backed away from his original claim, acknowledging that the Guard "had not confirmed that there was a sniper." No other explanation was at hand. Silence only fed confusion.

Batz's story told of Canterbury being pressed by reporters about his initial mention that he heard a single shot before the Guard started shooting.

"What is your evidence?"

"I'd rather not go into that," the general said.

"Can you tell us approximately how much time elapsed between the firing of this first shot and when the Guardsmen opened fire?"

"A split second," Canterbury replied.

He was asked what kind of weapon the first shot came from.

"I could not identify the weapon."

Other questions were posed:

Q. Do you feel the consequences of the shooting of these students by the Guardsmen is justified?

A. Obviously, when four people lose their lives, the con-

Gen. Canterbury testified during the Scranton Commission hearings. (Howard Ruffner)

sequences are never justified. The only justification is that the lives of the Guardsmen were in danger before the shooting began.

Q. Who gave the order for the Guardsmen to shoot?

A. No one gave an order. Each man made the judgment on his own that his life was in danger.

Q. Does this mean that some of the demonstrators were very close to the Guardsmen when the troops decided their lives were in danger?

A. Yes. Some of the students were within 10 or 12 feet of the Guardsmen.

Q. You were there. Did you feel your life was in danger, Gen. Canterbury?

A. Yes, I felt I could have been killed out there.

Q. How many Guardsmen were struck by stones thrown by the students?

A. Almost all of my men were hit.

Q. How many Guardsmen actually fired shots at the students?

A. Sixteen or 17.

Q. How many rounds were fired?

A. Thirty-five.

Q. Why didn't the Guardsmen stop to help the wounded students?

A. When the shooting ended, the crowd closed in. We returned to the campus Commons and immediately dispatched ambulances to the scene.

Q. Why didn't the Guardsmen fire over their heads or at least try to wound the students before they shot to kill?

A. I think you will find that many of the Guardsmen did fire over students' heads.

Q. If there was another campus disturbance in Ohio, would you recommend calling out the National Guard?

A. I certainly would.

The *Beacon Journal* continued to report on the National Guard rationale of a sniper and single bullet. On May 13, a week after the shooting, the newspaper published a front-page story confirming the assertion of the Kent police that they had seized from civilians four weapons — two handguns and two rifles — and turned them over to federal authorities for analysis. A National Guard spokesman said the confiscations "pointed to new indications of sniper fire that allegedly touched off shooting by Guardsmen."

The sniper theory was further amplified by an assistant to Del Corso that a Roman Catholic nun, doing graduate work at the university, claimed that a bullet came through her dormitory room window and hit a wall.

"The angle was such that the bullet had to have been fired from atop a roof or other elevated position, not from the ground where the troops were," according to Lt. Col. J.E.P. McCann, administrative assistant to the adjutant general.

The following day, Thursday, May 14, Lt. Col. Charles Fassinger, Canterbury's deputy, was the subject of a story alleging that a single shot was fired about 10 seconds before the National Guard volley. "I can't (say) if it was theirs or ours. But the reaction of the men supports the theory that it was fired from outside the ranks." Fassinger said police have a tape recording that proves there was a single shot, then a pause of 10 to 12 seconds and then a volley.

In an interview, Carringer drew from Dr. Robert Matson, vice president of student affairs, the prediction that "a number of arrests" will be made as a result of investigations of violence on the campus. "Hopefully, many of the radicals will be eliminated."

As the days rolled on, political voices began to be heard — loud, persistent and widespread.

On May 6, the *Beacon Journal* quoted Rabbi Balfour Brickner, an official of the Union of American Hebrew Congregations, who said, "The President has on his conscience four dead 'Bums.'" He was referencing a statement Nixon made at the Pentagon the previous week that "you see these bums blowing up campuses."

Gen. Winston P. Wilson, the top National Guard officer, was besieged the day after the shooting with calls from Capitol Hill, the White House, the Pentagon and reporters asking under what authority the Guardsmen fired. The *Beacon Journal* story said that Wilson referred to a pamphlet on the "rules of engagement" drawn up by the Ohio National Guard and approved by Guard headquarters at the Pentagon.

Wilson said that "When all other things fail," in putting down a civil disturbance, "rifles will be carried with a round in the chamber."

Stephen Young, a cantankerous Democratic senator, was never at a loss for words. He was not a man of quiet convictions. He was born on a May 4 long before, in 1889. Young told Bill Vance of the *Beacon Journal* Washington bureau that "trigger-happy National Guardsmen" killed four Kent State students after one of the Guardsmen "fired by reflex when struck by a thrown teargas canister." In his interview with Vance, the senator touched all the hot buttons. There were no gaps in his convictions.

A Young aide said the information about reflex or instinctive firing came from the senator's Ohio staff. "This is an outrageous occurrence on the part of these men," the senator said. His angry opinion was part of a tumultuous mix.

Vance also wrote of Young's "blistering President Nixon for calling student demonstrators opposed to his Vietnam policy 'bums.'" He described the president's response to the shootings as "coldly unfeeling."

Del Corso read Young's comments in the *Beacon Journal* and saw them as an opportunity to enter the fray. Reached by Vance in Columbus, he described Young as a "senile old liar." Del Corso, a solid Republican, labeled Young's opinion as "hearsay, intended to inflame the public against the military."

Over the next day or two, the brickbats flew. The 81-year-old senator fired back at Del Corso, threatening to "knock his false teeth down his gullet."

The controversy raged on. Differing points of view were heatedly expressed. Disagreement among neighbors grew strident. This was a moment when some parents became radicalized. In images of the dead students, they saw their own kids. Families were split. Those opposed to the Vietnam War tended to be empathetic to the students. Those who believed that defeating communism was a noble cause defended the actions of the National Guard.

In a story soon after the shootings, Sallot introduced an early assertion that a single shot came before the volley from Guardsmen's rifles. But not from a sniper. He quoted Richard Schreiber, a Kent State journalism teacher and self-proclaimed NRA member, who described watching a National Guard "officer fire a .45 caliber pistol over the heads of demonstrators." Schreiber told Sallot he watched this through binoculars from the veranda of Taylor Hall.

It has not been confirmed, but it is part of the Kent State lore and the subject of continuing arguments of when and why the Guard fired at students.

Gene Miller, a reporter for the *Miami Herald* — a sister newspaper to the *Beacon Journal* — traveled to a funeral home in the Squirrel Hill section of Pittsburgh to cover Allison Krause's funeral. In his story for the *Beacon Journal*, Miller described the rabbi praying in Hebrew and saying in English that the nation looks upon Allison as the symbol of the result of human violence. "Let us pray to stop this hatred and heal this wonderful country so that her tragic end is not in vain." Miller described Barry Levine, Allison's boyfriend who was with her when she was fatally shot, dropping "a red tulip on the casket and it rolled off and fell into the grave."

On May 7, memories of the horrors of war and the fruits of victory played out on an inside page in a story by Donn Gaynor on the 25th anniversary of the end of World War II in Europe. It included a large photograph of the *Beacon Journal's* front page from May 7, 1945. The huge banner headline on that day read: GERMAN WAR OVER!

The newspaper also noted the weekly toll of war dead in May 1970: 123 Americans, 450 South Vietnamese and 3,415 Vietcong and North Vietnamese; 997 Americans and 1,228 South Vietnamese were listed as wounded. These weekly news items were read avidly by opponents of the war who kept the toll of casualties.

On Page 6, where *Beacon Journal* daily editorials appeared, Bob Stopher wrote of Kent State as a national tragedy. "Repercussions of this campus riot and its deplorable climax have spread across the nation, not alone in anger but in mourning and grief that it could, that it did happen here."

The editorial called for Nixon to act on Senate Majority Leader Mike Mansfield's call for a high-level commission to investigate disorders at Kent State and elsewhere.

Just below the editorial was another that tied events together. It was an observation on the Pulitzer Prize that had been awarded on Monday, May 4, to independent journalist Seymour Hersh for his reporting on the My Lai massacre. "It was not the kind of constructive report that military and diplomatic officials prefer. In fact, it was one that has made Americans hang their heads in shame. But it had to be told." Hersh, the editorial said, "richly deserves this prestigious honor."

On Friday, May 8, the *Beacon Journal* gave front-page play to unexpected remarks attributed to Vice President Spiro Agnew, a frequent critic of the press. The story drew on an interview of Agnew with British television host David Frost that had been aired the night before in Los Angeles. Agnew said killing the four Kent State students was murder "if the Guardsmen fired without warning and without having been fired upon." The vice president said he did not condone the Guards' actions and "they responded with too much force."

The vice president's uncharacteristic comments stunned conservatives. Later, he was critical of *The Report of The President's Commission on Campus Unrest*, calling it "too permissive." During the fall of 1970, he campaigned vigorously for Republican candidates, attacking demonstrators but backing away from direct mentions of Kent State. In spite of repeated questioning by reporters, Agnew never again reaffirmed his comment that the Kent State killings were "murder."

The Kent State campus was now calm and quiet. It exuded a sense of abandonment as the week that began so violently finally wound down under the weight of Caris' order closing the campus "indefinitely." This peaceful feeling ran counter to alarming, heated pronouncements from politicians and university officials, as well as the general public.

In a speech to the Akron Bar Association on Thursday, May 7, Ohio's U.S. Sen. William Saxbe said students across America have something to say. "I think we should have listened to them."

Saxbe, a Republican, concluded that the Guardsmen had panicked when they fired at students. "For every student bent on violence, there is a brutal policeman waiting for him. They're meant for each other, and they'll find each other."

Saxbe's speech was set against a shocking background of widespread anti-war protests and reaction to the deadly shots fired at Kent State. Lack of clarity fanned confusion.

The Associated Press reported that 227 of the nation's 1,500 colleges had closed since May 4. That was a stunning number, reflecting the powerful impact on the public of the Kent State killings. Hundreds of colleges erupted in demonstrations. Strikes and demonstrations curtailed classes. Some were peaceful. Some violent. Some threatened to get out of hand. Rock throwing and, in response, teargas canisters and birdshot fired by law enforcement officers highlighted the confrontations and prompted university and college officials to act out of the fear of another Kent State.

Reporter Sanford Levenson provoked a wider discussion about the shootings in his Page 1 story on Saturday, May 9, reporting the assertion of an Akron physician that one of the wounded students was shot by something other than an M-1 rifle or a .45 caliber pistol.

The physician, Dr. J.W. Ewing, was a plastic surgeon and said to be an expert on ballistic wounds. He treated Donald MacKenzie, 21, at St. Thomas Hospital in Akron. MacKenzie was the only gunshot victim on May 4 to be treated at a medical facility other than Robinson Memorial Hospital in Ravenna.

Ewing described the path of the bullet that struck MacKenzie as entering "the back of his neck — about an inch left of the spinal cord — by a small-caliber bullet that came out through his jaw and cheek."

Ewing said the wound was made by a steel-jacketed, non-explosive bullet. "There were no steel fragments left in his face. If it had not been steel-jacketed, it would have shattered when it hit his jawbone. A military weapon would have blown his head apart." Instead, the doctor maintained, the bullet left a hole about the size of a nickel in MacKenzie's cheek.

Levenson described Ewing's expertise in ballistics, which grew from his experience during World War II in Europe. He was assigned to the 109th Evacuation Hospital and recalled performing plastic surgery on more than 27,000 wounded soldiers.

"I am not a stranger to these wounds," he said. "I can't tell you what the boy was shot by, but it was not with a military or police weapon. Those are too big to have left that small hole in his face."

No one came forward with corroborating evidence of any weapon that had discharged a steel-jacketed bullet. The doctor's vast experience in ballistics carried authority but in the moment was simply a lone voice that spoke through a newspaper story to describe the wound suffered by MacKenzie. By Friday, May 8, the student had been discharged from St. Thomas Hospital, an institution near downtown Akron run by the Sisters of Charity of St. Augustine (where Alcoholics Anonymous was founded in 1935).

On May 24, dissent appeared. The *Beacon Journal* reported that Dr. Robert J. Sillary, a Detroit forensic pathologist and an authority on gunshot wounds, "pointedly disagreed" with Ewing. Sillary described a situation when it would be "entirely possible for an M-1 bullet to cause a clear through-and-through wound without extensive damage." The story also quoted Dr. Joseph Davis, Dade County medical examiner, who disagreed with Ewing's interpretation. He suggested that the bullet that struck MacKenzie may have first passed through another person.

As authoritative as Ewing's account was in Levenson's telling, the challenges from the Detroit pathologist and Miami medical examiner effectively took the Ewing theory out of the discussion.

The big Sunday newspaper for May 10 loomed. It was Mother's Day. In spite of the fatigue that gripped reporters and editors, there was work to be done. Under Englehart's command, the staff took a deep breath and plunged ahead to craft what, in newsroom parlance, was known as a "take-out" — a major written reflection and analysis of the previous week's events.

The report — "3 Violent Days Then Tragedy" — was produced by Herzog, Levenson, McCrary, Carringer and Sallot. The package was edited by Hal Fry, one of the newsroom's sharpest intellects who had long anchored the copy desk. Fry, tall and thin, was a Lincolnesque figure. His hair was mostly gone. But his beard was full. He was beloved for his gentle ways and sharp eye for wayward uses of the English language in news stories.

The special report on Kent State opened on Page 1 and posed a series of questions:

It began on May Day — the international symbol of distress.

It was one of those perfectly sunny Spring days on the slopes of an ordinary midwestern college campus, but there was something about it.

The night before, the President had told the nation he was sending troops into one nation to shorten a war in another.

Start a war to shorten it? It was the topic of the morning at Kent State University.

And it was the focal point that touched off a chain of events that rocked the world 72 hours later.

What happened in those 72 hours is a matter of record and conjecture. But why did it happen?

Did supposed outsiders control the mobs in three successive nights of rioting? Were city and university officials lulled into thinking the Ohio National Guard was a cure-all for all troubles?

Above all, why were trained, armed soldiers called in when just a year before, similar demonstrations at Kent

State were handled efficiently by local law enforcement personnel?

The story jumped from Page 1 to a full page inside the newspaper. It did not answer "why?" That big question was on everyone's lips. Nobody had an answer at the time. The main story set the stage for several exclusive pieces and coverage to come in the following days and weeks.

Carringer had scored a late-week interview with Kent State president White. She quoted him as urging "those who believe in orderly change 'to speak out' and participate in making senseless violence impossible."

White said he was determined to press for "an investigation at the highest national level."

White told Carringer he identified the key elements in the tragedy. Among them:

A planned manipulation by a dedicated group of "destroyers."

An increased number of young people concerned about national policy and social values.

President Nixon's announcement of action in Cambodia that triggered the protests.

The dominant front-page piece of that Sunday edition was a report on a "resurgent peace movement" that brought 60,000 protesters to the edge of the White House grounds on Saturday afternoon. Almost one week after May 4, and "Kent State" had become a battle cry against the Vietnam War.

The story, by James Batten and Saul Friedman of the Knight Newspapers' Washington Bureau, described the protesters as "overwhelmingly white, young and anti-Nixon." They roared their demand, "Peace Now…Peace Now…Peace Now" — shouts that were within easy earshot of the troubled and angry president and his family.

Joe Rice, the *Beacon Journal* political writer, accompanied a group of Kent State students to the Washington rally. He described a sign scrawled on a small sheet of white paper bearing the single word KENT. Fifty years later, "Kent" still resonates, recalling images of a national tragedy, of a young girl's arms thrust in horror over the dead body of Jeff Miller.

The sign evoked "emotional, often angry, reactions," he wrote. The Kent State group stood shoulder-to-shoulder with students from across the country, listening to speakers decry the fatal shootings of the four Kent State students and victims in Vietnam and Cambodia.

Carringer and Batz collaborated in an effort to answer a question hanging over the now eerily silent campus: Was the violence the result of planning or a study in mob spontaneity? If it was planned, they asked, who did the planning — KSU students or off-campus revolutionaries? Why did they persist?

The pair interviewed university officials and one student who insisted that outside agitators were to blame. Other students who also claimed to have inside knowledge of the unrest said the violent events "just happened."

The poignancy of Mother's Day was evoked in an interview with Sarah Scheuer, mother of Sandra Scheuer, one of the four killed on Monday. The story, by John Askins of Knight Newspapers, was datelined Boardman, Ohio, Sandra's hometown.

"Mrs. Scheuer has a face that suggests a strong, vigorous personality," Askins wrote. "But the death of 20-year-old Sandra last week seems to have broken her, as it has broken the country."

She speaks bitterly about student radicals, the National Guard, college authorities, even the war in Asia. But in the end, Askins writes, "She can only stare at her living room carpet and say, hopelessly, 'I just don't understand.'"

Askins described Sandra's father, Martin, 59, as a "gentle man," with a firm German-accented voice that never wavered. "There is not much to say, except that we hope it will not be in vain for her to have died.

"We are conservative people. I voted for President Nixon. I was one of those who put him in office. But I sure wouldn't do it anymore."

CHAPTER SEVENTEEN

Visitors

On Wednesday afternoon, May 6, the telephone rang on my desk in the *Beacon Journal* newsroom. The caller was Kurt Luedtke, assistant to the executive editor of the *Detroit Free Press*. Kurt was a good, personal friend, smart and ambitious. He asked how the coverage of Kent State was going and how my staff was holding up. I gave him an update on the good stories our staff was producing and shared my fear that before long they would begin running on fumes.

Then he shifted to the purpose of his call: Knight Newspapers was sending a team of reporters to Kent to undertake an independent investigation of the shootings.

I was stunned. As he began to explain the rationale for the project, worry gripped me. Had Knight executives concluded that the *Beacon Journal* couldn't handle such a big story on its own? This was the first blow to my sense of pride in our work on this national tragedy. "You've got your hands full covering the daily story," Luedtke continued. "We are going to be working it on an investigative basis."

I listened quietly as Luedtke told me that he and Neal Shine, the *Free Press* managing editor and also a friend, originally were reluctant to take on a major assignment like Kent State. They assumed that at least one of the country's major newspapers would conduct its own independent investigation. But they had learned from Bill Schmidt, a *Free Press* reporter already at Kent State, that the big papers were "all pulling out. As far as they are concerned, the sto-

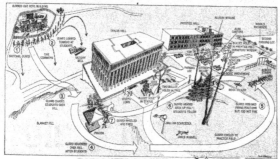

The special Knight-Akron Beacon Journal *report of May 24, 1970.*

ry's over." To Shine and Luedtke, this meant they wouldn't have to compete with papers like *The New York Times* or *Chicago Tribune*.

The *Beacon Journal* staff had noticed this as well. The declining presence of out-of-town reporters was a message that with hard work and enterprise, we could dominate the continuing story. It was a golden opportunity for us that energized the staff even more.

"So," I interrupted, "you're telling me this is a reflection on the *Beacon?*"

"Oh, hell, no. The guys in Miami think you are doing a great job."

I swallowed hard. Competition mattered to us. Even though Akron was a one-newspaper town, we measured ourselves against other Ohio dailies, especially Cleveland's *Plain Dealer*.

As one of the smaller papers in the Knight group, the *Beacon Journal* believed that the excellence of our Kent State coverage would win us recognition among the leading papers in the Knight organization.

This is not going to go down very easily in my newsroom, I thought. As we were ending the call, I told Luedtke that the *Beacon Journal* would welcome the Knight team and help in any way it could.

But I had some doubts. I understood that the ambition for this kind of journalism project had its origins in the Knight Newspapers headquarters in Miami. They wanted it done. My job was to smooth out any wrinkles in the cooperation between my staff and the Knight Newspapers team soon to alight in our newsroom. That's the path I chose.

I called Fitzpatrick and Englehart over to my office. When I finished telling them what was coming, they reacted with utter disbelief.

Englehart was the first to speak. "Shit." The news got Fitzpatrick's juices going. "It doesn't send a very good message to our troops who have worked so hard and done such a great job on this story." He shook his head. "The Detroit folks will see us at our best. We own this story and we are going to stay ahead." I knew I could count on Fitz to talk one-on-one to our Kent State team. He had a gift for honesty. He was good at smoothing ruffled feathers.

I envisioned the Knight team as a whirl of activity that would last about two weeks. And I agreed that the *Beacon Journal* staff was certain to be upset. "We have to make sure we stay focused on the story and continue to find exclusive developments. The Knight report won't be done for a couple of weeks. That gives us time to stay ahead on the story."

As the meeting ended, I sat at my desk and looked blankly out the window. This was a challenge I hadn't anticipated. I needed to shield the staff so they didn't feel like they were the junior varsity. And, I mused, I had to make sure no one mistook my quiet approach to managing this twist as being timid.

One by one, the seven members of the Knight team arrived in Akron. The newsroom watched with raised eyebrows and considerable skepticism as the visitors went to work. Lilly summed up the reaction from the staff: "I remember how other reporters and I felt somewhat daunted when what seemed like legions of *Detroit Free Press* reporters descended on our newsroom after the shootings. They kept taking our phone books, sending us on frustrating searches to retrieve them. Phone books were essential."

Space in our newsroom was tight. We found four metal desks in a corner of the newsroom near the Sports Department for the Knight team. They liked being among our staffers, mostly to ask directions and draw critical background from reporters who had been covering Kent State for months.

As the days wore on, the tight quarters encouraged the Knight team to spend more and more time in their rooms at the Akron Holiday Inn near downtown. That was an informal setting where they could have a beer or two in the evening as they typed up notes and swapped stories. Their rooms soon became piled with newspapers, documents, clips, photos, notebooks and countless Xerox copies. Tidying up the mess each day made life miserable for the hotel's cleaning women.

Shine, 39, was the team leader. He had started as a copy boy

Neal Shine led the Knight team.

at the *Free Press* in 1950 and had risen through the ranks to become managing editor. He was decent and fair, Irish through and through. He was beloved by his news staff, as much for his impish humor and funny stories as for his gifts as an editor.

He and I talked briefly each morning to ensure no conflicts were emerging that could undermine the project. He called his team together around 9, giving them the same stern caution. "You are here at the sufferance of our sister paper in Akron."

He stressed that *Beacon Journal* phone lines were not their private communication system. They were there to cooperate, not compete with the *Beacon Journal.* The practice of lifting scarce copies of Kent-area phone books and student directories from newsroom desks had to stop. There would be no territorial expansion, no occupying desks of *Beacon Journal* staffers out on assignment.

Still, the presence of the Knight team had upset the rhythms of our staff and its charge to push the Kent State story along every day. I tried not to show my anxiety about that reality.

Shine helped with his funny stories and outgoing nature. Englehart remained the point person for the *Beacon Journal* staff and increasingly became a valued resource for the out-of-town reporters. They knew his sources and memory were unmatched. Meanwhile, Fitzpatrick's comforting approach reassured our staff of the advantages of continuing to be aggressive on "our" story.

The *Free Press* reporters brought with them the shining legacy of the paper's coverage of the 1967 Detroit riots, for which the paper won the 1968 Pulitzer Prize. That Pulitzer citation recognized "both the brilliance of its detailed spot news staff work and its swift and accurate investigation into the underlying causes of the trag-

Gene Miller worked well with the Beacon Journal *staff.*

edy." Reporter Bill Serrin, 31, Shine and Luedtke were heavily involved in that enterprise. Serrin was known for his steady judgment and the tireless energy he brought to investigative work. The reputation of Gene Miller, 42, added luster to the group. He had his own Pulitzer at the *Miami Herald* for investigative reporting on a story that helped free two people wrongly convicted of murder.

Miller wore bow ties and was a master at unearthing small details that made for compelling stories. "Great stuff," he would exclaim, at digging out a new fact. At one point, Miller grew curious about the note sounded by the Victory Bell when the students rang it. He found a music teacher who went with him to listen to the bell's tone and declared the note as G sharp.

Shine had several lines of inquiry for the team to follow. Miller, Serrin and John Oppedahl, 25, a skilled interviewer, concentrated on the National Guard. Julie Morris, 23, had a passion for the truth and the growing impact of the women's liberation movement. Her assignment was interviewing young people. Bill Schmidt, also 23, joined Morris in chasing down and interviewing students living in town. Lee Winfrey, 37, was prized for his maturity and perspective as a reporter. He wrote one of the three main pieces for the special report.

Luedtke pushed the story from Detroit. He thought that urgency was critical. Immediacy was important. The special report had to seem fresh in readers' minds. After a few days, he drove to Akron to press the team for an early publication date — Sunday, May 17, instead of Sunday, May 24, the original target date. The reporters resisted strenuously. They needed more time to get the story together accurately. The original publication date held.

It was clear from the start that the Knight team wanted to replicate its success reporting the Detroit riot. They were determined to work the story as skillfully as they could. Some of the *Beacon Journal* staffers got an early sense that the Knight reporters envisioned the Kent State project as fodder for another Pulitzer.

Carringer, Herzog, Sallot and Englehart were attached to the Knight team. They were among our strongest reporters with knowledge and experience gained from months of covering unrest at Kent State. Those factors had considerable value in the eyes of the Knight team. Sallot said that his "worst fears were realized when it became apparent that his contribution to this project was to endlessly brief the out-of-towners, share phone numbers and contacts, and answer questions." But *Beacon Journal* staffers took a liking to Miller and gave him his first leads on the identification of Guardsmen.

Sallot reacted emotionally. "I was the kid, and I just had to suck it up, with a smile on my face. I did. I also learned an important lesson: Make sure you always treat with respect the local journalists on the scene whenever you are dispatched to some distant catastrophe. Gene Miller treated me as a colleague. He was a real pro, and I was always delighted to help him."

I kept an eye out for Sallot. He was the youngest, fresh out of journalism school but a veteran of observing unrest on the Kent State campus. His work was impressive, and he seemed to engage easily with the Knight team. I didn't trust Luedtke and Shine, who were known for their aggressive recruitment of young reporters for the *Free Press*.

After nine days in Akron, the corporate bean counters were beginning to get antsy over the mounting Holiday Inn bills. It was an expensive investment for Knight Newspapers. But it also was an effective statement that the company valued a great story and would invest in it. Shine, reflecting later on what he had learned, said, "There is no limit to what a newspaperman will eat and drink if he is not paying."

The Knight team returned to Detroit to write copy for the special section, still scheduled to be published on Sunday, May 24. As they departed, Lilly reflected on the experience. "We feared this team from the bigger paper and bigger city would big-foot us," throw their weight around, she said. "They didn't."

Luedtke and Shine thought it was essential to have an Ohio perspective in the report, and they asked me to come to Detroit to ensure that a Buckeye sense was maintained in the story. Privately, I thought that the two editors wanted it to appear that the *Beacon Journal* had a hand in wrapping up the special report. So, I drove to Detroit to help refine the copy in the final editing.

The Knight reporters had Sallot's phone number and he agreed to be available to them as a resource. As they wrote their first drafts, they rang him up night and day. He recalled, "I was gratified that I had steered them clear of some serious errors."

The copy started rattling into the Akron newsroom on the Knight wire on Friday, May 22, two days before the planned publication. Englehart was first to spot a quote from "KSU student Jeff Sallot." He made sure Sallot was identified as a *Beacon Journal* reporter, and that his name was in the credit box with the out-of-towners.

The report ran for 30,000 words. The *Beacon Journal* published a special eight-page section. The *Free Press* and the *Miami Herald* used it as the lead story in their editorial section. The *Philadelphia Inquirer* ran the report over three days.

Knight Newspapers was in it for keeps. Corporate news executives sensed that their team had produced a prizewinning special report. They wanted to make certain that it got good play in the company's major papers. The *Charlotte Observer* was handicapped by being in the midst of transferring to a new printing plant. It ran the section a week later using glossy proofs from the *Beacon Journal's* layout.

In its Page 1 story introducing the report, the *Beacon Journal* wrote that an "independent newspaper investigation has concluded that none of the four student deaths was necessary to satisfy any law enforcement purpose." The story said the report was based on hundreds of interviews by the Knight team with National Guardsmen, students, teachers, police, public officials and townspeople."

In the report, the Knight Newspapers team reached these conclusions:

> President Nixon's decision to invade Cambodia was identified as "the prime and immediate cause of the trouble."
>
> No sniper fired at the National Guard prior to the volley of rifle fire, which killed four students and wounded nine.
>
> The Guardsmen fired without orders to do so. Some fired at random while some aimed deliberately at students.
>
> The Guardsmen were not surrounded, and they could have taken several other courses of action rather than shooting the students.
>
> The four students who died had thrown no rocks at the Guard. The dead students were not politically radical.
>
> Governor James A. Rhodes was responsible for the order that the Guard was to break up any assembly at Kent, peaceful or otherwise.
>
> Gen. Del Corso championed the special Ohio Guard rule allowing Guardsmen to carry live rounds in the weapons.
>
> The Guard, despite increased training, still had no effective anti-riot equipment and no meaningful anti-riot training. Its equipment was limited to antiquated teargas canisters and the M-1 — a killer weapon with tremendous velocity and range.
>
> The Guard, in firing at the students, violated its regulations, which stress "restraint" and "minimum application of force."
>
> In escalating from teargas to bullets, the Guardsmen ignored several intermediate steps, which federal manuals say must be used before soldiers fire their weapons.
>
> Guard officers failed to inform students, faculty or the Kent administration that they had live ammunition in their weapons, although a 1968 statement by Del Corso said this was to be done as part of crowd-control strategy.

The Guardsmen violated the most important regulation of all: avoid death.

The report then posed these questions: Does the nation really oppose bloodshed in quelling a disorder? If it does, why is the Guard permitted to use equipment and tactics that escalate the risk of tragedy?

To the Knight team, the report was more than a recital of facts. The team hoped that its gathering of new facts would enable it to identify causes and to assess responsibilities.

For the editors, it was a balance of objectivity vs. interpretation. The team offered conclusions only if two requirements were satisfied:

Team members generally agreed on the conclusion.

They believed there was sufficient evidence to support it.

In listing its conclusions, the Knight report felt the need to refute the widespread but mistaken impression held by many people that the Guardsmen were "surrounded."

The report also acknowledged that the team was unable to answer two of the questions it pursued: the identity of the Guardsman who fired the first shot and why the first shot was fired.

Reading the eight-page special section on Sunday, May 24, *Beacon Journal* journalists took satisfaction in recognizing that the truthful narrative they had created, day after day in the pages of their newspaper, was sustained in the findings of the work of the Knight Newspapers team. We had the story. The special report enhanced it. The work of the Knight team was admired for its extensive detail, the power of its interviews of participants and victims, and the grace of its storytelling.

"But here's the thing," said Sallot. "It turned out that package was a hell of a great piece of journalism. It was impressive in its scope and detail. It was well-written and it broke some new ground. The central conclusion was that the Guard didn't need to shoot, and four students didn't need to die."

CHAPTER EIGHTEEN

FBI

It was a 27-mile drive east from Ray Redmond's modest home in the Fairlawn section of West Akron to Ravenna, the government center of Portage County. On clear mornings, Redmond wore sunglasses against the brilliant sunlight rising over the trees that gave neighboring Kent its name, the Tree City.

Redmond was a tall, modest man who had been making this journey for most of his 29 years as a *Beacon Journal* reporter. Olesky, his state desk colleague, said, "Ray was the Portage County Bureau forever, it seemed." Others thought of him as "sweet and kind" and "master of the understatement."

Wednesday, July 22, 1970, was a partly cloudy day, cool for summertime in northeastern Ohio. The parking lot at the courthouse was full, but an experienced reporter usually could find a spot to squeeze his car into.

Redmond began his daily rounds. Check with the cops, look at the court dockets and pick up intelligence from clerks and secretaries who had come to know him well. Redmond was welcomed in most of the offices. Over the years, he had become regarded as courteous, competent and fair-minded.

Around 2 p.m., Redmond walked into Ronald Kane's office. The Portage County prosecutor was in his first year in the job and had become a major figure in the aftermath of the shootings.

Kane had clashed with Gov. Rhodes during their meeting on Sunday, May 3, when he had insisted that the campus be closed.

Veteran Beacon Journal *reporter Ray Redmond. The county prosecutor leaked the summary of the FBI report and its finding that there was no reason for the Guard to shoot at the students. Below, the first page of the FBI report.*

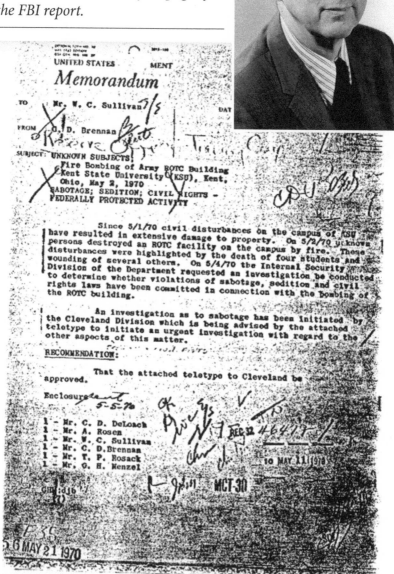

The governor refused. After the Guardsmen fired their deadly bullets on Monday, Kane called the governor at the statehouse in Columbus and again pressed for closing Kent State.

The governor delayed, and Kane turned to Portage County Common Pleas Judge Albert Caris. Caris was born and spent his life in Ravenna. His family could not afford the cost of college and law school was not a possibility. He was appointed probate judge in 1920 and was elected by popular vote to a full four-year term. While serving as probate judge, he quietly pursued his study of the law at home. He placed second in the state when he took the Ohio bar examination.

After listening to Kane's description of the governor's stubborn behavior, Caris quickly issued the injunction to close the university "indefinitely."

Kane's aggressive action in going around the governor fit his growing reputation of not backing away from controversy.

Redmond knew that Kane was helping arrangements to impanel a grand jury to take testimony on the shootings. The reporter had developed a good relationship with Kane through his brother, Herb Kane, a Ravenna lawyer the reporter had known for 20 years.

"What's new?" he asked the prosecutor.

Kane held out what looked like a report. "I'll show you something, but promise you won't tell anyone about it," he said. It was a summary of the FBI's investigation of the Kent State shootings. It was typed on heavy blue paper with an onion skin carbon copy attached.

"You can read it, but you can't have a copy."

As Redmond reached to take the papers, the young prosecutor's phone rang. Kane swung his chair away from the reporter and began to talk. "It gave me time to memorize parts of the FBI report. I realized it was dynamite," Redmond told me. Kane continued to talk and Redmond continued to read.

In it, a federal agency — the FBI — criticized the actions of a military organization, the Ohio National Guard. Redmond knew it would be vital to remember the report's details.

As Kane continued to talk, Redmond read the 14 pages of the summary over and over. After several minutes, Kane ended his call and reached for the report. Redmond handed it back to him without comment. He quickly left his office. "When I got out on the street, I jotted down as much of the information as I could remember."

Redmond ran to a pay phone. He called Englehart in Akron. "This is what I have," he blurted excitedly. I listened on another phone as he told us the amazing story of reading the report and what it revealed.

Redmond's voice rose as he related its contents. "The Guardsmen were not in danger. They had no reason to shoot the kids," he said. I took notes. When he finished the summary of what he remembered, I asked how quickly he could get back to the newsroom. "I'm on my way."

I turned to Englehart. "This is a real blockbuster." I had my own checklist and the first item was to get another source to confirm the FBI report. "Have someone call the Washington bureau and ask them to check with the FBI or the Department of Justice to make sure the report is the real thing."

I had to get the story started. I turned to my typewriter and began to shape the lede. "What a great story," I said to the news desk. "It's ours! Let's put a 'copyright' at the top of the story."

In 1970, a line that read "copyright 1970 Akron Beacon Journal" meant something about the important and exclusive nature of the story. It assured that we would get credit from other news organizations who used our exclusive story. In fact, this explosive story would get prominent play in newspapers across the country.

Redmond entered the newsroom and was greeted as a hero.

As he and I fleshed out the story, the Washington bureau called to confirm the document. It was a memorandum prepared for Ohio officials by the Justice Department. Signed by Jerris Leonard, chief of its civil rights division, the memorandum set forth various possible courses of action Ohio officials could take.

The Justice Department spokesman told our Washington bureau that federal action was being deferred to allow Ohio authorities to act on their own. He added, "We have not foreclosed federal action."

The Thursday, July 23, edition of the *Akron Beacon Journal* that rolled off the presses showed two lines of 72-point bold type across Page 1 that read:

FBI: NO REASON FOR GUARD

TO SHOOT AT KENT STATE

The FBI has concluded the campus shootings by the Ohio National Guard which led to the deaths of four Kent State University students was "not necessary and not in order."

And the Justice Department has advised Ohio officials that six Guardsmen could be criminally charged, the Beacon Journal has learned.

The FBI says the Guardsmen were not surrounded by demonstrators, had not run out of teargas and could have controlled the situation without shooting.

More than 100 FBI agents investigated the May 4 shooting on the KSU campus. Their findings are contained in a 7,000-page report and summarized in a 14-page report.

The Beacon Journal has learned that the summary says:

The shootings were not necessary and not in order.

About 200 demonstrators who were heckling the Guardsmen could have been turned back if arrests had been made or more teargas fired.

No Guardsmen were hurt by flying rocks or projectiles and none was in danger of his life at the time of the shooting. There was no hail of rocks beforehand.

One Guardsman fired at a student who was making an obscene gesture; another fired at a student preparing to throw a rock.

The report listed names, ranks, outfits and home addresses of the six Guardsmen who could be charged.

"It is understood," the story continued, "the report raises questions about whether the student-Guardsmen confrontation can be classed as a riot. The finding suggests that because there was no immediate threat to life or property, the demonstrators on the KSU campus were not rioters even though they were warned to disperse.

"Raising the question about whether or not there were riot conditions takes on considerable significance. Under law, if it is determined there was a riot, then no Guardsman would be prosecuted for his actions. In the absence of riot conditions, it could be that criminal charges could be filed."

An FBI spokesman in Washington told the *Beacon Journal* that the Justice Department, and not the FBI, had to decide whether anyone would be charged with a crime and what those crimes might be.

The story said the FBI report was expected to be used by *The President's Commission on Campus Unrest*. "The FBI report also could be used if there is a grand jury investigation in Portage County. Portage County Prosecutor Ronald Kane currently is seeking $100,000 from the state of Ohio to finance a grand jury probe."

The story created quite a stir among *Beacon Journal* readers and officials in Ohio and Washington. Readers called to cancel their subscriptions with such messages as, "How dare you!"

Denials and explanations were offered. An FBI spokesman was quoted as saying the FBI had released no reports of the Kent State investigation.

National Guard spokesmen took issue with the FBI finding that no Guardsmen were hurt by flying rocks or projectiles and none was in danger of his life at the time of the shooting.

In Columbus, McElroy said he didn't know if the "report was authentic or not. It doesn't sound like the FBI. They don't release reports like that."

Other officials said they had not received a copy of the report. Confusion grew over how and where the *Beacon Journal* got a copy of the FBI report. The newspaper protected the identity of its source, Ronald Kane. His role in "leaking" the report to Redmond was not known for several months.

Accusations, guess work, repercussions continued to flow.

In its Friday, July 24, editorial, the *Beacon Journal* said that of all the definitive views emerging about Kent State, the one "carrying the greatest weight of authority" was the FBI report.

"It is all too evident that the Guardsmen were over-armed and undertrained for the situation which they faced. For this, the top officers of the National Guard bear a terrible responsibility."

At 8:47 that same morning, President Nixon telephoned FBI Director J. Edgar Hoover to complain about what he called "the news leak."

According to one memo that Hoover sent at noontime to six of his top aides, "The President said that from what he had seen, although it was just a cursory examination of our report, it looks like the Guard had a lot of provocation. I said I thought they definitely had. The President said he told his people he was going to have it (the news story) 'shot down' as he was not going to have this student business erupting ...."

In a separate memo to four of his aides, Hoover characterized the Nixon request as an order. "The President was quite disturbed about the article in the paper and directed me to take steps to have it 'knocked down' insofar as the FBI was concerned. I told him I would see that this was done."

The tack the government chose was to point out an error in the lede of our story saying that the FBI had "concluded." That mistake was mine. I had inserted the word "concluded" as I wrote the story. My failure to recognize the limits of the FBI's investigative authority was personally embarrassing and eventually led to follow-up stories that wiped some of the luster from our enterprise.

The next day, Sallot reported details of the split reaction to the story about the FBI report. "There were those who said 'I told you so,' while those who weren't said 'I don't believe it.'"

Sallot observed that students and professors who had witnessed the bloody tragedy "beamed approval" over the findings and told the reporter, "Maybe somebody will believe us now."

His story explained that the report focused only on the seconds before the firing and the instant of the firing, and, at that moment, no Guardsman was hurt by rocks and none was in danger of his life.

Readers snatched up copies of the paper at newsstands, shook their heads and walked off to ponder what the FBI had found.

A week after the exclusive story was published, Zaidan wrote a piece explaining that the report, based on information gathered by 100 FBI agents, put the FBI in an unusual role. "The American left has never had much patience with J. Edgar Hoover and his cloak-and-dagger team; the American right has always found it convenient to quote FBI sources in assailing the left, but now seems to have broken faith with its favorite chronicler of subversion.

"An incredible aspect of the Justice Department memorandum is the heap of misinformation that the disbelievers unleashed to attack the contention that the shootings were unnecessary."

On Thursday, Aug. 6, a personal letter addressed to Jack Knight arrived in the *Beacon Journal* newsroom. It was from Hoover. It was his attempt to follow Nixon's dictate to "shut down" the newspaper's story on the FBI report.

Maidenburg gave me a copy of Hoover's letter and said Knight was writing a response. He suggested we package the two letters in the Friday paper.

Hoover wrote, "I thought you would want to know that this inaccurate article — which has been quoted by news media across the nation — has caused scores of knowledgeable and concerned citizens to write me inquiring whether the FBI has departed from its time-honored role of serving strictly as an investigative agency, and not as a prosecutor, jury or judge of the facts gathered by our Agents, such as you have strongly implied ...

"The results of our inquiries into the Kent State matter were furnished to the United States Department of Justice without recommendation or conclusion ...

"In view of the wide attention which your distorted article has received, I must request that this factual refutation and clear statement of truth be accorded an equally prominent position in the pages of your newspaper."

Knight's reply was vigorous and lifted spirits across the newsroom. He began with a forthright acknowledgement of the mistake. "We were in error in saying 'The FBI has concluded ...' rather than 'the FBI has reported ...'

"But an exercise in semantics," he continued, "must not be permitted to obscure the fact that our article was essentially correct and not 'distorted,' as you allege.

"It is interesting that you have not contested the pertinent information contained in our story, but only the notation that the FBI made a 'conclusion' about Kent State.

"Furthermore, I am surprised at the hostile tone of your letter, which is evidently intended to mollify public opinion.

"There is no occasion to lecture the editor for, as you know, we are quite as dedicated to the quest for truth as the FBI."

In the days and weeks following May 4, 1970, the Beacon Journal *published hundreds of letters about the Kent State shootings; many were critical of the newspaper's coverage. This was a special page filled with letters to the editor on May 9, 1970.*

CHAPTER NINETEEN

To the Editor

Within hours of the deadly shooting by National Guard troops on the Kent State University campus on May 4, letters began to pour into the *Beacon Journal* newsroom. Readers were upset and they wanted to have their say.

The letters spared no one. Guardsmen and their officers, students, university officials, Nixon, Rhodes and the *Akron Beacon Journal.*

> What is wrong with people that they will turn on those who protect them and support the element in our society that is destroying and plundering our colleges and communities?

> To believe that the Guardsmen, armed with bayonets, rifles and bullets, could be killed by stones is ridiculous.

> Freedom of speech does not give these students the right to destroy public or private property or endanger lives.

> "Murder" would be a more appropriate word to describe the killings.

> The blood spilled at Kent State University is in great part chargeable to the news media and much of it to the *Akron Beacon Journal.*

> The *Beacon Journal* has reached the peak of asininity. God in heaven, to what lengths you have continually gone to excuse or cover up for those bums that started the trouble? And when I say bums, you and the bums know damn well what bums I am talking about.

For the past 25 years, Tom Horner, a pleasant soft-spoken editorial writer, had edited reader submissions. Habitually, by 10 a.m. every day, he began to work his way through a tidy stack of letters addressed "to the editor" that had been dropped on his desk along the row of offices that housed the editorial page writers.

His task was an extension of a long tradition of democratic participation by readers in their local newspaper. The emergence of the British press in the early 18th century introduced a form of critical opinion essay that became known as a letter to the editor. In those days, it was a centerpiece of the newspaper. Some of the early contributors were well-known authors who wrote anonymously.

Increasingly, the early publications drew on letters from members of the public. This established the appearance of a dialogue between editors and readers.

As news, rather than opinion, became central to the mission of newspapers, letters to the editor were relegated to the inside pages. Over centuries, letters to the editor have survived significant changes in the daily newspaper. They continue to give voice to powerful individuals as well as those at the margins, whose concerns would otherwise be unheard.

Horner took pleasure sifting through the day's mail. He was proud of his work and, if asked, would slowly draw on his pipe and declare with a wry grin that the "Voice of the People" was the most cussed and discussed part of the *Beacon Journal*.

By early afternoon, in his thoughtful and careful way, Horner had chosen several letters as candidates for the next day's editorial page. He routinely presented his choices to Stopher, the editorial page editor.

Both Horner and Stopher were sensitive to community standards of fairness. They were especially protective of the newspaper's reputation and the public trust by which it was held. Stopher would patiently help Horner decide whether hard-edged letters exceeded the standards or simply invigorated the debate, and invited readers to join in. The two men were especially pleased when letters selected for publication expressed views that differed from the opinions of the newspaper.

The Kent State demonstrations and tragic climax had brought an avalanche of letters to the paper. More than a week after the shootings, Horner seemed overwhelmed. He felt moved to add his own thoughts on the task of sorting through submissions to the "Voice of the People." Letters to the editor, he wrote, were "a mighty chorus, sometimes loud and strident, occasionally in a lower voice, but at all times an accurate barometer of the opinions, the emotions, the hopes and goals of *Beacon Journal* readers."

"Never have so many written so much about a single situation," he continued. They came from people of all ages, ranging from a seventh-grader to an alert 80-year-old grandmother, from people in all social and economic strata. Some were typed, some scrawled, some crudely printed. But each carried a message. Every letter was read and evaluated. Anonymous letters and those without addresses were filed.

One of Horner's important tasks was to contact the author of every letter to confirm identities and quiz them briefly about the accuracy of their opinions. That practice established the validity of each letter the *Beacon Journal* published, whether it was signed or carried a tag like "Lucifer," or some other intonation.

The first Kent State letters were published on May 6, two days after the shooting. An older graduate student from Wadsworth, Ohio, recounted being with two of the students who were shot and killed. "Those who died weren't wild, SDS bearded hippies. They were kids like my sons and daughters. They came to the Commons for a peace rally. They wanted to know how to get the word to our government that the Vietnam War is immoral."

After the shooting, one young man said, "You think this bloody mess is awful, just imagine what these kids have to do every day in Vietnam — kill, kill, kill …."

"Listen to them. You know in your hearts, they're right."

A letter signed by two men who gave Akron addresses urged

that when human lives are at stake, guns should not be involved. Specifically, they "demanded" that "National Guard troops shall not carry guns on college and university campuses."

The number of letters grew. Increasingly, they reflected the deep division about Vietnam and the campus shootings at Kent State. The tone of many letters was vicious. In the minds of many readers, differences of opinion about the war and the students were not to be tolerated. Conversations among old friends grew ugly when Kent State was mentioned.

The next day, May 7, an assistant professor at Kent State who said he witnessed the shootings, wrote that "murder would be a more appropriate word" to describe the killings, "but so many people pulled the triggers that destroyed two sons and two daughters that I must say 'sacrificed,' instead. Through my many contacts with students, I ... have seen no professional agitators. I have seen and heard only young men and young women concerned about the war in Vietnam and Cambodia."

His letter drew a sharp rejoinder 11 days later from a professor of philosophy at the University of Akron. He wrote that the letter from a Kent State colleague "reveals shortsightedness and an attempt at preserving one's own interest that I have found prevalent among some of my own colleagues. Apparently, many faculty members feel that student unrest and the consequent gathering of power is something to condone, merely as a matter of self-preservation."

Letter writers over the next several days were quick to assign blame for the killings. A man from North Canton wrote, "I hope that students who participated in the riots will not attempt to absolve themselves of a large share of the responsibility for the deaths of four young people. The students were amply warned by Governor Rhodes that violence would not be tolerated .... The whole generation of older, supposedly wiser adults must stop pandering to our youth and continually apologizing for ourselves and our actions."

A woman from Akron asked, "Does peaceful assembly mean burning buildings, running through the city destroying property, endangering the health and safety of innocent citizens? Does peaceful assembly mean defying orders to disperse and then turning on the National Guard with rocks and bottles; shouting obscenities? … Did they think they could threaten the lives of the National Guard and suffer no consequences?"

Some writers prescribed restrictions on behavior as a solution. A woman writing from Akron suggested, "When students are accepted at a college or university, they should be given a statement of rules and regulations. If they cannot follow these rules, which all are expected to obey, they should be dismissed."

The range of deep divisions on the participation and actions of the National Guardsmen varied widely. A woman from suburban Norton wrote, "The National Guardsman are NOT responsible for the death of four KSU students." A woman from Kent added a counter opinion. "To believe that Guardsmen, armed with bayonets, rifles and teargas, could be killed by stones is ridiculous."

The *Beacon Journal* also was the target of criticism from the community for its coverage of Kent State. A writer who listed his address as the First National Tower in downtown Akron wrote, "The blood spilled at Kent State University is in great part chargeable to the news media and much of it to the *Beacon Journal*." Other writers also had the newspaper in their sights.

A call for reason was voiced by a man from Hudson. "What I mourn, more than the needless death of four young people, is the slow death of reason, understanding, compassion and respect in relations between people."

A college student from Cuyahoga Falls, a large Akron suburb, blamed the rioters for the fatal shooting. "Where property and human lives are endangered by subversive activity, our law enforcement agencies, whoever they may be, should be permitted to use whatever means necessary to put down such disturbances."

The volume of letters increased. On Monday, May 11, an editor's note explained, "Because of the flood of mail the *Beacon Journal* has received on the Kent State tragedy, letters have been drastically condensed."

Nearly two weeks after the Kent State shootings, Bob Kotzbauer, a veteran government reporter, sat in Horner's office to interview him.

Kotzbauer wrote that through Friday, May 15, the *Beacon Journal* had printed well over 100 letters, 75 percent of them carrying the writer's name and address. Identification was withheld by request on the others, but no letter was published that had been submitted without a signature. Kotzbauer explained that this was a longtime *Beacon Journal* policy.

In addition to the published letters, the *Beacon Journal* received about 400 others, some anonymous, some with inadequate addresses, and some copies of letters sent elsewhere. Extra space had been made available on May 9, 12 and 13 to publish as many letters as possible.

By late July the newspaper had received nearly 900 letters. Reader anger came to a boil a few days after the *Beacon Journal's* exclusive July 23 blockbuster story revealing details of a Justice Department memorandum summarizing the FBI's investigation of the May 4 shootings. That exclusive story on the FBI report brought the harshest reactions. Several of those letters, published on July 30, 1970, revealed the intensity of that anger:

A woman from Orrville, a rural community west of Akron, wrote, "Are you sure you are not one of those longhaired rioters? I have never seen such bias, untruthful and bad reporting as has appeared in the *Beacon Journal* lately …. We have bought our last *Akron Beacon Journal,* and we have been buying it for 28 years …. if enough of your readers would do the same, maybe you would get the idea that 'Free Press' means nothing if it isn't truthful.'"

"I'd like to know how many Communist parties are paying you off for our stories about Kent State," wrote a woman from Uniontown. "Why didn't you put the pictures in of the four darlings as they really looked when they died? Your paper is nothing but a scandal sheet …. Doesn't it ever enter your mind that you are really hurting the law enforcement officials with these rotten stories?"

If readers thought the newspaper was supporting the cause of Communists and rioters, it was a time for an explanation. The editors decided to respond to these attacks on the *Beacon Journal's* credibility. Horner's editorial was placed next to the angry letters from readers.

The editorial explained that the letter "writers are all furious that the U.S. Department of Justice should find the National Guard blameworthy" for shooting the students. "Most of them also are angry that the *Beacon Journal* last week revealed the contents of the FBI-Justice Department report on the incident."

"The letters were not chosen for their uniformity; they came that way …. We are aware that some readers hold quite different views from those voiced here. On any emotion-charged issue, those whose reaction is anger feel the strongest urge to write to a newspaper.

"Reporters are trained to subtract their opinions from what they write when they are reporting events 'objectively.' Any report inevitably involves something of the reporter's way of seeing. In the Kent State tragedy, we tried hard to minimize this. We put a large number of reporters of widely differing points of view on the story and tried to bring you as much of the truth as we could uncover. But we know that has been something less than the 'whole truth.' It had to be.

"We aim to report the news as accurately as we know how, and as fairly and as thoroughly as possible. We cannot always do this perfectly. But we're trying."

It was a daunting time for Horner. A devout Roman Catholic, the worry lines that etched his brow gave testimony to his struggle to select a mix of letters that expressed the sense of the community with an honesty that was truth-telling and still within the bounds of fairness. Horner recalled a previous period when the flow of letters was so strong: the 1964 presidential campaign. Then, the issue of "extremism" and the candidacy of Barry Goldwater were hot subjects.

Throughout the emotional period after May 4, students, activists and faculty generally felt that the news coverage was fair and accurate. An examination of the letters to the *Beacon Journal* by D. Ray Heisey, a professor of speech, revealed that about 50 percent of the favorable ones were from people associated with Kent State University.

The newspaper received more criticism than praise for its publication of the special Knight Newspapers report three weeks after the shooting. The *Beacon Journal's* exclusive story on the summary of the FBI's investigation "brought the worst reactions."

Heisey added his own conclusion to the sharp division in the public perception of the *Beacon Journal's* coverage.

"Whatever the outcome of the legal problems associated with the May disturbance, at least journalistic justice has been done. It is a rare thing when, in the face of what must be and have been enormous pressures — political, financial and so on — a newspaper and its editor demonstrate so graphically a commitment to informing its readers.

"It is not an overstatement to say that without your dedication, Kent may not have survived. A number of students who claimed to be eyewitnesses to the events in May wrote in the face of much criticism to support the newspaper's version of the Kent State tragedy."

The *Beacon Journal* weighed in with its own take on the matter: The paper "does not pretend that it has been able to tell 'the whole truth' on this or any other matter," said the editorial. "Truth ... has a number of sides."

CHAPTER TWENTY
Two Voices

Two men. Two voices. Arthur Krause. Peter Davies.

Each voice was distinctively different. Each reached out to me after May 4, 1970, in a different way with a particular purpose.

Arthur Krause, in his deep sadness over the loss of his daughter, Allison, sought me out as one who would listen. He understood the role and function of the newspaper. He was consumed by a powerful rage against Rhodes and others he held responsible. His bitterness was palpable.

Krause called me at home nearly every evening for many weeks after the shooting. The wall phone in our small breakfast room would ring soon after I arrived from work. I would stand leaning against the wall, listening while my family sat as quietly as they could and ate dinner.

In the beginning, he poured out parental anguish. He spoke of a great sense of guilt over his disapproval of his daughter's passionate opposition to the Vietnam War. Krause explained that he was from a generation that believed fighting wars was the way to save the American way of life.

He wept. And there were long seconds of silence on his end of the phone. I knew to be quiet and listen.

Then, Krause shifted his emotions from grieving his daughter to lauding her right to dissent without putting her life in danger. His voice would rise in rage as he spouted ideas for holding the government accountable. Constitutional rights became personal. In

During the weeks and months following May 4, Arthur Krause (above), father of Allison Krause, and Peter Davies (below) communicated with the author about the newspaper's reporting and their ideas for holding officials accountable.

his mind, they were written in his daughter's blood. There would be no justice; a "whitewash" of the Guard was already in motion.

After several weeks, the regularity of the phone calls waned. Krause had been urging me to put the powerful voice of the *Beacon Journal* to work as an activist partner in the crusade he was organizing to hold the government accountable. He seemed, finally, to be persuaded by my explanation that such a partisan role for the newspaper was both unethical and inappropriate.

In early July, Krause sent a gracious note to Jack Knight acknowledging the newspaper's coverage. In his reply on July 10, Knight wrote "You have our heartfelt sympathy on the tragedy which befell you. Your communication will serve as added encouragement for our efforts to be fair and objective."

One of those to whom Krause now turned was Davies, who would become a sympathizer and an advocate. Davies was born in England and, in 1957, settled on Staten Island. During the ensuing 13 years, Davies became involved in a number of causes.

He was an insurance broker by profession and a person of strong opinions. He had no prior connection with Kent State.

A few days after the shootings, Davies wrote a letter of protest to Nixon. He sent a copy to Krause in Pittsburgh. Krause called Davies to express his appreciation for the support. As they talked, Davies listened with deepening interest to Krause's explanation of legal suits and appeals being planned by the parents of the dead and wounded.

Davies became fully invested in the cause for justice that Krause had laid out for him. He assisted in preparing a legal suit against Rhodes and the officers and men of the Ohio National Guard.

He was relentless in his devotion to the investigation of what happened on May 4. He wrote hundreds of letters that are now part of the Kent State collection at the Yale University Library. Copies of those letters fill two boxes.

The letters are dense. Single spaced. Often filling two pages or more. The ones he wrote me focused on the *Beacon Journal*'s news stories and editorials.

His first letter to the newspaper, written Sept. 29, 1970, was addressed to Ben Maidenburg. He asked for clarification on the accuracy of different reports listing the distances the student victims were from the National Guard's line of fire. The FBI investigation and the Knight Newspapers' special report listed several differing measurements.

"I realize the question of distances may seem somewhat irrelevant in respect to the enormity of the losses," he wrote, "but as I have been following very intently every aspect of this disaster through personal involvement and consequently become engaged in correspondence with a few people who consider the actions of the Guard justified, I am most anxious to have the facts as concise as they possibly can be."

Maidenburg shipped Davies' letter over to me with a plea to "take it off my hands."

I decided to dig into the disparities in the two reports. On Oct. 7, 1970, I sent Davies a two-page reply. I acknowledged that I was uncertain "how the FBI agents determined where each of the students were when they were shot. Nor did I know how the FBI measured those distances. So I can't comment on the accuracy of its count.

"The Knight Newspapers team pinpointed the locations of each of the 13 students by using pictures and by interviewing witnesses. Then we hired a surveyor to measure each of those spots from the firing line." I attached a transcript of the portion of the testimony presented during the Scranton Commission hearings that detailed distances from the firing line to each victim.

Thus began an exchange of letters between Davies and me that extended into 1971 and finally ended in 1975. He had found an editor willing to take seriously his inquiries about the work of the *Beacon Journal*.

On Oct. 12, 1970, Davies sent me another detailed inquiry about an item in *Newsweek* magazine reporting that Allison Krause had "bits of concrete" in her jacket pocket. He presumed that the information came from the FBI report and asked if I could "enlighten" him on this point.

In my response, I acknowledged that no one on the *Beacon Journal* news staff had access to any personal effects of any of the victims of May 4. Because I had carefully read the Scranton Commission report, I knew there was an incidental mention of the concrete pieces with no explanation and no attribution.

The next letter on Oct. 21 opened with an expression of "bitterness and in a sense of despair." His target was a *Beacon Journal* editorial commenting on an Ohio grand jury finding that "the Guardsmen fired at the students in self-defense."

The editorial summarized the grand jury's three major conclusions:

> Sufficient evidence exists to indict 25 persons for 43 alleged criminal offenses.
>
> Members of the National Guard, over-armed and placed in an untenable position by their commanders, acted in self-defense and therefore cannot be prosecuted for the killing of four students and wounding of nine others.
>
> Major responsibility for the whole series of violent incidents rests with the administration of the university.

"In fairness, one must agree, no one can be indicted," the editorial continued.

Davies expressed his outrage to me. His scolding letter went on for three-and-a-half pages. He wrote, "I felt so certain that the *Beacon Journal* would never call on us to agree that no Guardsman can be indicted."

The logic of the editorial's conclusions was also upsetting to me. I showed Davies' letter to the editorial writers, which influenced them to write a second commentary with "some further reflections on the Kent State Affair." In my judgment, this editorial, published Tuesday, Oct. 27, was no more satisfying that the original that ran Oct. 20.

"Investigation by a federal grand jury would be of doubtful value," the editorial said. "Those seeking such a probe evidently believe that this is the last hope for obtaining some sort of criminal accusations against members of the National Guard who were exonerated by the state's grand jury."

During Davies' and my final exchange of letters, in April 1975, I expressed surprise that an attorney from the Ohio Attorney General's office, in an interview with me, seemed most interested in learning whether the *Beacon Journal* had paid Davies for information about Kent State.

I wrote to Davies that I had assured the attorney general's representative that we had not. Paying for information was unethical and not a practice in which newspapers typically engage. I did acknowledge that we had talked to Davies on many occasions, had exchanged letters with him and had published a number of letters to the editor authored by him.

My letter to Davies continued, "I had the feeling that the Attorney General's lawyer was seeking information that would permit him to make an argument in court that the *Beacon Journal's* news policy was anti-National Guard/pro-student and that this influenced our coverage of the shootings and the investigations that followed."

CHAPTER TWENTY-ONE

The Pulitzer Prize

In November 1955, near the end of the fall term at the Columbia Graduate School of Journalism, Prof. John Hohenberg stood before the full class of 70 and put out a call for volunteers to help him weed out several years of Pulitzer Prize entries. The work would be done on Saturday mornings and would pay $25 a week. My hand quickly shot up. It seemed like a rare chance to get a close look at excellence in journalism.

Hohenberg was administrator of the Pulitzer Prizes and a legendary teacher of a course called "Washington Reporting and Foreign Correspondence." The class opened for me a myriad of possibilities about what life as a journalist could hold. When I arrived on the Columbia campus in September 1955, I was a green kid from the Midwest. I had never been to New York. Everything that year was a new experience, including my introduction to the Pulitzer Prizes.

Hohenberg's class sat at a round copy desk-like table in the World Room in the Journalism School building. The room was dominated by a famous stained-glass window entitled "Liberty Lighting the World."

For years, the window had been in the New York World building in Lower Manhattan. It was New York's tallest building when it was completed in 1890. It also was known as the Pulitzer Building after its owner, Joseph Pulitzer. Earlier in 1955, the World Building

Beacon Journal *editors and staffers watching the* AP *wire machine move news of the newspaper's Pulitzer Prize. From left: Tim Smith, Abe Zaidan, Ben Madenburg, Robert Giles, Ray Redmond, John S. Knight, Al Fitzpatrick (behind JSK), Bill Schlemmer, Kathy Lilly. (Akron Beacon Journal)*

had been demolished for a new ramp to the Brooklyn Bridge. The window had been salvaged and sold to Columbia for $1.

Hohenberg was my favorite teacher that year. He was an imposing figure with a lively intellect and a generous view of his students. The morning light that filtered through the stained glass into the World Room was church-like and, for me, cast a feeling of reverence about Hohenberg.

He told stories of covering the 1935 murder trial of Bruno Richard Hauptmann, kidnapper of the Charles Lindbergh baby. He sent us to the United Nations to get a taste of diplomatic reporting. He imbedded in our memories such unforgettable commands as "Go with what you've got."

A small group of us worked through the winter and spring of 1956 in the Pulitzer Prize office tucked in a seventh-floor room crammed with folders containing Pulitzer journalism entries.

Hohenberg wanted us to comb through the stacks of old prize submissions, some dating back to the 1920s, seeking examples of excellence that reflected initiative and enterprise. We chatted as we shared stories of courageous reporting and powerful tales of conflict and tragedy. These files would be set aside to be returned to the Pulitzer Prize archive. The rest would be discarded.

As we worked, I discovered that most Pulitzer Prize submissions tended to be hefty, packaged in all manner of scrapbooks. Their bulk reflected the assumption of newspaper editors that, with prize entries, the more, the better. Scrapbooks were packed with documentation of the "exceptional" nature of the story being entered. Many nominating letters from editors were compelling statements articulating the belief that their newspaper's work merited a prize. As our assignment weeding old Pulitzer files ended, I was energized by fresh discoveries of journalistic excellence, and dreamed of putting that knowledge to work in the newspaper life that might lay ahead.

In December 1970, Lee Hills, president of Knight Newspapers, sent a memo to editors noting that many instances of editorial excellence during the year merited consideration for Pulitzer Prizes and other awards. He noted that "We won three Pulitzers in 1968 as well as many others. We do have the material for 1970, and if we nominate wisely, we should have rewarding results." His note was read by editors already eager to test their paper's best work against the competition from newsrooms across the country.

Hills was an elegant-looking news executive whose impeccable appearance evoked precision of thought. He had a personal interest in the Pulitzer Prize. He was the winner in 1956 for deadline reporting for his coverage of negotiations between the United

Auto Workers and Ford and General Motors that resulted in the guaranteed annual wage.

Several weeks before Hills' memo arrived, editors in Detroit and I, in Akron, were thinking "Pulitzer" and separately plotting submissions for the Feb. 1, 1971, deadline. I wanted our entry to reflect the *Beacon Journal's* exceptional coverage of Kent State. Logic persuaded me that editors at the *Detroit Free Press* were shaping their own sense of excellence around the extraordinary Knight Newspapers team's 30,000-word special report. The *Free Press* had mastered the process in 1968 with its winning entry for coverage of the 1967 Detroit riots.

Luedtke, assistant to the executive editor of the *Free Press*, and I had several telephone conversations trying to define a strategy for the Pulitzer quest. Disagreement quickly became apparent. Each of us was trying to advance our own self-interest in how the Pulitzer entries would be shaped. We also wanted to avoid involving the corporate executives.

Luedtke's idea was to wrap the *Beacon Journal's* coverage into a Knight Newspapers entry with the Knight team's special report and submit it in the National Reporting category.

I argued strongly that the *Beacon Journal's* reporting should stand alone in a Local General News category. We talked often but with no resolution.

Our indecision created a vacuum, and it wasn't long before the bosses filled it. On Nov. 3, 1970, Maidenburg stepped forward and took up the *Beacon Journal's* cause in a letter to Lee Hills.

"There have been several suggestions from here and there that the report done on the Kent State shootings and the subsequent large 'scoop' of ours on the FBI report, etc., could be candidates for the Pulitzer Prize.

"We admit, with no reservations, that the big What-Did-Happen job was done with the aid of *Free Press* and (Miami) *Herald* writers. (Creating hyphenated expressions was a peculiar style of Maidenburg's memo writing.)

"Just how the time and effort could be apportioned I don't know. But —

"The *Beacon Journal* has never won a Pulitzer Prize, though it has been able to bask in the glory that went to JSK on his Notebook (1968). And I wonder if it is possible for you to say to the *Free Press* and the *Herald*, 'Let the *Beacon Journal* make the pitch to the Pulitzer Committee.'

"I assure you that, should lightning strike us, we'll have no reluctance about sharing the credits."

On Nov. 6, Hills responded by writing a long letter to Jack Knight.

"I would like very much to see the *Beacon Journal* win a Pulitzer and am all for it if we can work it out," he began. "The approach to it on the Kent State story has some complications and a lot of facets.

"There are two reasons why I think we might have to make an entry as being from a team from the *Beacon Journal* and Knight Newspapers.

"1. If it were entered only from the *Beacon Journal*, someone who read over the material would be bound to spot the fact that six or seven of the people most prominent in executing this special investigative job were non-*Beacon Journal* people and might challenge us as representing it to be the work of a team from one newspaper when it actually was a broader group effort.

"2. I do not know whether there would be any personal complications with the seven or eight *Free Press* people who were heavily involved in the project if it were entered strictly as a *Beacon Journal*-only performance.

"The job itself was so outstanding that we should prepare the nomination very carefully and make sure it has the highest possible chance for success."

The two letters made me feel uneasy. I knew Maidenburg did not have the authority to be a steady and persuasive advocate for the *Beacon Journal*. I did not want corporate loyalties to sway the decision. Their interests lay with Knight Newspapers Inc., not a single entity like the *Free Press* or the *Beacon Journal*. I also knew that Hills worked in Detroit, which meant that Luedtke had easy access to him for one-on-one talks about the merits of the Knight Newspapers special report as the logical Knight Pulitzer entry.

My unease grew and I felt powerless to safeguard my staff's excellence in the eventual outcome.

I carried this burden of worry and uncertainty to Detroit in early December where Luedtke and I were attending a Knight Newspapers wire service meeting. At some point, we ended up in the bar. After a few drinks — Luedtke was drinking bourbon Manhattans with no fruit and I was nursing a Dewars on the rocks — we got serious about finding a solution. We both lamented that corporate had gotten involved. We clearly did not want the Pulitzer-entry decision to be made by Lee Hills or Jack Knight.

Our long, bar room conversation wandered toward a compromise that would give each of our entries an equal shot at a Pulitzer Prize. There would be separate entries. One would be the special report by the Knight Newspapers team, which would be entered in the name of Knight Newspapers in the National Reporting category. One would be the *Beacon Journal's* coverage of the shootings and the exclusive stories the paper developed in the tragedy's aftermath. This would be the *Beacon Journal* entry in the Local General News category.

While I was in Detroit, Knight asked Maidenburg for an update on the Pulitzer entry. When I returned, Maidenburg asked me to write a note with an update for JSK. I outlined the plan Luedtke and I agreed on. It apparently satisfied JSK, and that ended the discussion.

We turned to preparing the *Beacon Journal's* entry, with the Feb. 1, 1971, deadline in mind. Our entry consisted of a nominating letter and tear sheets with samples of the critical stories we selected to ask the jury and, hopefully, the Pulitzer Prize Board to read. Our entry consisted of 10 stories written by 15 staff reporters.

To write the nominating letter, I had in mind an independent voice, someone who had experience in the *Beacon Journal* news-room and understood its culture. At the suggestion of Fitzpatrick, the news editor, we decided to ask Murray Powers, who had been managing editor for 18 years. After retiring from the *Beacon Journal* in 1966, he had joined the Kent State faculty as a journalism professor.

Murray was a soft-spoken task master, a stickler for accuracy and truth. He was portly, good-natured and an effective mentor to young staff members. One of Murray's passions was the circus. He made sure it got abundant coverage when Barnum and Bailey came to town. We often thought of Murray as long suffering. He was a frequent target of Maidenburg's wrath. Murray knew that Maidenburg needed to vent from time to time. He viewed his role as carrying Maidenburg's message to the newsroom but serving as a buffer from his bursts of anger.

The package nominating the *Beacon Journal* for the Pulitzer Prize went in the mail to Columbia in January 1971. I breathed a deep sigh of relief.

As I began my research for this book, I remembered I had never read Power's letter or seen the *Beacon Journal*'s nomination entry before it was sent off. (That might seem odd now, but back then, I was intensely busy running the newsroom and somewhat naive about the importance of the letter's quality in a Pulitzer bid.) In September 2018, with help from an old friend, Sig Gissler, a retired administrator of the prizes, my wife Nancy and I visited the Pulitzer Prize offices at Columbia. They were still on the seventh floor of the Journalism School building. The tables were still crammed with entry files and stacks of books, signs of a pending move to remodeled quarters. Momentarily, the sight gave me the same feeling of wonderment that I felt during those Saturdays in the winter of 1956.

Bud Kliment, the deputy administrator, was waiting for us. He introduced us to Dana Canedy, the new Pulitzer Prize administrator and a Pulitzer winner from her days at *The New York Times*. They were exceedingly gracious as we chatted about the experience of our Pulitzer project and my desire to look at the *Beacon Journal's* Pulitzer Prize file.

The Pulitzer Prize Collection is housed in Columbia University's Rare Book and Manuscript Library. The collection consists of the original prize-winning exhibits. In many cases, the exhibit is accompanied by an entry form, a nominating letter, a photograph of the winner and/or a biography of the winner.

Getting access to the Pulitzer Prize newspaper files was an elaborate process. We were accompanied to our destination in the university's Butler Library. Our first task was to establish our identity. The librarian explained the limits on material that could be taken into the "reading room." This was even quieter than most library spaces, with 10 tables and two chairs at each table. Glass doors gave a full view into the reading area.

The librarian gave each of us a pair of white gloves to wear in our search of the material. She explained that we had to use a No. 2 lead pencil to write notes from our research. Soon, she reappeared with a large tray holding an over-sized black scrapbook.

I was thrilled to see this signally important exhibit that had such an impact on my life and that affirmed the professional integrity of people who had worked so hard with me.

The sparseness of the file's contents surprised me. As I turned back the bulky cover, I saw the nominating form. On the next two pages was the nominating letter from Powers. Next came a letter of support from William J. Miller, president of Federated Department Stores Inc. in Cincinnati, and a column of his from the *Cincinnati Enquirer*. This was a head-scratcher. I had never heard of Bill Miller. The 10 stories in our exhibit were pasted on the large, black pages that followed.

Wow, I thought, *this is a pretty thin exhibit. The power of our stories must have carried the day with the Pulitzer jury and board.*

I was eager to read Power's letter. It was simple and straightforward.

"The stories reflect the shared belief of the reporters and their editors that Kent State deserved more than routine reporting.

With the national mood quickly fragmenting, and the tendency to explain the shootings with slogans, accusations and epithets becoming dominant, the *Beacon Journal* staff responded to the mandate for thorough, accurate reporting that would reveal the truth about Kent State.

"What distinguishes the *Beacon Journal's* work is that the nature of its disclosures, all under the pressure of a deadline, contributed to a common understanding of what happened May 4.

"Many of the gathered facts in these stories were exclusive and later became part of the larger investigative reports prepared by the FBI and other agencies."

I thought it was a wonderful letter. I loved Powers' phrase, "the *Beacon Journal* staff responded to the mandate for thorough, accurate reporting that would reveal the truth about Kent State." I gave him a huge virtual hug.

The path of the *Beacon Journal's* Pulitzer Prize entry was not an easy one. The first stop was the jury, which meets in the World Room. On March 4-5, 1971, some 45 journalists, most of them senior editors, gathered for their work as Pulitzer jurors. It is considered to be an honor to serve. Five journalists were assigned to each of the 10 journalism categories. At the end of two days, each jury submitted to Hohenberg a report ranking three finalists along with brief explanations for the jury's decisions.

In those days, the work of selecting Pulitzer winners was a closely guarded secret. At the beginning of the judging, Hohenberg gave the group a stern admonition to not gossip or share information about the entries with others sitting in the World Room or with colleagues back home.

As I finished my examination of our nomination file, the Pulitzer Prize office had another document for me. It contained details of the work of the General Local News jury in 1971. And it held a surprise: that year, the General Local Reporting jury was deadlocked. The members reported to Hohenberg that there was a tie for first place: the *Beacon Journal* and James V. Healon of the Hartford bureau of United Press International.

The jury recognized Healon for "reporting police cover-up of the facts in the killing of two burglars, his persistence in seeking rectification of the injustice, and the final successful conclusion of his efforts."

The jury's summary stated that the *"Akron Beacon Journal* reported the Kent State killings fast and completely, maintaining commendable balance in the face of strong local emotions and incorrect rumors which beset the area. It also obtained a major exclusive in publishing the contents of the FBI report later."

Members of the deadlocked jury included Evarts Graham Jr., managing editor, *St. Louis Post-Dispatch*, chair; Louis Guzzo, managing editor, *Seattle Post Intelligencer*; A. Edward Heins, managing editor, *The Register & Tribune*, Des Moines; Charles O. Kilpatrick, executive editor, *San Antonio Express & News*; William E. Giles, assistant general manager, Dow Jones & Co. (William Giles and I were not related.)

The Pulitzer Prize Board in 1971 was comprised of 12 senior editors; the president of Columbia, William J. McGill, and the dean of the journalism school, Edward W. Barrett. It was all-powerful. It was not uncommon for the board to overturn a jury's recommendation.

The board met at Columbia on April 8, 1971, and actively asserted its prerogatives in awarding Pulitzers. It overturned jury recommendations in three categories, awarding prizes to entries it thought more deserving.

One of the reversals was for the National Reporting prize. The jury ranked the Knight Newspapers special report second behind William Woo, a reporter for the *St. Louis Post-Dispatch*. When the board met on April 8, they passed over those top two finalists to designate a different winner, Lucinda Franks and Thomas Powers of UPI, for a documentary on the life and death of a 28-year-old revolutionary, Diana Oughton.

How the board chose between the *Beacon Journal* and Healon is not known. Hills was on the board in 1971. But his role with Knight Newspapers would have compelled him to follow the long-standing Pulitzer tradition of stepping out of the conference room when the board took up the tie. Pulitzer records show that Hills did not participate in the discussion and did not vote.

The Pulitzer Prizes were announced during the afternoon of Monday, May 3, 1971, just a year after the Kent State shootings. Anticipation in many newsrooms was rampant. Intense competition often led to small cracks in the secrecy surrounding the prizes. That morning, Maidenburg called me into his office and shut the door. He confided that he had learned from Hills that the *Beacon Journal* was being awarded a Pulitzer. He swore me to secrecy. We wanted the staff to be surprised when the prizes were announced that afternoon.

Around 3 p.m., Knight and Maidenburg joined a small group of staffers crowding around the AP wire machine, watching a series of Pulitzer stories roll out at 66 words a minute. When the machine began to tap the words "*Akron Beacon Journal* and Kent State" the celebration began. Shouts, hugs, handshakes, smiles and the pop of champagne corks followed. I was soon pulled away to take the first of a series of phone calls from the wire services seeking comment.

The AP quoted me this way, "We received a good deal of criticism from public officials and our readers at the time many of our stories were published. I think all of our stories stood the test of truth."

The UPI story quoted me as saying: "We used a variety of methods in obtaining our information. The first-day story, of course, was hastily put together with all the information we could get ...."

"The paper had a number of exclusive stories developed by reporters wherever they were able to dig stories out.

"The principal one, I imagine, was the story of the FBI report on July 23 in which we discovered the FBI investigation had found it had not been necessary for the Guardsmen to shoot the students."

I was grinning as I talked to a number of reporters, trying to focus on lucid answers to their questions while my mind was back in the newsroom where the staff was celebrating this extraordinary milestone for the *Beacon Journal*.

Bob Stopher's editorial the next day, May 4, 1971, captured what we all felt. The headline read, "A Pulitzer Prize We Wish We'd Won Some Other Way."

> We never thought to see the day when the Beacon Journal was sorry to win a Pulitzer Prize. We're seeing it today.
>
> Yes, newspeople on the staff worked hard and well and fast that day — with zero time for thinking about the implications or the impact of what they were doing.
>
> Instead, there was a terrible awareness of how fragmentary and incoherent were the bits of information we could sort out and get into print that chaotic afternoon.
>
> We were not satisfied then, or in all the trying we have done in the months since, that we were bringing you enough of the whole truth so that you could understand — and even we could understand.
>
> Obviously, many in the community were less satisfied than we. By critics firmly convinced that they possessed both the truth and the understanding — and the poles of difference in their convictions as to what that truth and its "correct" meaning were — we have been repeatedly and loudly accused of deliberate distortion.
>
> The only unbridgeable difference between us and the critics is this: We know how hard we were trying and are still trying. And we will go on trying to tell it to you straight. That's our job — the only way we can be worth anything to you.

CHAPTER TWENTY-TWO

Resistance and Loss

The four students killed at Kent State became victims of the consequences of a nation deeply divided by the chaos of the Vietnam War. Countless arrests, month after month, turned college students into rebels as a new counterculture of opposition to Vietnam took hold.

Americans were accustomed to supporting wars as acts of patriotism. However, the increasingly critical news coverage from Vietnam was confusing. Stories of mounting casualties and failed jungle engagements with the Vietcong were not welcome news — not what the country was accustomed to reading. Americans prided themselves in the belief that their nation had never lost a war. And yet, the growing reality that the country was failing in its mission to protect South Vietnam and stop the Communist takeover of Southeast Asia seemed to herald defeat.

On April 30, 1975, television images of the last helicopters lifting off the roof of the U.S. Embassy in Saigon told Americans the undeniable truth: Our country had lost the war.

In 1982, seven years after that rooftop evacuation and 12 years after the campus killing of four Kent State students, the Vietnam Veterans Memorial Wall was dedicated in Washington to honor members of the U.S. armed forces who died in service to their country in Vietnam/Southeast Asia. The Wall marked the beginning of the war, 1959, when the first American fell, to its bitter

Visitors share a quiet moment at the May 4 memorial. (Kent State University Press)

end, 1975, when the last casualty was recorded. It is a simple, elegant statement that honors American casualties but not the war. It stands in silent tribute to individual sacrifice. The names now number 58,276 and include eight women. They are a measure of the impact on a nation that persisted for 16 years in a failed military enterprise halfway around the globe.

The design for the wall was chosen in a competition from among 14,000 submissions. The result is a compromise borne of controversy fueled by its unconventional design, its black color and its lack of ornamentation. The chosen design was created by Chinese-American architect Maya Lin, a 21-year-old undergraduate at Yale University. Since its unveiling, it has become Washington's most frequently visited memorial.

The names of Allison Krause, Jeffrey Miller, Sandra Scheuer and William Schroeder are not among the 57,939 names that were originally etched on the two long walls of polished black granite. Yet, memories of the Kent State Four are as keen as for any of the men and women who died on the battlefield.

The sacrifice of the defenseless students was, in its own right, an expression of freedom guaranteed under the First Amendment to the Constitution of the United States. On May 4, 1970, believing they were safe on their own college campus, the rallying stu-

The light-post memorial to Jeffrey Miller on the Prentice Hall parking lot. (Robert Giles)

dents were exercising three of the basic freedoms protected by that amendment: freedom of speech, the right to peaceably assemble and the right to petition the government for a redress of grievances.

In the years immediately after May 4, 1970, a community of survivors struggled to honor the fallen at Kent State, dead and wounded. Initially, the university sought only to erase the memory of the killings. One early concession was its sponsorship, from 1971 to 1975, of an official commemoration each May 4.

In 1976, the university announced that it would no longer sponsor such commemorations. Ending university funding was intended to stifle future gatherings. Instead, the move inspired students and community members to organize the May 4 Task Force. The group's initial purpose was to organize an annual commemoration at Kent State. Each year since 1976, thousands gather on the campus for a silent march around the campus, a candlelight vigil, music, speeches from family, eyewitnesses, a leading voice and a ringing of the Victory Bell on the Commons in memory of those killed and injured.

Through the years, divisive emotions continued to run high. The May 4 Task Force's tightly knit community was resolved to challenge the university administration's stubborn resistance to the idea of creating an enduring memorial honoring the fallen. The Task Force expanded its initial purpose of supporting families affected by the shootings. They began educational programs and gradually raised awareness of the wide impact of May 4.

After years of contentious debate and discussion, and the continuing influence of incoming students who became engaged in the tradition of student activism, Kent State set aside a 2.5-acre wooded site overlooking the Commons. The university held a national design competition and chose an environmental concept by Chicago architect Bruno Ast.

The memorial was dedicated in 1986. It is constructed of carnelian granite, a stone associated with strength and time. The granite blocks are placed in a plaza measuring 70 feet wide, bound by a granite walkway that merges with the sidewalk winding from residence halls to the heart of the academic campus. The plaza extends to the hillside, ending in a jagged, abstract border symbolic of both sharp disruptions. It is an expression of the conflict of ideas. Many see in its form a suggestion that what happened at Kent State tore at the fabric of society.

The words "Inquire, Learn, Reflect" are engraved in the plaza's stone threshold. The inscription was agreed upon by the designer and Kent State University, affirming that the memorial site is meant to provide visitors an opportunity to pause and think about the dead and wounded. It encourages reflection on how differences might be resolved peacefully. In such a peaceful place, one cannot help but wonder how such savage violence could have occurred.

In 1999, at the urging of relatives of the four dead students, the university constructed individual memorials for Allison Krause, Jeff Miller, Sandy Scheuer, and William Schroeder. Raised rectangles of granite have been placed in the Prentice Hall parking lot approximately where each fell, mortally wounded. Each memorial space is framed by six light posts about 4 feet high with each victim's name engraved on a triangular marble plaque in one corner.

The effort to declare the shooting site a National Historic Place began soon after the May 4 Task Force was organized. Early applications to the National Park Service, which manages historic landmarks across the U.S., were turned down. It was thought that not enough time had passed to suitably evaluate the historical impact of the Kent State shootings. Forty years later, in 2010, the shooting site was registered on the list of National Historic Places as "Kent State Shooting Site." The completed site now covers 17 acres and includes landmarks associated with the shooting, including the Victory Bell, Taylor Hall, the Pagoda, and the Prentice Hall parking lot. Kent State is now one of 90,000 locations associated with impactful events that contributed significantly to U.S. history. The designation by the Secretary of the Interior came in 2016 and finally, on May 4, 2018, the site was officially recognized as a historic landmark, one of a select group of 2,500 historic places to share that distinction.

Initially, 58,175 daffodils were planted to bloom around the May 4 anniversary, to honor the number of American war dead. Daffodils still bloom there today, evoking an enduring connection between an unpopular war that dominated the news for more than a decade and the senseless killing of young college students.

On May 3, 2007, just before the yearly commemoration, an Ohio Historical Society marker was dedicated by KSU president Lester Lefton. It is one of 1,600 Ohio Historical Markers.

The front side of the Ohio Historical Marker reads:

May 4, 1970

In 1968, Richard Nixon won the presidency partly based on a campaign promise to end the Vietnam War. Though the war seemed to be winding down, on April 30, 1970, Nixon announced the invasion of Cambodia, triggering protests across college campuses. On Friday, May 1, an anti-war rally was held on the Commons at Kent State University. Protesters called for another rally to be held on Monday, May 4. Disturbances in downtown Kent that night caused city officials to ask Governor James Rhodes to send the Ohio National Guard to maintain order. Troops put on alert Saturday afternoon were called to campus Saturday evening after an ROTC building was set on fire. Sunday morning in a press conference that was also broadcast to the troops on campus, Rhodes vowed to "eradicate the problem" of protests at Kent State.

The back side of Ohio Historical Marker reads:

Kent State University: May 4, 1970

On May 4, 1970, Kent State students protested on the Commons against the U.S. invasion of Cambodia and the presence of the Ohio National Guard called to campus to quell demonstrations. Guardsman advanced, driving students past Taylor Hall. A small group of protesters taunted the Guard from the Prentice Hall parking lot. The Guard marched back to the Pagoda, where members of Company A, 145th Infantry, and Troop G, 107th Armored Cavalry, turned and fired 61-67 shots during thirteen seconds. Four students were killed: Allison Krause, Jeffrey Miller, Sandra Scheuer, and William Schroeder. Nine students were wounded: Alan Canfora, John Cleary, Thomas Grace, Dean Kahler, Joseph Lewis, D. Scott MacKenzie, James Russell, Robert Stamps, and Douglas Wrentmore. Those shot were 20 to 245 yards away from the Guard. The Report of The President's Commission on Campus Unrest concluded that the shootings were "unnecessary, unwarranted, and inexcusable."

In 2008, Kent State University announced plans to construct a May 4 Visitors' Center in a room in Taylor Hall. The center was officially opened in May 2013, on the 43rd anniversary of the shootings.

The Song That Changed a Nation

OHIO
Tin soldiers and Nixon coming,
We're finally on our own.
This summer I hear the drumming,
Four dead in Ohio.
Gotta get down to it
Soldiers are cutting us down
Should have been done long ago.
What if you knew her
And found her dead on the ground
How can you run when you know?
Gotta get down to it
Soldiers are cutting us down
Should have been done long ago.
What if you knew her
And found her dead on the ground
How can you run when you know?
Tin Soldiers and Nixon coming,
We're finally on our own.
This summer I hear the drumming,
Four dead in Ohio.

Music so often finds its voice as an expression of a nation's sorrow or outrage in a time of deep loss.

After the Kent State massacre, Neil Young wrote "Ohio." In a very short time, his lament, "Four Dead in Ohio," became the epic musical statement of anger toward President Nixon and the shock of Ohio National Guard soldiers taking up arms against citizen protest.

When Young saw the horrific image conveyed in Howard Ruffner's photo on the cover of *Life* magazine, he is said to

From left, Neil Young, David Crosby, Graham Nash and Stephen Stills. (CMA-Creative Management Associates/ Atlantic)

have disappeared for several hours and then returned to his band mates — David Crosby, Stephen Stills, and Graham Nash — with his song.

On May 21, 1970, the foursome went into the Record Plant Studio in Los Angeles and recorded it live in only a few takes.

After its release the following month, the song was banned from some AM radio stations because of the challenge to the Nixon administration in the lyrics. It soon received airplay on underground FM stations in larger cities and college towns.

Years later, *The Guardian* described the song as the "greatest protest record." For many, it remains a vivid remembrance of the awful tragedy on that warm, spring day in Ohio.

CHAPTER TWENTY-THREE

The Scranton Report

Drama that had been building for more than two months anticipating a hearing on the Kent State shootings began to play out
on Wednesday, Aug. 19, 1970. The stage was Cunningham Hall, a
1960s-era classroom building on the Kent State campus. Members
of *The President's Commission on Campus Unrest* gathered for the
opening session of their public investigation of the May 4 shootings.

The 250 seats were quickly filled, about three-quarters with
students. The air conditioning pumped chilled air as the hearing
began, but before long the audience was baking under the television klieg lights. The somber mood was a mix of sorrow and tragedy. Press from across the nation brought note pads, film and tape.
Over the next three days, an overflow crowd sat jammed on the
floor of a hallway outside the hearing room, listening intently as
the sounds of testimony were piped to them over a speaker system.

It was serious business for what was to become known as the
Scranton Commission. Its mandate was to reconstruct the events
that climaxed with the May 4 killing of four and wounding of nine.

William W. Scranton was appointed by President Nixon to chair
the commission. Known as a moderate Republican, Scranton was
a descendant of Mayflower colonists and the founders of Scranton,
Penn. The former governor was heir to a fortune in railroads and
utilities. His management of the hearing on the Kent State campus
reflected a soft-spoken, amiable, patrician style.

The Scranton Commission opened with Kent State University president Robert White as the first witness. He sits at the table in the lower right of the photograph. (Kent State University Press)

Sallot interviewed Scranton, who told him the commission's role did not include a criminal investigation. Its objectives were different from those of the FBI or law enforcement agencies. It would be seeking to learn the causes of the trouble, not just what happened.

The opening session of the commission on Aug. 19 was well-staffed with *Beacon Journal* reporters, eager to capture the tense mood as testimony of key witnesses began.

The newspaper was prepared to lead Page 1 with a running account of the early testimony. The first witness was Kent State University President Robert I. White. He wore his trademark dark suit, white shirt and tie. He sat on a folding chair and spoke into a large microphone placed in front of him on a makeshift table. As

*William W. Scranton
(Howard Ruffner)*

he spoke, he looked into a sea of photographers and television cameras. Commission members sat in a row at a table to his left.

The *Beacon Journal* had obtained a copy of White's prepared opening statement and published it on the front page of its first edition on Aug. 19. "I realize only too well," he began, "that the general public holds campus administrators responsible for much of our grief and that I am no exception, as my mail proves." He suggested to the commission, "You have had access to more solid evidence than I and I make no slightest pretense of knowing all the answers."

White was questioned by Kenneth "Red" McIntyre from Detroit, the commission's chief investigator. McIntyre was a veteran of federal investigations, having worked on the 1965 murder of three civil rights workers in Neshoba County, Miss.

Sallot and David Hess of the *Beacon Journal's* Washington bureau, observed that during his 40 minutes of testimony, White appeared at ease, puffing occasionally on his pipe.

Lt. Gen. Benjamin O. Davis, U.S. Air Force (ret.), asked whether faculty members participated in the disruptions. White's answer was emphatic. "I know of no faculty member who acted in the interest of the disruption ... the mass of our faculty was a tremendous, stabilizing influence."

Asked by the commission who was in control of the campus on May 4, White replied tersely, "The National Guard."

White was quizzed about Rhodes' decision to ban a campus rally at noon on May 4. He clarified, "It was not really an open question whether peaceful rallies would be permitted." In effect, he said, "The National Guard had decided to prevent any student groups from forming."

White was followed as a witness by Del Corso. The adjutant general had a military bearing and was proud of his long service in the U.S. Army. He became a commissioned officer in 1937. As a battalion and regimental commander in World War II, he saw action in the Pacific from Guadalcanal to the Philippines. Rhodes appointed him adjutant general in 1968.

It was Del Corso who had maintained that a sniper had first fired at National Guard troops and had then backed off on his statement. This was the first question posed to him. "Was he quoted correctly that the National Guard's own probe turned up no evidence of a sniper?"

His attorney, Charles Brown of Columbus, refused to allow him to answer. The question was rephrased. Del Corso then said the National Guard report "stated we never identified a sniper as such as defined by the military."

As the hearing adjourned on Wednesday, Hess approached Del Corso to inquire how he defined a "sniper." Was it someone "who is shooting from ambush — such as a rooftop — as distinguished from someone who may be firing while attacking from the front?"

The reporter continued to press the adjutant general, "Do you mean, sir, that the Guard report concludes that students were shooting as they approached the Guard formations?" Brown would not let him answer that question, either.

Del Corso finally responded as he ended the interview: "Our troops reported they thought they heard shots from other than military weapons."

During his turn on the stand, the adjutant general was grilled on National Guard policies on the use of lethal weapons. He said a National Guardsman is permitted to fire weapons only in self-defense to protect the life of another individual, and he is permitted to fire only single shots aimed at identifiable targets.

Del Corso added that each soldier must ultimately be his own judge of when he considers his life in danger or when he is in danger of being seriously injured.

During the first day's testimony, it was revealed that Rhodes had made a last-minute but unsuccessful attempt to postpone the start of the hearing. The governor said he feared that the commission might "taint" the work of the state grand jury investigation that he planned to impanel. The governor declined an invitation to testify before the commission. He claimed that he had no additional information to give.

Hess and Zaidan wrote a piece reflecting on Wednesday's testimony. The two reporters began with the observation neatly captured in the Page 1 headline: "In May, Everybody Shouted, But No One Was Listening."

They noted that panel members repeatedly asked witnesses for recommendations on how to resolve complex differences that "ripped the campus apart," leading to the shootings that still weighed heavily on the school's future.

"And repeatedly, the witnesses groped for answers that gave a hint of the scope of the problem. Perhaps the most significant commission finding will be a simple reinforcement of claims that both sides do a lot of talking but very few on either side seemed to listen."

Steve Sharoff, a graduate assistant in history — who helped stage the ritual burial of the Constitution on the Commons — testified that, "The channels of communication between the students and the administration are terrible and always have been."

The students, Sharoff implied, "are embarked on a moral crusade to right the wrongs they perceive and will not be deflected from their goals."

The report devoted 410 pages of its 537 pages to Kent State.
The remainder focused on the killings at Jackson State University.
(Doug Weaver)

His claim of inattentiveness by the KSU administration was challenged later in testimony by professor Glenn Frank. He contended that the channels of communications to air grievances and discuss problems are open "if the students will take the initiative and use them."

In its first-edition story on Thursday, Aug. 20, the *Beacon Journal* reported the exchange between Canterbury and McIntyre that revealed a conflict between the testimony of the Guard commander and President White.

Canterbury said his authority to disperse students gathered on the Commons before the shooting came from a directive issued on May 3 under Ohio law. It "gives state militiamen the power to disperse crowds during a clear and present danger." He also stated it was White "who informed us of the impending rally and asked that it be forbidden."

Canterbury asserted that White's request came at a meeting with Guard, university and city officials at 10 a.m. May 4. He denied that Rhodes' press conference statement on Sunday was an order to break up campus assemblies. "His proclamation gave us the authority to do what we had to do."

In fact, the decision to ban the rally can be traced to Rhodes. In his statements on May 3, the governor said he would be seeking a state of emergency declaration from the courts. He never did this. But it was generally accepted that the Guard was now in charge of the campus and all rallies were illegal.

On Monday morning, 12,000 leaflets were distributed on campus indicating that all rallies were prohibited as long as the Guard was in control of the campus.

Carringer found White willing to talk about his own testimony. He insisted that he did not ask Canterbury to disperse the planned May 4 rally.

White argued to the reporter that, "From past history, all my associates know that my response to whether the students should be allowed to assemble would have been affirmative."

"The record is clear," White said, "and if the commission wants clarification, I shall be happy to comply."

During his testimony Canterbury testified that the first sound he heard was a single shot "closely followed by a volley fired by Guardsmen."

Asked directly by McIntyre if he had given an order for the Guardsmen to turn and fire on students, Canterbury replied "no."

"We canvassed all the officers to determine if anyone had given an order to fire. The answer was negative."

Frank was a witness of high interest because of his powerful role after the shootings in easing tensions between the demonstrators and the Guard. He was considered by many to have performed a heroic intervention.

Extensive excerpts of his testimony ran in the *Beacon Journal* on Thursday, Aug. 20, describing his activities on May 4. He said he was sitting in the Student Union building where he could see students leaving the building. He left his lunch and went to the front of the Commons to see what could be done.

"A student came running down over the hill saying someone had been shot and they needed an ambulance immediately. I then ran back down to where the National Guard was stationed and there was a Kent State University ambulance there. I hopped in and we went to where the shooting had occurred.

"It was quite a chaotic situation. People were screaming — everything from 'Kill the Pigs' to 'Get the Guard off the Campus' — even telling me to stay the hell out of the way. A number of students recognized me and asked what they could do, and I said just try to keep the crowd back. They did an excellent job."

After the ambulance left, Frank said he returned to the National Guard area. "At that time a number of instructors were very heatedly telling General Canterbury things ... that they were murderers and so forth...."

"I ran up to the major (Harry Jones) who was in command. I told him, 'For God's sake, don't come any closer.'

"He said, 'My orders are to move ahead.' I said, 'It'll be over my dead body.' And he, thank God, stopped. I returned back down to the Guard area and asked if we could have time to get the students off. I was informed by General Canterbury that we had five minutes to disperse the group. I went to the group and made an impassioned plea, which apparently helped."

The commission concluded its hearing on Friday afternoon, Aug. 21, with Rhodes' decision to not testify as the dominate angle in the story. Sallot and Hess probed for an explanation for the governor's absence. Scranton told them the panel wanted to talk to Rhodes. "We asked him to come — and he refused."

Why didn't the commission use its subpoena power to compel Rhodes' testimony? Scranton replied, "We had only a limited time to conduct our investigation and ... (the governor) could have stalled us on this issue for a considerable length of time" in the courts.

Scranton, in his closing remarks, bore down on the commission's effort to avoid taking testimony that might compromise the upcoming grand jury investigation. He said, "We have no power to implement any recommendation we make, except the power of persuasion."

The Scranton Commission issued its report to President Nixon on Saturday, Sept. 26, 1970. Its conclusions drew mixed reactions. The expectation among many was that other legal forums would act more forcefully in laying blame, assigning responsibility for the murder and injury of students on an American college campus. Advocates for punishing the shooters and expelling students spoke more loudly than the calm, measured voice of the Scranton Commission as it shared its findings with the White House and a nation still reeling from the violent outburst on May 4.

Legal actions did follow — lawsuits, grand juries, two rulings by the U.S. Supreme Court among them. They were regarded by many as inconclusive.

"America, heal thyself," is how David Hess began his lead story on the Scranton Report in the Sunday *Beacon Journal,* Sept. 27, 1970.

Sadly, after all these years, there still is no justice from the Kent State killings.

The report, in its plaintive language, understood that the crisis on American campuses had no parallel in American history. It stated that only the president, by exerting his moral leadership through example and instruction, could effectively calm the rhetoric of both public officials and protesters.

In 1970, Richard Nixon commissioned the Scranton Report for a good purpose. Tragically he lacked the moral leadership to influence action, to create a movement to carry forth its straightforward ideas. In fact, he ignored its urgent plea that "nothing is more important than an end to the war in Indochina."

The report scolded a "small minority of extremists" and faculty who engaged in or led disruptive conduct. "They have no place in the university community."

The report also struck a strong First Amendment note, urging students to protect the right of all speakers to be heard, even when they disagree with the point of view expressed. "Dissent is a healthy sign of freedom and a protection against stagnation."

Therein is a message for today's activists, where a rise in reports of hate crimes on campus have prompted colleges and universities to implement bias-response teams, igniting a pushback from conservative students, controversial speakers and followers of the alt-right movement to claim that colleges are sanitizing campuses of dissent.

Finally, the commission was prescient in addressing the community of law-enforcement officers, discouraging the "issuance of loaded weapons to law-enforcement officers engaged in controlling disorders."

The *Akron Beacon Journal* gave its readers the most comprehensive and complete coverage of the hearings during the summer of 1970. But even those newspaper pages of notable explanatory journalism could not begin to do justice to the hearings.

As I re-read our stories describing the work of the Scranton Commission and its recommendations, I am mindful of how, in the 21st century, the United States became a nation in turmoil. The accounts from 1970 have value today in the truthful, transparent manner by which they conveyed the work of independent-minded citizens acting in the best spirit of a non-partisan inquiry.

The report the commission wrote and delivered to the president of the United States is a document to be lauded. It was meant to be read by the "American People." It is the work of a large staff of serious-minded women and men.

Their full report, published in book form, is a model for exploring the Kent State shootings, to be sure. But its penetrating assessment on the causes and origins of strife and violence afflicting college campuses was meant for the country at large — as a cautionary lesson for our future.

National Guard defendants, from left, James McGee, James Pierce, Larry Shafer and Ralph Zoller were acquitted in 1974. (Akron Beacon Journal)

CHAPTER TWENTY-FOUR

The Quest for Justice

The shootings at Kent State symbolize a great American tragedy. It is remembered by many people as much for the denial of justice as it is for violence and death.

The President's Commission on Campus Unrest was formed soon after May 4 and completed its report by the end of September 1970. It is important to note a fundamental reality: The work of the Scranton Commission was not a legal activity. It was intended to be an inquiry by a group of citizens over a limited time. It fulfilled its presidential mandate as a broad inquiry into the history and causes of campus unrest.

Those who remained aggrieved and angry could take little comfort in the commission's conclusions other than, perhaps, its vigorous support of dissent under the First Amendment and its harsh criticism of the Guard's action as "unnecessary, unwarranted and inexcusable."

Nothing changed. Four students dead. Nine injured. Countless thousands grieved, sharing a sense of pain, fury, and bitterness. The road ahead in pursuit of justice would be long and winding.

In addition to the Scranton Commission, other nonjudicial investigations were carried out immediately following May 4 by the FBI and Ohio Highway Patrol.

The Highway Patrol reported its findings in a 3,000-word document presented to Portage County prosecutor Ronald Kane on

July 22, 1970. The report was stamped "Confidential" and intended for use by a grand jury.

It was revealed later that the report placed blame for the shootings on the students. In effect, it exonerated the National Guardsmen who fired a barrage from their weapons into the demonstrators.

The Highway Patrol's report became the major resource for a special state grand jury that met in secret in the fall of 1970.

The FBI investigation was conducted by more than 100 agents. The initial wave of investigators arrived at Kent State within 24 hours of the shootings. Its 7,500-page report was sent to the U.S. Justice Department in late July 1970.

A summary of the FBI report was the basis of an exclusive story published by the *Beacon Journal* a day later, on July 23, 1970. The newspaper reported from the FBI's 14-page summary that the shootings "were not necessary and not in order" and that no Guardsmen were hurt by flying rocks, and "none was in danger of his life at the time of the shooting." The story and the meaning of its summary — one government agency blaming another — was a thunderbolt that overshadowed the previous day's news of the Highway Patrol's report.

Soon to follow these investigations was a series of court cases that would stretch over nearly a decade. Together, they were said to be the most complex and costliest series of courtroom trials at that point in American history.

The first of the criminal cases was a special state grand jury that drew on the findings of the Ohio Highway Patrol probe. Its purpose, the *Beacon Journal* reported, was to determine "if the fatalities should be classified as accidental or homicidal."

The jury was impaneled on Sept. 15, 1970. To begin the process, Portage County Common Pleas Judge Edwin Jones met outside the courthouse with the 15 jurors and a group of journalists. Before inspecting the shooting scene, they were given instructions. The proceedings were secret. Demonstrations at the courthouse were banned.

Then the jurors, trailed by reporters and photographers, walked over the Commons and inspected the Pagoda, the metal sculpture next to Taylor Hall, and the Prentice Hall parking lot where the four dead students fell.

Testimony began the following day when the first of more than 300 witnesses were called. Most of those who testified were students.

One month and one day later, on Oct. 16, the *Beacon Journal* reported that the grand jury had issued secret indictments against 25 people — mostly Kent State students — and one professor.

Coming just six months after May 4, nerves and emotions were still raw. A *Beacon Journal* story by Jeff Sallot and Ray Redmond reported that tight security was in place at the courthouse as the grand jury report was made public. As word of the grand jury's report began to spread, a crowd estimated at 600 began to form on the Kent State campus. The gathering remained peaceful at the urging of student marshals wearing orange-and-white armbands.

Sallot and Redmond itemized the jury's conclusions from its 18-page report. It exonerated the National Guard in the shooting deaths of four students and wounding of nine. It also assailed the Kent State administration for a "too-permissive policy toward radicals," criticized campus police for its "shocking inability" to stop demonstrators attacking firefighters as the ROTC building burned, and called the Guard's use of M-1 rifles to quell a campus disturbance "not appropriate."

The reporters noted that the "jury's report contrasted sharply" with those of the FBI and the Scranton Commission. The grand jury also concluded that the National Guardsmen who "fired the fatal volley May 4 acted in self-defense and cannot be prosecuted under Ohio law."

More than a year passed, however, before criminal trials began. During that time, public reaction to the grand jury report continued to be "intense and polarized."

The delay in the start of the trials resulted from efforts by lawyers for the "Kent 25," as the defendants were known, "to destroy the grand jury report and overturn the indictments." Judge William K. Thomas of the U.S. District Court for the Northern District of Ohio ordered that the jury's report be expunged because it "irreparably injures" the indicted plaintiffs — the Kent 25 — and would continue to do so as long as it remained in effect. However, Thomas allowed the grand jury indictments to stand but ordered the actual report to be expunged.

Appeals to the U.S. Sixth District Court of Appeals and, finally, the U.S. Supreme Court upheld Thomas's rulings. The lone dissent on the Supreme Court was Justice William Douglas, who wrote that Ohio anti-riot laws are "over broad."

Two official copies of the grand jury report were destroyed the week before the trial of the Kent 25 began. This seemed to only be a symbolic act. The report was now officially removed from public access, but the widely reported details of the report were indelible.

Even the weather complicated the dynamics surrounding the opening of the trial.

The front page of the *Beacon Journal* on Monday, Nov. 22, 1971, led with a story describing huge traffic delays from a 12-inch snowfall driven by "gusty winds" across the Akron area including Ravenna where the trial was to begin.

Reporter William Hershey's story at the bottom of Page 1 reported the opening of the trial. He began by explaining a series of "far-reaching gag rules" issued by Portage County judges Jones and Caris, noting "no cameras and a prohibition on artists' sketches of the court proceedings."

The first to go to trial was a student, Jerry Rupe, 23, charged with arson, striking a firefighter, interfering with a firefighter and first-degree riot in the burning of the ROTC building the evening of May 2. He was convicted of a misdemeanor, but the trial jury could not agree on a decision on three more serious charges.

The Rupe trial set a pattern of difficulty that plagued the prosecutors. Charges were dismissed against the second defendant. The third and fourth defendants pled guilty to first-degree riot. Jones ordered the fifth defendant, Mary Helen Nicholas, be acquitted for lack of evidence.

That ruling led to the bombshell two weeks later. At 2:06 p.m. Tuesday, Dec. 7, 1971, a state prosecutor, John Hayward, dramatically asked that charges be dismissed against the remaining 20 defendants. The *Beacon Journal*'s story by Herzog and Clark cited the far-reaching effects:

"It ends a major chapter in the Kent State affair, further discredits the work of the special state grand jury and brings to a close all but the civil suits that grew out of the Kent State disorders."

The defendants' relief and joy were understandable. At the start of the trials, the Kent 25 and their supporters were skeptical whether justice could be served for the dead and injured. The *Beacon Journal* editorial on Dec. 8 observed that the action taken by the prosecution to dismiss the remaining 20 cases "indicated that the system does work."

Still, legal accountability for the killings remained elusive. The question now was whether responsibility for the shootings could be found at the federal level. In late 1971, few could have predicted that federal courts would be preoccupied with Kent State issues for nearly seven years more.

Legal twists and turns kept the quest for Kent State justice on the front page: In 1971, the U.S. Justice Department decided it would not convene a federal grand jury. Two years later, the Justice Department changed its mind and opened an investigation.

On March 29, 1974, a federal grand jury, meeting in Cleveland, issued indictments against eight enlisted men of the Ohio National Guard. However, it found no conspiracy among the Guardsmen to fire into the crowd of demonstrators on the Kent State campus.

Beacon Journal reporter John Dunphy summarized the work of the federal grand jury. Its 23 members were sworn in by chief U.S. District Judge Frank J. Battisti on Dec. 18, 1973. During 39 sessions, the jurors heard from 173 witnesses including most of the 28 Guardsmen who fired their weapons.

Following their acquittal, from left, Guardsmen Barry Morris, William Perkins, James Pierce and Matthew McManus autograph a trial exhibit photo of them shooting students. (The Associated Press)

Following a long-standing practice in the federal judicial system, the federal grand jury did not issue a written report. Dunphy wrote that the lack of a report "leaves unanswered the question of who fired the first shot and what prompted the Guardsmen to turn 180 degrees almost in concert and fire a 13-second barrage into the crowd." The absence of a report fueled further confusion and ambiguity in the public mind.

Reporter Terry Oblander interviewed the parents of the slain students and described them as "relieved and glad that the truth about the shootings may come out of the grand jury indictments." It was an indication that hope had a firm grip on those who believed that inevitably there would be justice.

This optimistic expectation was to be short-lived. The federal criminal trial against the eight Guardsmen lasted only 10 days. On Friday, Nov. 8, 1974, Dunphy captured the end of the trial in his *Beacon Journal* story.

> Thirteen seconds of gunfire. These sounds began and ended the government's case.
>
> As the jury, lawyers, defendants and spectators sat hushed within the ornate courtroom of Federal Judge Frank J. Battisti Friday, a tape recorder filled the room with the sound of the fatal volley that erupted from Ohio National Guardsmen on May 4, 1970.
>
> It was the last piece of evidence offered by government lawyers before Judge Battisti turned to the chief prosecutor Robert Murphy and asked, "What specifically have you proven?"
>
> Murphy responded: "We have shown the shooting was unjustified and there was no danger posed to the Guardsmen's lives."
>
> Judge Battisti agreed, but added, "We need go no further in this case."
>
> With that he turned to the jury and read a 17-page opinion acquitting the Guardsmen because the government failed to prove its case beyond a reasonable doubt under the law. The sound of the gavel was an ominous note of finality.

The verdict was deeply satisfying to the eight Guardsmen. For the parents of the dead students, the nine wounded survivors, and their supporters, it was a bitter setback. They now saw only one remaining chance for justice in a series of federal civil suits — a total of 13 individual cases.

These cases were intended to compel Rhodes, National Guard officers, the enlisted men they commanded, and former president White to stand as defendants before each set of parents of the dead students and the nine survivors.

The plaintiffs pursued their cases on two tracks. One sought to sue the state of Ohio and its officials, hoping to find a jury that would hold Governor Rhodes and the National Guard responsible for the deaths and injuries. The second was to sue Guardsmen and officials as individuals, an approach that brought a moment of success.

The plaintiffs were repeatedly rebuffed because the courts, including the Ohio Supreme Court, ruled that the Guard and the governor were protected under the ancient doctrine of "sovereign immunity." This meant that Ohio, as a sovereign entity, could not be sued without its own consent.

After a series of appeals, the case, *Scheuer v. Rhodes,* reached the U.S. Supreme Court. In April 1974, the court ruled that the doctrine of "sovereign immunity" was not absolute and ordered the federal district court to hear the plaintiff's claim. The decision was unanimous, 8-0. Justice William Douglas did not participate.

More than a year later, Judge Don Young from Toledo and the U.S. District Court for the Northern District of Ohio was assigned to the trial. The mood was somber as the court convened at 10:37 a.m. on Monday, May 19, 1975.

Spectators craned to view Arthur and Doris Krause, the parents of Allison Krause. Rhodes created a stir as he arrived, barking a firm "no comment" to journalists. Down the marble corridor leading to the courtroom were Del Corso and Canterbury. The trio appeared to be unyielding and aggrieved that, once more, their actions were being challenged.

The wrongful death suit asked for a judgment of $46 million. The trial lasted 15 weeks, exceedingly long for a civil trial. The jury heard the testimony of 101 witnesses. The trial transcript ran over 12,000 pages.

Late in the afternoon of Aug. 27, 1975, the jury of six men and six women ended 33 hours of deliberation and returned to the courtroom to announce their decisions.

The bailiff trembled as he read each of the 13 verdicts. The packed courtroom sat stunned as it listened to the exoneration of Rhodes and the National Guard officers and soldiers for the shootings. Three of the women jurors wept. They had voted to hold the officials accountable.

"The bitterness of families and survivors could not be restrained," Dunphy wrote:

> "This is an outrage. There is no justice," yelled Alan Canfora, who had been shot through the wrist by a Guard bullet.
>
> "Murderers," shouted Thomas Grace, Canfora's Kent State roommate, who was felled at the time when a bullet tore through his ankle.
>
> Arthur Krause moaned, "My God."

It was inevitable that the verdict would be appealed. On June 21, 1977, after a year-and-a-half of preparation, oral arguments were heard by a three-judge panel of the Sixth Circuit Court of Appeals in Cincinnati. Three months later, the court ordered a new trial.

Its opinion also stated that all claims against former president Robert White should be dropped because he had no control over the National Guard on May 4, 1970.

As Judge Thomas gaveled the start of the second federal civil trial on Dec. 11, 1978, talk of a settlement was in the air.

The *Beacon Journal* reported that plaintiffs in the case "tentatively have agreed to drop their suit if they receive a total of $600,000 and a public apology from the defendants."

The final settlement was $675,000, announced on Jan. 4, 1979. The largest share went to Dean Kahler, who was paralyzed below the waist from a National Guard bullet and would never walk again.

The *Beacon Journal* reported that the main stumbling block in negotiating the settlement was the wording of the statement. The key was achieving language that the plaintiffs could call "an apology" and the defendants could claim was nothing more than an expression of "regret."

The statement was signed by 28 defendants. It acknowledged that "the tragedy of May 4, 1970, should not have occurred....We deeply regret those events and are profoundly saddened by the deaths of four students and the wounding of nine others." Among the signatories were James A. Rhodes, Sylvester T. Del Corso, and Robert H. Canterbury.

The out-of-court settlement ended a long and painful judicial examination of the terrible wounds from May 4. Editorialists expressed hope that it would initiate a period of healing. In reality, that was a false hope. The settlement of cash and a statement of regret cannot undo what happened 50 years ago. Annual commemorations every May 4 honor the memory of the victims and decry the failure of our judicial system to hold officials responsible.

One actor in this tragedy who, at the most critical moment, could have prevented the killing of students by the Ohio National Guard was Brig. Gen. Robert Canterbury.

He was the highest-ranking officer on the Kent State campus on May 4. He was in command of the troops. During his testimony in the 1975 federal civil trial, he denied responsibility for several command responsibilities.

He said he had had no direct responsibility for the weapons used and whether they were loaded. He denied responsibility for the tactics of his troops and the methods of dispersing students protesting against the United States invasion of Cambodia, as well as their expressions of anger at the presence of his soldiers on their campus.

According to a story in *The New York Times*, Canterbury said he knew that the Guardsmen had been armed with rifles, .45 caliber pistols, and bayonets and had assumed that the weapons had been loaded but that he did not discuss this with his junior officers. He said the decision to carry loaded weapons was up to the unit commanders and not him.

Canterbury's testimony demonstrated the extent to which the

Families and victims listened to details of the settlement in November 1979 that ended nearly a decade of legal cases. Dean Kahler is in the left foreground. An unidentified man is seated to his left. Next to him are Martin and Sarah Scheuer, parents of Sandy Scheuer. Next to the Scheuers are Elaine Miller Holstein and Artie Holstein, parents of Jeff Miller. Arthur Krause stands against the back wall (holding a cigarette). In front of him is Doris Krause. (Kent State University News Service.)

National Guard sought to sow confusion and avoid responsibility in its effort to thwart justice and shift the blame to the victims. The finger-pointing appeared to be circular.

Canterbury was the product of a long career in the military. He knew that tradition and military law define the authority a military officer exercises over subordinates by virtue of rank or assignment.

On May 4, 1970, his failure to effectively direct the troops under his command was a serious breach of leadership. It served to stigmatize his units for generations.

Dunphy's story detailed the effort of Robert Blakemore, the plaintiff's attorney from Akron in the federal district court, to draw from Canterbury an admission that the ultimate responsibility for the troops and command decisions was his and his alone. Blakemore's further line of questioning was blocked by Judge Young during the trial in U.S. District Court that began in May 1975.

Canterbury's testimony, reported in *Beacon Journal* news stories and captured in court transcripts, show that he failed to exercise the qualities of command and leadership that are indispensable to an officer.

It is fair to wonder how he avoided accountability for his failure to control his soldiers when others were charged with committing crimes for their acts at Kent State. How did he avoid being held accountable for his leadership failures in a court-martial under the Uniform Code of Military Justice?

The law is clear. Pursuant to both the UCMJ and federal law, members of the Army National Guard are subject to court-martial only when they are placed in federal service. Thus, if the Ohio National Guard units (Companies A and C and Group G) and their officers had been ordered to duty at Kent State by President Nixon, they would have been "federalized" and subject to the UCMJ. They could have been court-martialed. Instead, their assignment in Kent was at the call of Gov. Rhodes responding to a formal request from Kent Mayor Leroy Satrom. At Kent State, the Guardsmen and their officers were in the state of Ohio's service and not subject to the charges and punishment of the UCMJ.

Moreover, the special state grand jury concluded that the National Guardsmen who "fired the fatal volley May 4 acted in self-defense and cannot be prosecuted under Ohio law." This verdict provides the explanation why Canterbury was never charged under the laws of the state of Ohio.

It is fair to say that Canterbury did not intend for his troops to shoot and kill students. But they did. Moreover, it was his failure of leadership and command that contributed to the deadly actions that day.

It also could be said that Canterbury was a victim of Rhodes' irresponsible leadership. However, this does not excuse his failures at Kent State.

In the military, a commander is responsible for the actions of those he or she commands. It is their responsibility to ensure that those under his or her command act in a manner consistent with proper military judgment and decorum. Canterbury failed. As the officer in command, he paid no legal price for his failures of judgment and leadership at Kent State. He was the individual who was in command of those Ohio National Guard soldiers, yet his official military record is unblemished.

May 4, 1970, will continue to weigh heavily on those who remember, including, perhaps, on the general.

Visitors to Kent State leave constant reminders that Flowers are better than bullets. (Doug Weaver)

CHAPTER TWENTY-FIVE

The Meaning

The quest to understand Kent State, to give it meaning, has persisted for nearly 50 years.

Its impact begins with the Vietnam War. The war changed America as a country. We still carry the scars left by the loss of more than 50,000 fighting men and women and the deaths of millions of Vietnamese. Within the puzzle of that war, Kent State is a unique, complicated, distinctive, tragic event.

The Kent State shootings have helped define the limits of political and moral tolerance for state violence.

Never before had U.S. soldiers purposely shot and killed American college students on their own campus. "They killed our children" is a common refrain I heard whenever I talked about this book.

National Guard bullets trampled our sacred First Amendment protections to speak and demonstrate against the war without fear. Many of those gathered on the campus on May 4, 1970, also were making a statement of resentment that a military unit was occupying their university. The campus was their turf. The anger at men in uniform toting guns ran very deep. These staggering realities set the Kent State massacre apart from other anti-war protests. It marked a loss of innocence.

At the same time, across our land, men and women in uniform were returning home from service in Vietnam. Tragically, their welcome was disrespected and dishonored. Hometown parades were rare. The nation was not in a mood to acknowledge their courage, dedication, and individual sacrifice. Doing one's duty in the service of our country was not enough. In the minds and hearts of many Americans, our combat units bore responsibility for a failed war waged by politicians.

Shooting at human targets with "malice aforethought" is the common-law definition of "murder." After 50 years, it is evermore clear that the Ohio National Guard committed acts of murder that have gone unpunished. On that fateful day, four Guardsmen fired M-1 bullets with malicious intent and killed Jeffrey, Allison, Sandra, and William.

The consequences of that moment influenced a series of critical outcomes that affected the larger society, immediately and over time. These must be acknowledged to define the *meaning* of Kent State:

The campus shootings forced a change in the Ohio National Guard regulations. No longer would live ammunition be permitted to be carried by units patrolling campus demonstrations. Other National Guards across the country followed suit.

Anti-war protests blossomed across the country in the days after the shootings and became the largest national student strike in American history. The demonstrations rolled on, giving unity to generations well beyond Vietnam. Today, especially, we witness young people taking to the streets demanding political action on guns or women's rights.

Kent State had a direct influence on national politics. In his book, *The Ends of Power*, H.R. Haldeman, a top aide to President Nixon, wrote that the shootings began the slide into Watergate two years later, eventually destroying the Nixon presidency.

The voting age was lowered from 21 to 18. The proposal was approved by Congress in March 1971 and was ratified as the 26th Constitutional Amendment in July 1971. It was the quickest constitutional ratification in American history. It invited millions of new voices to help elect our leaders.

In June 1973, Congress passed legislation that prohibited the use of additional funds in Southeast Asia starting two months later

... after Aug. 15. It marked the first time both chambers had agreed to withdraw funding from the war.

The draft was ended when the existing draft law expired in 1973. In 1968, as a presidential candidate, Richard Nixon promised to end selective service. He calculated that young people would lose interest in protesting the war if they knew they would not have to go to Vietnam. An all-volunteer military was introduced.

In a 1974 Kent State case, *Scheuer v. Rhodes,* the U.S Supreme Court ruled that public officials acting in their official individual capacities could be brought to civil trial for their actions.

First Amendment privileges were strengthened in the market-place of ideas. Over time, an increase in court decisions protected the freedoms it guaranteed. Many of the cases reflected the interests of young people stubbornly challenging the status quo, advocating a new counterculture, and bravely making public statements against the war.

The meaning of Kent State embraced a growing recognition that the government was fallible. The war and its consequence bred cynicism. Citizens mistrusted their institutions. Adults lost the will to act when change was needed after school shootings and other tragic events. The spirit of young people speaking out for what they believed began to make a difference. Youthful activism replacing adult complacency continues today.

John Filo's photograph of anguished Mary Ann Vecchio screaming over the dead body of Jeffrey Miller has achieved iconic status. Still today, it is symbolic and influential, touching off strong emotional responses. It will always endure as the most recognizable and remembered image of Kent State.

To this list, I add this concluding thought:

Reconstructing the Beacon Journal's coverage of the Kent State shootings offers important touchstones for today's citizen struggling to discern who and what to believe. The newspaper's work argues for the power of good journalism.

I will explore the values of 1970 and how to recognize them, even in today's partisan media environment.

First, let's find the reality in today's media landscape by posing a question:

If Kent State happened tomorrow, what would the news coverage look like?

That question persisted for me as I reconstructed the *Beacon Journal*'s work in today's time of dramatic change in newsgathering technology and practices. My own career had encompassed many of these defining changes in journalism while always holding steady on truth as an unshakeable value.

As I puzzled over my own question, it seemed immediately clear that if four students were killed at Kent State tomorrow by troops of the Ohio National Guard, the *Akron Beacon Journal* would not influence the telling of the story to the degree it did in 1970.

Today, the images and sounds from the Kent State campus would burst into view on the power of the internet. The ubiquity of hand-held devices would enable many among the thousands of witnesses to capture the tragedy unfolding before them. The desire to serve a culture of impatience —*I want it now* — would be prevalent. Urgency would be the enemy of accuracy and care.

Horror and fear — as in 1970 — would be etched on the faces of these witnesses as nimble fingers and thumbs struggled to tap out the news on their phones. The avalanche of sounds, voices, and images would be overwhelming. Many on the campus would be sickened as they recorded the bloody chaos, struggling to make sense of a world changing before their eyes. Others would follow the human instinct to aid the wounded scattered among them.

Command of Twitter, Facebook, Instagram, and email would send the stunning news on a near-instant global journey: "Four Dead at Kent State!"

The wire services soon would file the first professionally crafted bulletins. The public's eyes would be fixed momentarily on digital accounts urgently popping up on cell phone screens and office computers. Repeated bulletins and fresh updates would keep a nation transfixed.

Initially, the crush of digital information would be unmanageable for editors and news directors to sort out as they scrambled to give the public an accurate, focused picture of what had happened.

Before long, though, differences would emerge. Common facts would no longer be universally accepted. The cultural wars of the time would twist reason and truth in the emerging search for blame. Each witness would possess personal evidence they would carry with them for a lifetime.

The digital images would shape memories; some would become weapons for taking sides, framing opinions, and inserting bias.

If Kent State happened tomorrow, competition would multiply. Algorithms would create a moment in which hundreds, maybe thousands, would be clicking, trying to tell the story. During the early hours and days, digital forms of communicating details of this tragedy would give rise to misinformation. Eventually, the public would turn to legacy news organizations that remained "old school" in their reliance on traditional reporting protocols.

Cable channels and analysts would be on air within hours, parsing selected footage intended to serve their audiences: Guardsmen's lives were truly in danger. Or not. Protesters were innocent victims acting within the bounds of a peaceful, constitutionally protected demonstration against the Vietnam War. Or not. Voices of protest were honorable. Or not.

Ebb and flow. Twists and turns. Attitudes would begin to harden.

If Kent State happened tomorrow, would it be possible to extract a truthful narrative from such a jumble of information and misinformation?

The sad reality is that the *Beacon Journal's* capacity today to tackle a huge story like Kent State is but a shadow of what it was in 1970. It is gamely publishing a daily newspaper with a staff of 35, as compared with 150 in the mid-1970s. The shrinkage of its newsgathering resources follows a national trend. It is left without the reporting resources that could devote months to closely track the growing campus unrest — to observe each demonstration as it played out on the Kent State campus.

The proud, professional legacy of Jack Knight and Knight Newspapers is just a memory. The company whose newspapers excelled for so many years was sold to the McClatchy Company in 2006. It was a sad ending for the nation's second-largest newspaper publisher and a move that reflected growing uncertainty in the industry.

Soon after McClatchy became the owner of the *Beacon Journal,* the company decided that Akron did not fit its vision of a growth market. The *Beacon Journal* was sold to Black Press Ltd., a Canadian firm with limited experience in running medium-sized newspapers.

In April 2018, the *Beacon Journal* was bought by GateHouse Media, a holding company and one of the largest publishers of locally based print and digital media. In a series of cost-saving measures, the number of journalists at the newspaper has fallen sharply. Its future will soon be defined by a publishing strategy in the joint enterprise of GateHouse Media and Gannett.

In spite of these reversals and in keeping with a trend reflecting the changing world of local newspaper journalism, the *Akron Beacon Journal* remains the major source of local news in the greater Akron area.

The paper's local news dominance matches the findings of a Knight Foundation-Gallup poll, released in late 2019, showing that local news media are more trusted than national media.

The study concluded that "Americans still believe local news outlets are doing many things right" in informing their communities. Local journalists are seen as more caring, trustworthy, and unbiased.

The Knight-Gallup study warns, though, that the trust of local news outlets is more fragile than previously understood — and vulnerable to the same perceptions of partisan bias that threaten confidence in the national news media.

The reader may feel disheartened after reading my imagined scenario of a "Kent-State-Shooting-Today" and how it might be covered in social and mainstream news media.

But hope is not lost. There are, in fact, lessons here that remain vital in the interest of helping readers become better news consumers and making our republic stronger. It is also comforting to know that today's readers *know* this. They understand the consequences of social media, the partisan bickering, the twisting of the truth, claims challenging the validity of "facts." They live it daily.

At heart, the premise of this book is to reinforce the values of journalism a half century ago and suggest how they might serve us all today. Facts did matter in the most profound way as the *Beacon Journal* news staff's reporting shaped a narrative by which the public could begin to understand the terrible tragedy at Kent State. Day after day, the stories set an accurate framework that influenced other reports, documentaries, and studies. Readers trusted the *Beacon Journal's* accounts; for many, it became their truth.

So, here are those lessons. Consider them a toolbox for understanding today's news events.

Be wary of rumors, misinformation, and disinformation

Rumors were plentiful after May 4. They were not dismissed out of hand. Instead, they were carefully examined and given their due, if justified, by the paper's reporters and editors. Our journalists had been taught to check the data, search papers of record, talk to people in a position to know, and publish stories that were anchored in the best available version of the truth. We did not print rumors. We vetted them and sifted out what was true.

The best example of misinformation was how National Guard officials worked to shift blame on the students for threatening the lives of their troops. Guard commanders apparently were convinced that a sniper had fired on their troops. This was their truth. For a few days, this rationale was widely accepted and used to deflect criticism of them while focusing fault instead on the demonstrators.

The *Beacon Journal,* though, waited to judge. It conducted its own investigation, demonstrating that the suspect bullet hole in the metal sculpture could not have been caused by a bullet fired at the Guard. Only after the *Beacon Journal* reported the details of a test firing proving that no evidence existed of a sniper bullet, did the sniper theory fade from public discussion.

Unfortunately, in today's political climate, misinformation is repeated as true again and again, even after it's been proved false. This becomes *dis*information — a deliberate tactic of lying in the face of well-documented truth. It works because lazy news consumers allow it to work.

Welcome the scrutiny of the powerful

Today's partisans tend to offer blind affinity to their top leaders — and label as "fake news" any report that questions those leaders. They shouldn't.

Gov. Rhodes' intemperate remarks on Sunday, May 3, for example, were given a full, straightforward account by the *Beacon Journal*. His was the voice of authority, able to redirect the mission of Ohio's National Guard. So, we could not ignore his scornful statements labeling student demonstrators as violent hippies, as "worse than brownshirts."

This wasn't fake news. This is what Rhodes believed as the elected chief executive of the state of Ohio. His words *were* news. In turn, stories about him and his angry remarks, including his refusal to close the university before May 4, were based on extensive reporting.

Careful readers of all persuasions recognized that the *Beacon Journal's* breadth of coverage was holding him responsible — as much as a daily newspaper could hold a high public official responsible.

In the end, he was the one who set the stage for state violence on May 4. Our scrutiny of Rhodes was fully justified.

Beware the journalist bearing opinions

Our journalists did not have the freedom to speculate or write news analyses. Opinions and commentary were published on the editorial pages, where they belonged. The op-ed page, now a staple in daily newspapers, was not introduced until later in 1970. Knowing facts, creating a truthful narrative, and being objective empowered the staff. Fair, balanced reporting gave a voice to the truth.

Unfortunately, today, too many journalists have merged fact-finding with their opinions of what is true. You see that daily on cable news stations. In newspapering, the line between fact-finding and opinion remains strong. *The New York Times*, *Washington Post* and *Wall Street Journal* have different opinions on their editorial pages. But all boast excellent newsrooms staffed by informed, fact-finding reporters and editors.

Those newspaper standards are what you should seek out in other media — including cable shows, podcasts, websites, blogs, and the many forms of social media.

Pay attention to those journalists with deep sourcing

Beacon Journal reporters tested sourcing in a string of breaking news reports. How deep did a source's knowledge go? Did the source have a solid track record of speaking the truth, of providing an accurate account of events? Talking with sources required a degree of skepticism.

We knew the challenge of deciding which sources were credible. We understood that sources were critical to obtaining timely information, whether from a person, publication, record, or document. We often fell back on sources' willingness to go on the record and be public. Anonymous sources were scarce in our Kent State coverage.

Today, with the social-media rush to judgment, too many news consumers are impatient to wait for the facts. That's understandable but unfortunate. A remedy is to identify early those reporters with good track records in terms of sourcing and being consistently factual. Then give them the benefit of the doubt on breaking news. Chances are their deep level of sourcing and their own standards of reporting are at work within that news.

If a reporter ever fails in that measure, drop him or her like a bad habit.

Seek out those who seek objectivity ...

We practiced objectivity in the original sense of the word. Objectivity was the ultimate discipline of journalism then, the rock-bottom imperative requiring that all news writing deal objectively with the facts. There was no room for subjectivity. It was recognized that complete objectivity might be unattainable but striving for it was the grail of journalism. Objectivity could always be improved upon. The daily emphasis on this quality earned the trust our readers accorded us. Truth mattered.

... but beware of false equivalencies

The expression "false equivalence" was not part of the journalism vocabulary in 1970. Neither was the imperative for "he said, she said" balance in stories. Our reporters were taught to give each side, *all* sides, an appropriate voice. That didn't mean an equal voice. Over the years, that lesson has been hard learned on the topic of climate change. Today, the deniers no longer are accorded equal treatment in the news columns of responsible daily newspapers.

Beacon Journal editors and reporters had been taught to recognize when one point of view lacked substance or could not yield facts, just opinions. They understood that deep reporting, asking hard questions, looking at records and finding sources who knew the facts would eventually yield the truths that readers expected.

Don't get sucked into conspiracy theories

Conspiracy theorists were quick to contend that Students for a Democratic Society (SDS) or the Black United Students (BUS) might have been outside agitators and influential forces behind the May 4 rally. But news stories quickly provided evidence that the Kent State demonstrations were homegrown.

Citizens with strong anti-communist sentiments continued to believe that radicals were to blame — some still do — but as *Beacon Journal* stories pointed to other possible causes, the passion for seeing a communist threat on the campus killing field seemed to diminish. Even the National Guard's continuing reference to a sniper or soldiers made fearful of rocks hurled by students began to vanish under the weight of hard-nosed reporting and intense questions of the journalists.

Our newsroom recognized that the conspiracy theorists were generally misinformed. Over time, our commitment prevailed to discover and publish the truth.

Always be skeptical of what you hear

A final tool: Embrace skepticism.

Gone are the days when we could find comfort in a shared and equally respected news media. At Kent State, there were no ideologies to face in shaping our coverage. Some Democrats supported the Vietnam War, and Republicans were among those in opposition to Nixon's policies. Partisan news outlets were not as influential in 1970 as they are today.

Careful news consumers should be prepared to watch and listen with some degree of skepticism — even if those sources routinely reinforce your values and beliefs.

The *Beacon Journal* news staff got Kent State right the first time. So did the young student photographers. So did Glenn Frank, the brave geology professor. And, yes, so did the Kent State students who wanted the Ohio National Guard off their campus so they could freely express their opposition to the Vietnam War.

My thoughts often go to John Darnell's brilliantly timed and accurate image that captured the moment when Guardsmen were shooting to kill.

The soldiers were clustered under the Pagoda next to Taylor Hall. Their faces hidden with gas masks ... steel combat helmets on their heads. They aimed their M-1 rifles right at their targets, demonstrators on an American college campus. They murdered four college kids.

Among those Guardsmen are four killers. They fired the fatal bullets that took life from Jeff Miller, Allison Krause, Sandy Scheuer and Bill Schroeder.

A remembrance, held by the Victory Bell in 1995. (Kent State University Press Service)

The military worked hard to protect the identity of those killers. Finally, the U.S. Justice Department produced a roster of 29 men by name and rank who admitted to shooting. Five other men denied firing and were omitted from the list. A roster of those Guardsmen has been published. The specific identities of those who fired the fatal bullets remain uncertain; they are killers, unpunished — tragic examples of what war does to decent men.

It was more than 40 years after May 4 that the U.S. government acknowledged to the United Nations that the killings were "murder."

In 2010, the family of Allison Krause organized the Kent State Truth Tribunal, with financial support from filmmaker Michael Moore. Its purpose was to "reveal the truth and establish a clear and correct historical record from the collective voices of Kent State."

Laurel Krause, Allison's sister, is cofounder and director. She says, "Telling the truth about what happened at Kent State is at the political heart of this barbaric incident. They took our family members, but we will not let them take our truth."

In her speech at the 45th May 4 Commemoration in 2015, Krause reported that the Kent State Truth Tribunal in 2014 had brought Kent State before the United Nations Human Rights Committee in Geneva.

"There, something remarkable happened," she said. "The U.S. delegation at their formal treaty hearing and review admitted, 'In 1970, four students were killed, were murdered and nine injured.'

"In a simple phrase, and for the first time in 45 years, our government finally admitted what we all knew to be true — this was government-executed murder.

"Our response was also simple," Krause continued, "Now that our government has established that Kent State was murder, we demand they treat Kent State as murder and immediately examine the evidence in the forensic digital findings that captured the order to shoot. We know the statute of limitations never expires for murder."

Even after admitting to murder, the Justice Department declined to open a new inquiry into Kent State.

After 50 years, Kent State is woven into the fabric of our national conscience. May 4, 1970, became a movement of its own, anchored in the belief that truth does matter.

The movement must continue.

Afterword by Mitch McKenney
Getting Truth to Matter Again

It definitely would have live coverage.

That's the first difference you would see if — as author Robert Giles imagined in this book's final chapter — the events of 1970 at Kent State University happened instead in 2020. At each demonstration ahead of May 4, some in the crowd would be holding up phones, sharing live video.

Imagine that happening with images of a burning ROTC building on a Saturday night, or the police officer on a bullhorn ordering everyone to disperse that Monday. If 3,000 demonstrators and spectators were in the Commons area, how many would be documenting it live? Several hundred?

If it were happening now, a cable network might switch to a live feed of Northeast Ohio around the time of the tear gas canisters, with a BREAKING NEWS banner underneath and guests on set to analyze campus unrest nationwide. Viewers unwittingly would see fatal shootings live on their screens, and even if they didn't see it live, the video would certainly get repeated in wall-to-wall coverage — though perhaps without the most graphic moments.

Over the next few pages, this essay considers how changes in the news ecosystem would affect coverage of a similar incident today, what journalists are facing as their industries fight for survival, and what those interested in truth can and should do now. In short, how can we make sure truth still matters?

My personal connections to this are as someone who grew up reading the *Beacon Journal* in the 1970s, who learned journalism at Kent State 15 years after the shootings, and who in 1998 started a decade editing local news and features at the *Akron Beacon Journal*. By then Giles had already left to be editor in Rochester, N.Y., and then Detroit. Knight had died in 1981, though the newsroom keeps his silhouetted image on a door, and its journalists still hear from readers who remind them – usually when pointing out an error – that Knight never would have stood for that. I left to join the Kent State University journalism faculty in 2008.

In 1970, as Giles put it, "journalism was done differently, when there was no internet, cable TV and social media to shape stories or fan points of view." That was a time when people expected you to know what was in the paper. Now media messages come at the audience whether it wants them or not — and plenty have decided they hear enough news and don't need to go looking for more. Newspaper penetration, the percentage of Akron-area people seeing what their hometown journalists produce — even counting online views — doesn't come close to what it was in 1970.

And no longer does someone deliver the editor's lunch on a silver platter.

What else is different? The *Beacon Journal* newsroom and printing presses aren't at 44 East Exchange Street anymore. Over the past decade, owners of legacy newspapers realized the value of their downtown real estate had grown while their need for vast square footage had shrunk, prompting owners to sell their buildings and presses and rent offices and time on a press. In the *Beacon Journal's* case, the new digs are down the street in a renovated building where B.F. Goodrich used to make tires. The newspaper itself gets printed and trucked in from a neighboring county.

Fifteen journalists shared in the *Beacon Journal's* 1971 Pulitzer Prize, a fraction of the vast newsroom at the time. In contrast, while packing for their office move in October and taking final pictures before leaving, staffers counted their entire newsroom at 40, including part-time sports statisticians.

When considering how local journalists might cover a similar incident today, it's likely the reporter would be expected to post updates of the scene upon arrival, probably a couple of images and live video, and thus devote less time asking questions. This has been the norm for sports and spot news — that reporters have to stop and file while the story's still going on. The upside to doing this in the digital age is the reporter doesn't have to leave the scene to find a working pay phone or friendly secretary.

It's also conceivable that much of the initial reporting wouldn't look all that different: Reporters at the scene, following up with police, witnesses, families, officials and others, looking to get the immediate story right. Any journalist then or now will recognize the challenge of learning the victims' identities before the authorities wanted to release them. Not necessarily to publish them before their families are told, but to understand as much as possible. I haven't known a newsroom that didn't take pride at rallying on the first day of a big story.

Following a weekend with the apparent arson of a campus building, the governor's choice of words the next day and the National Guard's presence on campus, it's likely at least one reporter and photographer would be assigned to cover the planned rally. Maybe a pair of modern-day Kent State journalism students like Jeff Sallot and Paul Tople.

On the *Beacon Journal*'s end, the editors could see for themselves what's happening — both from their own reporters' postings and what other media (particularly television stations) post. But it's worth noting that by 2019, with sales of papers and mergers of newspaper companies, the *Beacon Journal*'s editor now has a corporate role in which he oversees the *Record-Courier* in Kent and seven other daily newsrooms in Northeast Ohio. In our hypothetical, it is possible there would be collaboration between the *Beacon Journal* and *Record-Courier* newsrooms and staffs.

It's the reporting on the days following the shootings that might look different.

The account from 1970 describes a phalanx of editors directing a roomful of reporters to get answers and provide context. They would attend meetings and hearings and trials, work to pry public records loose and insist officials answer their questions. Today, once the shooting stopped, how many reporters would have deep sourcing or even name recognition of the people involved?

As Giles put it, "Most journalists today hold passionately to the values of their craft, just as they or their predecessors did in May 1970. ... Over time, shoe-leather reporting, good sources and deep knowledge of the subject at hand builds trust — trust between reporters and their sources, trust with readers in knowing that a story has been exhaustively reported, carefully edited and focused on the truth."

Of course he's right that the trust is under threat, and let's add that the crisis started long before Donald Trump decided to make "the dishonest media" a target. Even setting aside the oft-rehearsed arguments over biased reporting in a story or on a network, it's inarguable that the public's trust and confidence in news organizations is nowhere near what it was in 1970. (Look up reports from Gallup, Pew, Knight, Kettering and others to see for yourself.)

That trust started falling before cable news arrived in 1980 and continues to fall in nearly every telling, tracking with a wider distrust of public institutions. So certainly it's vital that tomorrow's journalists be taught to build trust by developing good sources, asking the right questions, cherishing accuracy and getting righteously angry at those who lie to them. I'm happy to say that's my current job description.

My duties also include teaching media literacy each year to hundreds of students from across the university by managing a popular course called *Media, Power and Culture*. It does some things you might expect from a class like this, such as explore the news business and show why we have free speech and press freedom in the First Amendment. But more broadly, it demands that students think critically about who's behind the various media messages that barrage us — whether it's in news, entertainment, advertising or tweets — and explore the motivations for them.

In short, citizens can't be passive mass media *users* anymore. No matter how old they are, what work they do or where they live, they need to scrutinize the stories they see and hear. They need to challenge dubious claims on social media and show they care about truth. Often, I show them the altered version of John Filo's image of Mary Ann Vecchio kneeling over the body of Jeffrey Miller, next to the real one that ran on The Associated Press wire. The altered one doesn't include the fence post that appears to come out of the teenager's head. It's unclear how Filo's original image was manipulated to eliminate the pole. It has been a controversial topic over the years. We talk about whether an altered photograph can still be true.

To show how to be a news consumer, I show them one of the various online grids that rank news outlets by quality of news content on the y-axis (ranging from high to poor), and political bias (far left to far right) on the x-axis. The most partisan of students usually want to argue their favorite sites' placement, and it's good debate to have.

I also make them watch and react to *Spotlight*, the 2015 film detailing *The Boston Globe*'s Pulitzer-winning investigation that uncovered how the archdiocese covered up child sexual abuse by priests. The film won the Oscar for Best Picture, and the cast includes Mark Ruffalo, Rachel McAdams, Liev Schreiber and Kent State alumnus Michael Keaton. In their response, students are to explain the journalism and ethics issues involved. Examples: Deciding on whether to use anonymous sources, sorting out conflicts of interest, and holding the story even though additional people could be victimized in the meantime.

Each time, I have students who offer an additional comment about how much they liked it. One said she watched it a second time with her family. Others have said thanks for making them do the assignment. I like that the *Globe* journalists relied on shoe-leather reporting — interviews and documents — and following leads until they found documents exposing the coverup. They faced resistance from the community, the church and even within their own newsroom, but in the end they got to the truth.

I ask students to do the same as what I would ask of any adult citizen: Don't take what you hear at face value. Find out who said so, and why. Use online tools that let you check for faked photos, made-up stories and other hokum. Better yet, don't share anything on social media that doesn't come from a source you know well. And stop going around the paywall and buy a subscription so that the news source can keep paying its employees. Good journalism doesn't come cheap.

Finally, here's a slightly revised version of the original question that raises more questions: If the events of 1970 happened now, how would today's journalism affect the outcome? Would smartphone video of the events of a similar May 1, 2 and 3, shared in real time, bring attention that somehow would alter the climactic events of May 4? Would knowing there was live coverage that day affect decisions by protesters or Guardsmen? Presumably having social media video of the events would make it possible to offer the public a better view of what happened after the fact. But as America's recent history with police confrontations shows us, even video can be misleading without additional information.

Today's audience scrolls through a social media news feed with good information right next to misinformation, from sources of varying quality and motivation, and no grownup in charge. The threat to journalism that Giles referenced goes beyond what newsroom employees control. We also need a population that values truth and doesn't mind working to discern it.

You could get lost in what-if's of how such an event in 2020 would play out now in local media and on the national stage — if National Guard troops, called to a campus amid antiwar protests, turned around and fired into a crowd — and what the reporting might look like in the hours and days that followed.

May it remain just that — a thought experiment.

Mitch McKenney is an associate professor of journalism and mass communication at Kent State University

About the Author

Robert Giles was curator of the Nieman Foundation for Journalism at Harvard University from 2000 until 2011. He came to Harvard after a newspaper career of nearly 40 years that included editorships at *The Detroit News*, *Times-Union* and *Democrat & Chronicle* in Rochester, N.Y., and the *Akron Beacon Journal*. Before coming to Harvard, Giles was a senior vice president of the Freedom Forum and executive director of its Media Studies Center in New York City.

Giles is a member of the American Academy of Arts and Sciences. He is a graduate of DePauw University and Columbia Graduate School of Journalism. He was a Nieman Fellow in 1966 and received an honorary doctorate from DePauw in 1996. He was a Pulitzer Prize juror eight times.

Giles and his wife, Nancy, a psychologist and a specialist in trauma, live in the Traverse City area of northern Michigan, where he is active in several civic organizations, including serving on the editorial board of the Traverse City *Record-Eagle*. The Giles have three children and four grandchildren.

The Beacon Journal newsroom circa 1970 looking across to the City Desk and the News Desk.

Celebrating the Pulitzer Prize, May 1971. From left, Ray Redmond, Bob Giles, John S. Knight, Pat Englehart, Jim Herzog and Kathy Lilly.

Truth Tellers

Dear Reader,

The journalists you meet on the pages of *When Truth Mattered* were my colleagues at the *Akron Beacon Journal* in 1970. A few were friends. But for most, our relationship was shaped by the reality that I was the boss. My memories of them in that extraordinary time run deep. I think about them with great affection and appreciation. It was rewarding to work with them. They created the *Beacon Journal's* truthful narrative of an American tragedy. I want you to know about their lives before and after May 4, 1970.

AL FITZPATRICK

Al was born in Elyria, Ohio, the seventh of 12 children. In 1956, at age 28, he graduated from Kent State. He was the first person of color at the paper at a time when the *Beacon Journal* newsroom had lots of rednecks, hillbillies and drunks. Al began on the state desk and worked his way through critical editing roles. By 1970, he was news editor responsible for directing the editing functions of getting out the paper each day. His was an indispensable role in keeping the paper running while the focus was on the Kent State shootings. Al succeeded me as managing editor in 1973, when I became executive editor. It was a proud moment for all of us to recognize that Al had become the highest-ranking black newspaper editor in the country. Al blazed many trails during his 29-year-career at the *Beacon Journal* and beyond. In 1979, Fitzpatrick became coordinator of minority affairs for the Knight-Ridder group. He later served as assistant vice president. He has won many awards for his distinctive and directive actions in advancing the cause of journalists of color in U.S. newsrooms. He is retired and lives in Akron with his wife, Derien.

PAT ENGELHART

Pat was born in Zanesville, Ohio, and began his newspaper career at the hometown paper, the *Zanesville Signal*. After graduating from the Medill School of Journalism, he worked in Fairmont, West Virginia, and Evansville, Indiana, before being hired to fill an opening on the *Beacon Journal* wire desk in 1954. He worked for 10 years as a copy editor, then left the paper in 1964 for an opportunity on an industrial magazine. He returned in 1968 as state editor. He and his wife, Marge, lived in the small town of Mogadore. Kent State gave Pat a mission. He was a fiery, whirlwind commander of the state desk in the late 1960s and 1970s. He drove reporters and editors to be the best that they could be. His quest for the truth was unquenchable. Or, as a colleague said, "He had a lust for Rolling Rock and the truth." Those who cussed him for cracking the verbal whip also loved him for his dedication. Pat retired from the *Beacon Journal* in 1990 and moved to Ocala, Florida. He died there in 1995 at 70 from T-cell lymphoma.

RON CLARK

Ron, a native of Smithville, Ohio, was a graduate of Kent State and earned a master's degree from the Medill School of Journalism at Northwestern University. After service as *Beacon Journal* city editor and metropolitan editor, he became editorial page editor. Ron left the *Beacon Journal* in 1981 and moved to St. Paul as chief editorial writer of the *Pioneer Press*, a position he held for 21 years. He was diagnosed with non-Hodgkin's lymphoma in

October 2001 and the following June took a leave from the paper to fight his cancer. He had hoped to return to the paper, but reconsidered after a case of shingles sent him back to the hospital. "It's not good for me and not good for the newspaper to have that uncertainty," he said. "I just wanted to bite the bullet, end my association with the paper and go to work trying to get the cancer behind me." He died at the age of 60 in 2003. His obituary described him as the "gentle man of the editorial page."

HARRY LIGGETT

Harry was born in Dennison, Ohio, a small community midway between Columbus and Pittsburgh. He graduated from Ohio State in 1953 and, after military service, became city editor of *The Evening Chronicle* in Uhrichsville, Ohio. Eventually, he left his life-long home in Dennison and moved to Akron after he landed a job at the *Beacon Journal* in 1965. He became an assistant state editor and was admired as a mentor to young reporters. John Olesky, who worked alongside him as an assistant editor, recalls that Harry was determined, quietly ferocious and gruff. Harry was remembered by others as a no-nonsense guy who wanted to do the right thing. Harry was a strong-willed president of the Newspaper Guild unit at the *Beacon Journal*. Once he stormed out of a bargaining session with management, slamming the door with such vigor that the sound could have been heard at the Knight Newspaper headquarters in Miami. It did resound; he won the concession for his co-workers. After his retirement in 1995, Harry created an online scrapbook, BJ Alums. It chronicles the passing of former colleagues and posts updates on the activities of living retirees. Harry died of cancer at 83 in January 2014.

HAL FRY

Hal Fry, a native of Washington, D.C., and a graduate of the University of Michigan, served in World War II and received the Legion of Merit for his work with photo reconnaissance. When he joined the *Beacon Journal* in 1949, he was fluent in four languages and spoke seven. Recalling his fatherly influence as a copy editor, one of his colleagues said of him, "If you ever had a question, you went to Hal. If you were smart, you went to him first." Precision and conciseness were two principles that characterized his influence over 34 years at the paper. At the time of the Kent State unrest, Fry worked on the main copy desk. He anchored the editing of many of the difficult and complex stories produced by the reporting staff. When he retired in 1983, he also had worked as a reporter, feature writer and, finally, as an editorial writer. In retirement, he wrote "Publish It!" a history of the *Beacon Journal* as it marked its 150th anniversary. He liked to travel and to work with his hands. He built two large additions to the family home in Cuyahoga Falls, Ohio. He died in November 2004 at 86 after a long struggle with Alzheimer's disease.

CHUCK AYERS

Chuck Ayers graduated from Kent State with a degree in graphic design. He began his cartooning career as a staff artist at the *Beacon Journal*. Later he became the newspaper's editorial cartoonist. Chuck's experiments with an idea for a comic strip emerged as "Crankshaft" about a cranky old bus driver. He also drew a second strip, "Funky Winkerbean." Both strips are loosely based in Northeast Ohio and contain local references. The comic strips are syndicated in U.S. newspapers and across the globe. Ayers has taught cartooning at Kent State and the University of Akron. His work has been printed in *The New York Times*, *The Washington Post* and school textbooks. His sketches of the aftermath of the campus shootings on May 4 were published the following day and contributed unique elements to the *Beacon Journal's* coverage of the tragedy. In 2010, Chuck and Tom Batiuk, who created the story lines for "Crankshaft" and "Funky Winkerbean," dedicated illustrations from the two strips in the Kent State student lounge.

HELEN CARRINGER

Helen, a native of Canton, Ohio, came from a family with a strong work ethic and limited resources. In 1943, she entered the journalism program at Ohio State but was unable to continue her studies. Her determination took her to New York, where she worked as a secretary and took night writing classes at Columbia. She moved home to become editor of an employee publication and then was hired by the *Canton Repository*. She was women's editor for 14 years before coming to the *Beacon Journal* in 1966. Her assignment as education writer took her often to the Kent State campus. She was a fine writer who poured enormous energy and dedication into everything she tackled. Helen was always polite when dealing with public officials. That open and genuine exterior often disguised the solid steel underneath that drove her to get at the heart of the story. She was appointed an editorial writer in 1976. She won a number of prizes for her stories on education, her columns and editorials. Helen was 59 when she died in September 1982 after a long illness.

JOHN DE GROOT

John is a native of Philadelphia and a journalism graduate of Kent State. He worked on the staff of the *Record-Courier* in Ravenna and Kent before joining the *Beacon Journal* as a reporter in 1965. His gifts for story telling won him admirers among *Beacon Journal* readers. He was metropolitan editor at the time of the Kent State unrest but volunteered for reporting duties and contributed exclusive stories about Gov. Rhodes' activities on the campus in May 1970. Soon after Kent State, deGroot left Akron to accept a reporting position with the *Miami Herald*. Later, he became city editor of the *Fort Lauderdale News*. He was a key part of a *Fort Lauderdale News* series that exposed government corruption in the 1970s. When the *News* folded in 1992, he moved to the *Sun-Sentinel*. Later in his career, his column was one of the most-read features in the *Sun-Sentinel*. He was a highly gifted writer who wrote a Broadway play about Ernest Hemingway. He lives in Fort Lauderdale.

JIM HERZOG

Jim, a native of Stamford, Connecticut, was a graduate of Grinnell College in Iowa and the Columbia Graduate School of Journalism. He served in Tunisia with the Peace Corps before joining the staff of the *Beacon Journal* in 1970. He won a conservation writers award for his coverage of strip mining. In 1972, Herzog moved to the Louisville *Courier-Journal* where he was an investigative reporter. The newspaper sent him to its Washington bureau in 1976. In 1977, he went to work for Scripps-Howard. He covered the White House from the start of the Reagan administration. He was on a presidential trip to the G-7 Ottawa Summit in July 1981 when he discovered the first symptoms of cancer. He continued to work until June 1982. Following Jim's death in August 1982 at 39, President Reagan sent a letter to his wife, Margot. "Jim exemplified the best of his profession. We'll miss him, his sense of humor, his warmth and most of all, friendship."

DAVID HESS

David was up from "the hollows" of West Virginia. His father, Willard, was a newspaperman, and David soon became curious about the stories his father covered. His love of people and the world around him defined his military, professional and personal life. He earned a degree in geology and a master's degree in political science from Ohio State University. David served in the U.S. Army during the Korean conflict He retired from the U.S. Naval Reserve in 1989, having achieved the rank of commander. He took pride in his life's endeavor, writing about government. He developed a serious pursuit of journalism in an alliance with Abe Zaidan. Together they produced a thoughtful, provocative liberal magazine in Columbus, the state's conservative capital. David didn't mind the long hours and accepted the low pay as the price of writing about complex budgets and the quest for evidence of deception. After the magazine closed, he followed his colleague, Zaidan, to Akron. In 1971, he was named Washington correspondent for the *Beacon Journal*. He was president of the National Press Club in 1985. Zaidan remembers that David was "an awful poker player. Just awful." David moved back to Columbus in 2013 to be with family and friends. He died in July 2017 at 83 after complications from a series of strokes.

SANFORD LEVENSON

Sandy Levenson was born in Lyndhurst, a suburb of Cleveland. He received his journalism education at Ohio University. After graduation, he found work as a copy editor on the *Indianapolis News*. He joined the *Beacon Journal* in 1966 where, for 35 years, he held a variety of roles including editor of *Beacon* magazine and features writer. He was a gentleman and a gentle man, widely appreciated for his skill in writing headlines. A colleague described him as "a gem!" Following his retirement from the *Beacon Journal*, Sandy worked as news editor at the *Medina Gazette*. He passed away in July 2008.

Photo by Will Englund

KATHY LILLY

Kathy is a native of Cleveland and a journalism graduate of Ohio University. She worked on the staff of the *Herald-Dispatch* of Huntington, W.Va., before joining the *Beacon Journal* in 1969. She left the paper in 1975 and became a foreign correspondent for the *Baltimore Sun*. During 29 years at the *Sun*, she spent many years working in the Soviet Union and witnessed its coup and fall. She took a buyout from the *Sun* and was hired by *The Washington Post*, first as an editor and, then in 2010, she became Moscow bureau chief. After Kathy Lilly divorced her first husband, she began using her maiden name, Lally, and her bylines in *The Post* now read "by Kathy Lally."

LACY MCCRARY

Lacy is a native of Johnson City, Tenn., and a 1960 graduate of the Kent State School of Journalism. He studied at the Air Force Acad-

emy. He joined the *Beacon Journal* in 1961 and worked as a reporter and assistant city editor before moving to Columbus to head the newspaper's statehouse bureau. After retiring from the *Philadelphia Inquirer*, Lacy moved to Murrells Inlet, S.C.. Soon after relocating, Lacy suffered a stroke in 2015. A colleague was looking for a photograph to post on BJ Alums. He examined more than a dozen photos and reports he had no luck finding one in which Lacy was not showing a wide smile or a laugh. That's the way Lacy rolls.

BOB PAGE

Bob was a journalism graduate of Kent State who joined the *Beacon Journal* in 1968. Among his reporting beats were the cities of Barberton and Cuyahoga Falls, the major suburban news bureaus. He left the paper in 1973 to study for the ministry. He earned master of divinity and doctor of ministries degrees from Trinity Evangelical Divinity School in Deerfield, Illinois. After graduation, he began a new career at an Evangelical Free Church pastoral ministry. For 37 years, Bob served congregations in Nebraska and Fargo, N.D. Bob came to Live Oaks, Fla., in January 2013 after 20 years at the Evangelical Free Church in Crystal Lake, Ill. Among his retirement activities are golf, pickleball and walking.

RAY REDMOND

Ray was born in Warren, Ohio. He began his career in journalism at the *Akron Times-Press* near the end of the Great Depression. He enlisted in the U.S. Army and served as an information officer in

Gen. George Patton's 3rd Army. He was in France on D-day, June 6, 1944, a day that he celebrated with a drink throughout his life. Patriotism was a big theme in Ray's life. After the war, he returned to Akron and resumed his career, this time at the *Beacon Journal*, which had acquired the *Times-Press* in 1938. He covered Portage County and over the years proved more than once that he had a reporter's gift for being on the scene for the big stories. Ray was a mentor to young reporters, who came to think of him for his kindness, his capacity for understatement and his sense of humor. He was a humble man who rarely talked about his critical role in breaking the story of the FBI and its perceived influence on the *Beacon Journal's* Pulitzer Prize. He retired from the newspaper in 1975 after 34 years as a reporter. Ray and his wife, Nea, traveled widely and were deeply involved in the Annunciation Greek Orthodox Church in the heart of Akron. He died in April 2008 at age 90.

DON ROESE

Don is a native of Akron. He joined the *Beacon Journal* as a photographer in 1957 and was an eyewitness to the shootings on May 4. His first-person report phoned from the campus helped the *Beacon Journal* get to press quickly with an accurate account of what happened as National Guard troops shot at protestors. In retirement, Don became an avid camper, traveling to Alaska for months.

JEFF SALLOT

Jeff was born in Cleveland and is a journalism graduate of Kent State. As a student, he was a summer intern and campus stringer for the *Beacon Journal*. He became a full-time member of the news staff in May 1970. He continued to report the Kent State story into 1971, when he was hired by the *Toronto Star*. He moved from the *Star* to the *Globe and Mail* in 1973. He was the paper's Moscow bureau chief from 1988 to 1991 and covered the collapse of the Soviet Union. Jeff served as the Globe's diplomatic correspondent and reported from more than 30 countries. In 2007, he joined the journalism faculty at Carleton University, where he developed a multi-media reporting course. His coverage of a scandal in the Royal Canadian Mounted Police led to a book, *Nobody Said No*. In retirement, he lives in Ottawa, continues to travel and produce online journalism.

BOB SCHUMACHER

Bob Schumacher's 40 years in newspapers were a fulfillment for his love for sports and an aspiration for being in charge of small newsrooms. He was born in Parkersburg, W.Va., and was intensely loyal to the Mountaineers and the Thundering Herd, teams of his two colleges, West Virginia University and Marshall College. Before arriving at the *Beacon Journal* as a state desk reporter, Bob had stops as a reporter at newspapers in Beckley and Huntington, W.Va., and Charlotte, N.C. He left the *Beacon Journal* in 1971 and held several reporting positions at *The Dayton Journal Herald*, including as two years as beat reporter covering the Cincinnati Bengals. He later became editor of the Michigan

City (Indiana) *News-Dispatch*, the *Tribune-Star* of Terre Haute, Indiana, and the *Sheboygan Press*. In 1998, he was diagnosed with Parkinson's disease. He successfully battled the disease until 2014, when he died at age 72.

PAUL TOPLE

Paul was a life-long resident of the Akron area who graduated from Kent State with a degree in photo journalism. At 14, his parents gave him a photo processing kit that he thought was the "dumbest gift" ever. In fact, it was a forerunner of his destiny. After graduating from Kent State in 1970, he began a career of 42 years at the *Beacon Journal*. Paul shared in three Pulitzer Prizes won by the *Beacon Journal*. He was known for his compassion, gentleness and demeanor that typically drew out the best in his photo subjects, often in difficult circumstances. Boy Scouting was a major influence in his life. He became an Eagle Scout in 1965 and, as a recognition of his life-long devotion to scouting, was later awarded the coveted Silver Beaver Award. He was 70 when he died of cancer in May 2018.

ABE ZAIDAN

Abe is a graduate of the University of Illinois and the University of Pittsburgh. He has worked for several newspapers and magazines during his long journalistic career. During his time at the *Beacon Journal*, he was the political editor, senior editor and columnist. He later spent seven years with Cleveland's *Plain Dealer* as a reporter and columnist before leaving to devote full time to writing. His columns and articles have appeared in nearly all major U.S. newspapers and the *International Herald Tribune*. *The Washington Post* published some 300 of his articles. He also was a political columnist for *Ohio Magazine* for three years and later a monthly columnist for *Northern Ohio Live*. Zaidan has authored five books, including *Portraits of Power*, with Dr. John Green, director of the Bliss Institute for Applied Politics at the University of Akron. It was published in 2007 and contains 90 essays that reflect Zaidan's witty and vivid style of reporting on Gov. James Rhodes and the wrenching events of the shootings at Kent State University. In retirement, Abe created two blogs for sharing his thoughts: "Plunderbund" and "Grumpy Abe." He lives in the Fairlawn district of West Akron.

Acknowledgements

There is little mystery to writing a book. An idea. Hard work. Lots of help. A bit of luck.

For this story about the tragedies at Kent State, the help began at home. Dr. Nancy Giles, my wife and loving companion of 60 years, was a true partner, the first reader-in-chief. With my draft of a fresh chapter in hand, she would sit at the kitchen counter, bent over the manuscript. She would ask, "Can I read with a pencil in my hand?" Her gift of language introduced expressive passages that brought life and important meaning to my initial takes. I knew the story, but often she had a better feel for how to tell it. We discussed her suggestions, line by line. We didn't always agree that her feedback had improved on my newspaperman's style. Eventually, I would retreat to my computer in our second-story loft and incorporate the changes that seemed to fit.

My luck also included a team of friends, wise mentors, skilled readers, well-wishers and trusted allies. They believed in me and encouraged me to keep on. "You have an important story to tell," was a common refrain.

Martha Bebinger, a Nieman Fellow, class of 2010, who covers health care for radio station WBUR in Boston, was an early reader who faithfully responded with long email messages packed with smart reactions and instructive commentary. She was a great fan, typically ending a note with upbeat comment like, "applauding from afar."

Doug Weaver, my editor at Mission Point Press in Traverse City, was an inspiration. He brought a deep newspaper background to the task and a sense of story that strengthened the text and directed the production over the course of the project.

I keenly recall an August evening in 2017 when two accomplished Michigan authors, John Bacon and Doug Stanton, sat with me in a Traverse City fish house urging me to "write this story. Most of your reporters from that time have passed. You have one of the few surviving memories. You have to preserve the story and the lessons of journalism from 1970."

Truth is illuminated by facts and in Bob Campbell, retired politics editor of the *Detroit Free Press,* I was fortunate to have a fact-checker who brought rich details and a passion for accuracy to his task. His wife, Ruth Campbell, who worked with me as a copy editor at *The Detroit News,* closely combed the manuscript to ensure that the i's were dotted and t's crossed, and style usage was consistent throughout.

The three Giles children had significant roles. Dave, a First Amendment lawyer with E.W. Scripps in Cincinnati, provided guidance on copyrights and photo permissions. Megan had endless ideas for marketing *When Truth Mattered,* and Rob, a lawyer with the Navy JAG, guided me through the thickets of military law to explore whether National Guard officers could be court-martialed.

Other members of the team at Mission Point Press brought their many and varied talents to the book's writing, production and release. Heather Lee Shaw provided superb design of the front and back covers and the interior pages; Anne Stanton offered continual and needed encouragement from the project's beginning; Jodee Taylor oversaw our promotions rollout; Noah Shaw created a sterling author website; Nick Loud oversaw our video trailer; Colleen Zanotti created our interior graphics; and C.D. Dahlquist was our proofreader.

Tony and Debbie Demin spent a sunny November afternoon with camera lenses and keen eyes capturing images of the author.

Extraordinary help also came from the staff at the May 4 Special Collections at the Kent State University Library. Amanda Faehnel and Katie Clements chased down photos and documents. Cara Gilgenbach, administrator of the Special Collections and Archives, made sure that we had access to the material we needed. Virginia Dressler, digital projects librarian, and Anita Clary, special collections librarian, dug out numbers documenting Kent State enrollment and campus expansion. Kate Medicus, special collections cataloger, invited me to contribute to the May 4 Oral History Project.

Thank you, too, to Phil Rajala, whose scans brought fresh life to old photos.

At the Pulitzer Prize offices in the Columbia Graduate School of Journalism, I was assisted by an old friend, Sig Gissler, former administrator, and warmly welcomed by Dana Canedy, current administrator of the prizes, and Bud Kliment, deputy administrator.

Jessica Dooling of the Yale University Library generously helped us locate critical correspondence from its Kent State collection.

Interviews with Susan Knight, associate professor at the Walter Cronkite School of Journalism at Arizona State University and Elizabeth Smith, assistant professor of journalism at Pepperdine University, sharpened my understanding of how social media would influence coverage of a Kent State tragedy today.

Laurel Krause, sister of the victim, Allison Krause, welcomed a telephone call from me and described with appreciation the impact of my telephone talks all those years ago with her father, Arthur Krause.

A generation of Nieman Fellows in Journalism at Harvard provided aid, comfort and guidance of all sorts. These included Beth Macy, author of *Dopesick* and *Factory Man;* Lisa Mullins, WBUR's Boston host for All Things Considered; Amy Goldstein of *The Washington Post* and author of *Janesville;* James Scott of Charleston and author of *Rampage* and *Target Tokyo;* Alfredo Corchado, award-winning American-Mexican journalist; and Tommy Tomlinson, who wrote *The Elephant in the Room.*

Geneva Overholser, Guy Raz, Sandy Rowe, Alfred Corchado,

Amy Gajda, Jim Tobin, Hank Klibanoff, James Scott, Doug Stanton and John Bacon — gifted authors, journalists, teachers, scholars — read the finished manuscript and generously evaluated my efforts to tell this story 50 years afterward.

Other friends along the way offered good ideas and words of encouragement. James Williamson, a fount of information and contacts about Kent State; Gene Policinski, president of the Freedom Forum Institute; Mary Kay Blake, long-time friend and associate through the Gannett and Freedom Forum years; Bob Haiman, an old colleague from our days together as editors; Kurt and Eleanor Luedtke, who talked me through the idea for *When Truth Mattered*.

Michael Shearer, current editor of the *Akron Beacon Journal*, was accessible and generous in enabling me to use the newspaper's archives and in granting permission to use images from its important photo collection.

Tim Smith and Jan Leach, both former *Beacon Journal* editors, gave me important guidance from their present roles on the Kent State Journalism School faculty. Heather White, in charge of groundskeeping, identified the northern red oak tree near Taylor Hall where a Guardsman's bullet lies embedded.

Charlie Sennott, another colleague from my Nieman years, collaborated with me to ensure that a portion of the profits from *When Truth Mattered* would be shared with his bold project, *GroundTruth*.

Early readers of the first chapters had a common reaction: put more of yourself into your story-telling. It was hard for me to do, but I think I came to accept their guidance in ways that are reflected through the pages of *When Truth Mattered*.

Finally, thank you to so many others who expressed keen interest in this sad story from another time and encouraged me to keep writing.

Notes by Chapter

Foreword

xvi **At least 61 times...** Over time, the bullet count has not been definitive. I have used the investigation for *The President's Commission on Campus Unrest* as a reliable source. Its count is 61; 28 soldiers acknowledged firing from Blanket Hill. Of these, 25 fired 55 shots from rifles, two fired a total of five shots from .45 caliber pistols, and one fired a single blast from a shotgun. 61 shots.

Other sources state that 67 bullets were fired. Among these is a book titled *67 Shots* by Howard Means. He writes, "When the Guardsmen began firing at 12:24 p.m. on May 4, 1970 — 67 shots in 13 seconds — all but six rounds" were M-1 bullets. Means accounts for 28 rounds "known to impact objects or people." He details where each bullet ended its flight. Beyond that, I am uncertain how to use his description to reach a total of 67 bullets fired.

In writing this book, I have relied on the report of *The President's Commission* as the most reliable source — in addition to the *Akron Beacon Journal* — of what happened at Kent State. That logic explains why I decided to use 61 as the number of shots fired on May 4.

CHAPTER ONE

21 **By August 1970 — 11 years after U.S. armed forces became engaged in Southeast Asia...** The Vietnam Conflict Extract Data File of the Defense Casualty Analysis System (DCAS) Extract Files contains records of 58,220 U.S. military fatal casualties of the Vietnam War.

26 Thomas R. Hensley, professor emeritus of political science, and Jerry M. Lewis, professor emeritus of sociology at Kent State, edited *Kent State & May 4th — a Social Science Perspective*. It is an important addition to the Kent State literature, exploring particularly the extended aftermath of May 4 that took place in state and federal courts.

CHAPTER FIVE

50   **When he died in 2011, his old bureau chief...** *St. Paul Pioneer Press*, May 7, 2011.

CHAPTER SIX

55   **The bitter aftertaste of these two protests...** During May 1970, according to *The Report of the President's Commission on Campus Unrest*, "National Guardsmen were activated on 24 occasions at 21 universities in 16 states, including Kent State University."

CHAPTER EIGHT

73   **And in one memorable encounter, Allison Krause...** William A. Gordon, *Four Dead in Ohio*. (Laguna Hills, Calif.: North Ridge Books, 1995), p 28.

77   **The story said the governor had arrived at Kent State...** Gov. James Rhodes' speech on campus disorders in Kent, May 3, 1970. Kent State University Libraries Special Collections.

CHAPTER NINE

The recollection of the critical details of *Beacon Journal* reporter Jeff Sallot's coverage of the Kent State shootings are drawn from a long memorandum he prepared for me on Dec. 31, 2018; a talk he gave to journalism students at Carleton University in Ottawa, Ontario, on May 4, 1990, the 20th anniversary of the shootings, and telephone conversations with him.

81   **Among the growing number were students, teachers.** Thomas M. Grace, *Kent State: Death and Dissent in the Long Sixties*. (Amherst, MA: University of Massachusetts Press, 2016), p. 217.

81   **When someone asked him for a definition...** *ibid.*

84   **On Monday morning, Tople returned to his role as a student.** Paul Tople, *Akron Beacon Journal*, Sunday, April 30, 2000, p. J10.

87 **The Guardsmen were clearly outnumbered.** Thomas M. Grace, *Kent State: Death and Dissent in the Long Sixties.* (Amherst, MA: University of Massachusetts Press, 2016), p. 220.

87 **He said some of the Guardsmen were armed...** "Blooper" and "Thumper," according to Gordon L. Rottman, *US Army Infantryman in Vietnam 1965-73.* (Oxford, UK: Osprey, 2005), p. 31.

89 **Specifically, Tom Grace and William Schroeder are slightly mispositioned.** Thomas M. Grace, *Kent State: Death and Dissent in the Long Sixties.* (Amherst, MA: University of Massachusetts Press, 2016), p. 272.

92 **Sallot looked to his left and saw that the Guardsmen next to the Pagoda.** The Pagoda was a square bench made of 4-by-4 wooden beams. *The Report of The President's Commission on Campus Unrest*, p. 272.

95 **Minutes after the horrific sound of rifle volleys...** United Press International. *The Observer*, Notre Dame and Saint Mary's College, p. 3. "Seek to Determine Guard Motive."

100 **At that moment, Sallot held in his hand a phone receiver...** *Akron Beacon Journal*, Monday, May 4, 1970.

61 Bullets

106 **During its investigations, the FBI collected rocks...** *The President's Commission on Campus Unrest.* (New York: Arno Press, 1970), p. 285.

107 **What happens when bullets enter...** Jason Fagone, *What Bullets Do to Bodies*, Huffington Post Highline, April 2017.

CHAPTER TEN

107 The details in the chapter about Robinson Memorial Hospital are drawn from a memo on Feb. 9, 2019, sent to me by Bob Page, the reporter on the scene. I have added my own recollections from having been in the *Beacon Journal* newsroom on the afternoon of May 4 as we strove to confirm the names of the dead and wounded Kent State students.

CHAPTER ELEVEN

117   **Controlled chaos prevailed among the Guardsmen.** *The Report of The President's Commission on Campus Unrest.* (New York: Arno Press, 1970), pp. 278-9.

117   **The Guardsmen looked "scared to death ... a bunch of summertime soldiers."** *The Report of The President's Commission on Campus Unrest.* (New York: Arno Press, 1970), p. 278.

118   **Glenn Frank shuttled between...** Thomas M. Grace, *Kent State: Death and Dissent in the Long Sixties.* (Amherst, MA: University of Massachusetts Press, 2016), p. 230.

119   **He had 23 years of military experience...** ibid, p. 265.

119   **Maj. Harry Jones of the National Guard...** *The Report of The President's Commission on Campus Unrest.* (New York: Arno Press, 1970), p. 278.

121   **With Sallot hanging on to the only open line to the Kent State campus...** Memorandum explaining the use of the Ohio Bell Telephone Co. written by Ron Clark to the author, Aug. 11, 1970.

122   **Several hands of authority were involved...** *The Report of The President's Commission on Campus Unrest.* (New York: Arno Press, 1970), pp. 285-86.

127   **The first piece that revealed fresh, substantial information...** James Herzog, *Akron Beacon Journal*, May 5, 1970, p. A2.

128   **Canterbury held a news conference on the edge...** Robert Batz, *Akron Beacon Journal*, May 5, 1970, p. A2

129   **Helen Carringer, 46, had covered education...** Helen Carringer, *Akron Beacon Journal*, May 5, 1970, p. A8

130   **Kathy Lilly had another story to tell.** Kathy Lilly, *Akron Beacon Journal*, May 5, 1970, p. A9.

131   **Chuck Ayers, 22, ... worked part-time as an artist...** Chuck Ayers, *Akron Beacon Journal.* May 5, 1970, p. A23.

133   **It took years for Krummel to talk openly about the Kent State shootings...** Art Krummel, "Ex-guardsman recalls how close he came to fateful act." April 30, 2000, p. J13.

133   **Ray Redmond was the last Beacon Journal reporter...** Ray Redmond, *Akron Beacon Journal*, May 5, 1970, p. A8.

133   **On the editorial page for the May 5 edition...** James
        Jackson, *Akron Beacon Journal,* May 5, 1970, p. A6.

CHAPTER TWELVE

137   **The bullet burrowed into a nearby tree.** The tree was
        identified as a northern red oak from information supplied
        by Heather White, Kent State University grounds manager.
        She found an overhead screen-capture from the university's
        campus tree inventory that identified each of the tree species
        near the Don Drumm sculpture. In 1970, the tree had a
        slender trunk; it was not much more than a sapling. A
        separate photograph shows the bullet hole as it appears today,
        nearly 50 years later, embedded in a mature tree. That image
        can be seen in the Kent State University Library Special May
        4 Collection.

        Kyle McDonald, *"Full History of Familiar Kent State Sculpture
        Comes to Light after Decades,"* Record-Courier, April 21, 2014.

137   **Canterbury ... was not willing to say...** William A. Gordon,
        Four Dead in Ohio. (Laguna Hills, Calif.: North Ridge Books,
        1995), pp. 49-50.

138   **Claims that Guardsmen were responding to a sniper
        shooting...** *The Report of The President's Commission on
        Campus Unrest.* (New York: Arno Press, 1970), p. 279.

139   **On the afternoon of May 4, Mickey Porter, a local
        columnist...** "Tells How He Saw KSU Campus Battle." *Akron
        Beacon Journal.* May 5, 1970, A27.

139   **He surrendered his revolver.** *The Report of The President's
        Commission on Campus Unrest.* (New York: Arno Press,
        1970), p. 279.

139   **Porter was the only reporter...** "Kent State — a New Look."
        Janis Froelich, The *Tampa Tribune.* May 31, 2018.

139   **It was sustained by such reports as contained in a front-
        page...** Howard Means, *67 Shots: Kent State and the End of
        American Innocence.* (Philadelphia: Da Capo Press, 2016), p.
        108.

141   **Lilly described the newspaper's reporting...** Kathy Lally,
        memo to the author, Feb. 16, 2019. (Kathy Lilly's marriage
        to Russ Lilly ended after she left the *Beacon Journal* and she
        now uses her maiden name, Kathy Lally.)

145 **The Ohio Highway Patrol investigated the shooting…** *The Report of The President's Commission on Campus Unrest* (New York: Arno Press, 1970), p. 279.

CHAPTER THIRTEEN

147 **Photo images of Vietnam's atrocities haunted the nation's conscience.** Loren Ghiglione, *The American Journalist: Paradox of the Press.* (Library of Congress: Washington, 1990), p. 83.

147 **In 1968, AP's Eddie Adams captured the…** *Breaking News: How The Associated Press has covered war, peace and everything else.* (New York: Princeton Architectural Press, 1990), p. 329.

147 **Ron Haeberle was a U.S. Army photographer…** Evelyn Theiss, photos by Ronald L. Haeberle, "The Photographer Who Showed the World What Really Happened at My Lai." *Time* magazine. March 15, 2018.

147 **The starkness of the atrocity…** How reporter Seymour Hersh uncovered a massacre. CBC Radio. Posted at 8 a.m. June 14, 2018.

150 **Filo spent a couple of days before May 4…** Sam Roe, "Thirteen Seconds. Dozens of bullets. One explosive photo." *Columbia Journalism Review.* June 1, 2016.

151 **Filo realized there was only one camera body left…** Bill Lilly, "Pulitzer Winner John Filo, Photo's Subject, Reunited at Kent State." *Akron Beacon Journal.* May 5, 2009. Lilly reported that Filo thought his famous photo had ruined Mary Ann Vecchio's life. "It took me 25 years before I could talk to her." They first met in 1995. Vecchio said the picture "haunted her for quite a while, but she finally came to terms with it. I have a much better appreciation today for my place in history."

151 **Filo snapped the shutter.** *The President's Commission on Campus Unrest.* (New York: Arno Press, 1970), p. 270.

152 **During a talk at Kent State in 2009, Filo said…** From remarks by John Filo at the 30th Commemoration of the Kent State Tragedy, Kent State University, May 4, 2009.

154 **He squinted through the eyepiece of his Nikon camera.**
Andrew Putz, "The Shootings: The Art of Violence," *The Scene*, May 4, 2000, pp. 4-6.

155 **When he returned to his campus flat on Sunday evening...**
Andrew Putz, "The Shootings: The Art of Violence," *The Scene*, May 4, 2000, pp. 4-6.

155 **His picture ... was taken "one or two seconds after the firing began."** "Camera Caught Action at KSU." Interview with John Darnell, published in the *Akron Beacon Journal*, May 13, 1970. p. 1.

155 **In front was a sergeant crouched in a firing position...**
John Fitzgerald O'Hara, "The man who started the killings at Kent State: The Myron Pryor lie detector test." *The Sixties: A Journal of History, Politics, Culture.* Published online Aug. 1, 2016, pp. 79-114.

Abstract. This article re-examines the role of Ohio National Guard Sgt. Myron Pryor in the Kent State shootings. Pryor first came under suspicion as a key perpetrator of the shootings in the words of early Kent State conspiracy theorists, and subsequently in official investigations and prosecutions. Though he was not indicted and is now deceased, Pryor remains a lightning rod in Kent State conspiracy theories and is often portrayed in the context of guilt. Recently, Pryor's role has been rehashed after May 4 victim and activist Alan Canfora unveiled new audio evidence in 2010 pointing to Pryor as a possible catalyst in the shootings. By looking at countervailing evidence, including not-before-released evidence from the private files of Pryor's defense attorney, C.D. Lambros, the author calls into question Pryor's alleged role in the May 4 shootings, and argues for a careful reevaluation of evidence in assigning responsibility for the Kent State shootings to Pryor.

158 **Cleary...had been standing near the sculpture...** William A. Gordon, *Four Dead in Ohio.* (Laguna, Calif.: North Ridge Books, 1995), p. 188.

158 **The five photographs...** Tragedy at Kent. *Life.* Time, Inc. May 15, 1970. Cover photo by Howard Ruffner. Photos by John Filo, John Darnell, pp. 30-37.

158   **Filo, Darnell and Ruffner received high journalism honors for their pictures.** Sam Roe, "Thirteen seconds. Dozens of bullets. One explosive photo." *Columbia Journalism Review.* June 1, 2016, pp. 1-12.

160   **Most unsettling to me was a backstory involving Filo.** On June 6, 2016, I sent a letter to Sam Roe at the *Chicago Tribune* complimenting him on his "thoughtful and authoritative" piece in CJR on how Filo came to take the iconic photograph of the Kent State shootings. In my letter, I filled in some details about how the *Beacon Journal* missed getting Filo's famous photograph. I was with Filo at a gathering of Pulitzer Prize winners at Macalester College in Minnesota the following year. He gave me the detailed backstory of how he decided to take his rolls of film back to his hometown newspaper in Pennsylvania for processing. Filo has been very gracious over the years in not focusing on how an earlier unhappy experience with the *Beacon Journal* photo lab helped him decide he did not want to entrust his film to us.

       In 1999, when Filo was working for CBS in New York and I was executive director of the Freedom Forum's Media Studies Center in the city, he and I presented a public showing of his images from May 4, along with my description of the *Beacon Journal's* coverage. Among the images he showed that afternoon were several that had never been seen by the public. In July 2019, the Freedom Forum Institute generously granted permission to use comments by Filo from a video of that program as it was shown on May 4, 2000.

CHAPTER FOURTEEN

163   **Joe Rice, the Beacon Journal's political writer, reported that Taft...** Joe Rice, *Akron Beacon Journal*, May 6, 1970, p. 1A.

163   **Many people felt that the governor's remarks worsened...** *The President's Commission on Campus Unrest.* (New York: Arno Press, 1970), pp. 254-55. Of Gov. Rhodes' role, the national commission's report said: "Many persons felt that the governor had spoken firmly and forthrightly. Others felt that his remarks were inflammatory and worsened an already tense situation. Some, including many Kent students, believed the governor was hoping that his words and actions

at Kent would win him additional votes in the primary election. ..."

165   **Kane, 34, explained to Rhodes that he wanted to close...** Kane grew up in Cleveland. We were baseball teammates at John Marshall High School on the city's west side. He graduated from Baldwin-Wallace College and Cleveland State University Law School. Kane's request for an injunction closing the university stated that: "A state of emergency exists on campus ... and the continued operation of the university poses a threat to many students not involved in the riots and the townspeople of the city of Kent ... and that a clear and present danger exists." His petition for the injunction further stated that while the administration of Kent State had earlier that afternoon announced the closing of the campus, "that could be rescinded and the university reopened before conditions merit it."

165   **Monday afternoon, after the shooting...** Judge Caris' order barred "all students, faculty, administration, employees and other persons from entering the campus without the authority of the National Guard." President Robert White and the school's Board of Trustees were specifically named as being barred.

166   **Lacy McCrary, 36, chief of the newspaper's statehouse bureau...** Lacy McCrary, *Akron Beacon Journal*, May 8, 1970, p. B1.

167   **Abe Zaidan had a special love for politics.** Abe Zaidan, with John Green, *Portraits of Power.* (Akron: The University of Akron Press, 2007), David Hess, Forward, pp. IX-XI.

167   **Rhodes had assumed control of the confusing situation.** Abe Zaidan, *Akron Beacon Journal*, May 8, 1970, p. 2A.

168   **McCrary's widely read commentary...** Lacy McCrary, "View From Columbus," *Akron Beacon Journal.* May 10, 1970, p. A15.

CHAPTER FIFTEEN

171   **He was remembered by some as Kent State's "last teacher president."** Thomas M. Grace. *Kent State, Death and Dissent in the Long Sixties.* (Amherst: MA: University of Massachusetts Press, 2016), p. 66.

171   **White was well-liked for his laissez-faire style.** Howard Means, *67 Shots: Kent State and the End of American Innocence* (Boston: Da Capo Press, 2016), pp. 188-189.

173   **The university president and the governor had a brief meeting at the airport around noon...** Howard Means, *67 Shots: Kent State and the End of American Innocence.* (Boston: De Capo Press, 2016), pp. 46-47.

173   **White learned that control of the campus...** *The President's Commission on Campus Unrest.* (New York: Arno Press, 1970), pp. 240-241.

176   **He sent a telegram to President Nixon renewing a plea...** Western Union telegram from President Robert I. White to President Richard M. Nixon sent 2:45 p.m., May 11, 1970.

176   **On May 5, the National Guard gave White permission to hold a press conference...** President Robert White's press conference, May 5, 1970. Text excerpted with permission from the Special Kent State Collection, Kent State University Library.

176   **The faculty meeting lasted 90 minutes...** "Audio Recording: President White Meeting with KSU Faculty," Kent State University Libraries. Special Collections and Archives, accessed May 20, 2019, https://omeka.library.kent.edu/special-collections/items/show/227.

176   **In a statement mailed to Kent State parents on May 7...** Statement from President Robert I. White addressed to Kent State parents, May 7, 1970.

CHAPTER SIXTEEN

183   **It was owned and published by Robert C. Dix.** Tear sheets from editorials and news coverage of the Kent-Ravenna *Record-Courier* are used with permission of the Special Kent State Collections in the Kent State University Library.

193   **The editorial called for Nixon to act.** This became *The President's Commission on Campus Unrest* chaired by former Pennsylvania Gov. William Scranton.

193   **Unexpected remarks attributed to...** "Agnew: Kent Was Murder." The Associated Press. *Akron Beacon Journal*, Friday, May 8, 1970, page 1.

195   **The Beacon Journal reported that Dr. Robert J. Sillary...**
        Special Report on Kent State, published by the *Akron Beacon
        Journal,* May 24, 1970, p. A24.

196   **The package was edited by Hal Fry...** Hal Fry; introduction
        by *Beacon Journal* associate editor David Cooper, *"Print
        It!" 150 Years of the Akron Beacon Journal.* (Akron Beacon
        Journal, 1989.) Hal Fry was a sensitive writer, house
        grammarian, and an excellent editor who handled most
        of the Kent State stories. He also was a friend and wise
        counselor to generations of *Beacon Journal* journalists.

CHAPTER SEVENTEEN

The story told in this chapter is drawn from several sources.

The special eight-page sections written and edited by a team
of journalists from Knight Newspapers and published in the
Akron Beacon Journal, May 24, 1970. Quotes from the text
with permission of the *Beacon Journal.*

A booklet, *Reporting the Kent State Incident,* about how the
special project was produced by Knight Newspapers at the
request of the American Newspaper Publishers Association
and the Committee on Education in Journalism, ANPA
Foundation, New York: 750 Third Ave., 10017, 1970. The
booklet is an account of the reportorial techniques and
problems the Knight team encountered. The booklet was
intended as a teaching aid in college journalism programs.

Quotes from Kathy Lilly and Jeff Sallot, *Beacon Journal*
reporters, are taken from electronic communications with
the author, 2019.

CHAPTER EIGHTEEN

211   **Caris was born and spent his life in Ravenna...** A
        biographical sketch of Judge Albert Caris was found in a
        summer 2019 bulletin of the Reed Memorial Library in
        Ravenna, Ohio.

211   **The reporter had developed a good relationship with Kane
        through his brother...** Details of Ray Redmond's meeting
        with Prosecutor Ron Kane are taken from an undated private
        note Redmond wrote to me describing his experience in
        obtaining information from the FBI report.

215   **The next day, Sallot reported details of the split reaction** ... William A. Gordon, *Four Dead in Ohio: Was There a Conspiracy at Kent State?* (Laguna Hills, Calif.: North Ridge Books, 1995), pp. 100-101.

215   **At 8:47 that same morning...** Details of President Nixon's telephone call to J. Edgar Hoover early on Aug. 24, 1970, and subsequent memos sent by Hoover to his top aides came from declassified FBI files.

CHAPTER NINETEEN

220   **The emergence of the British press in the early 18th century...** Karin Wahl-Jorgenson, *Journalists and the Public: Newsroom Culture, Newsrooms and the Public* (Cresskill, N.J.: Hampton Press, Inc., 2007), p. 31.

220   **As news, rather than opinion, became central to the mission...** ibid, p. 29.

222   **The tone of many letters was vicious.** *The President's Commission on Campus Unrest.* (New York: Arno Press, 1970), p. 254.

226   **Throughout the emotional period after May 4...** D. Ray Heisey, professor of speech at Kent State, presented his research paper, *University and Community Reaction to the News Coverage of the Kent State Tragedy*, at an educational conference in Cleveland in April 1971. Prof. Heisey wrote, "Probably the greatest criticism from the community was directed at the *Akron Beacon Journal*. In the letters to the editor which commented on May 4 coverage, and particularly on the newspaper's special report on the shootings, 67.5 percent condemned the newspaper as "yellow," "irresponsible," "garbage," "idiotic," "too sensational and dramatic." For their special Kent State report, published less than three weeks after the shootings and which won the George Polk Memorial Award for national reporting, the *Beacon Journal* acknowledged that criticism outweighed praise. On July 29,1970, the *Beacon Journal* indicated it had received in excess of 900 letters."

CHAPTER TWENTY

William A. Gordon, *Four Dead in Ohio: Was There a Conspiracy at Kent State?* (Laguna Hills, Calif.: North Ridge Books, 1995), pp. 133-134.

A Kent State archive in the Yale University Library contains the papers and letters of Peter Davies. Included in the collection are copies of our letters about the *Beacon Journal's* coverage of Kent State and its aftermath.

In his book, Gordon writes, "From the day of the shootings, Davies launched into a holy crusade — a never-ending battle for 'truth and justice' the American way."

229   **He was an insurance broker by profession ...** Peter Davies, in collaboration with the Board of Church and Society of the United Methodist Church, *The Truth about Kent State: A Challenge to the American Conscience.* (New York: Farrar, Straus and Giroux, 1973), pp. 4-5.

CHAPTER TWENTY-ONE

235   **In December 1970, Lee Hills, president of Knight Newspapers...** Memorandum from Lee Hills, president of Knight Newspapers Inc., to editors, executive editors, and managing editors. Subject: Pulitzer Prizes. Dec. 15, 1970.

236   **It wasn't long before the bosses filled it.** Letter from Ben Maidenburg to Lee Hills, Nov. 3, 1970.

237   **On Nov. 6, Hills responded...** Memo to John S. Knight from Lee Hills responding to Ben Maidenburg's letter to Lee Hills, Nov. 6, 1970.

238   **While I was in Detroit, Knight asked Maidenburg for an update...** Letter from author to John S. Knight, Dec. 11, 1970.

240   **The Pulitzer Prize Collection is housed in...** This information is found in a document describing the Pulitzer Prize Collection, which is part of Columbia's Rare Book and Manuscript Library located in the Butler Library on the Columbia campus.

240   **The sparseness of the file's contents surprised me.** Pulitzer Prize nominating letter from Murray Powers, professor of journalism at Kent State, to John Hohenberg, secretary of the Board on the Pulitzer Prizes, Columbia University, Jan.

26, 1971. Reprinted with permission from the Pulitzer Prize Collection, Butler Library, Columbia University.

242   **How the board chose...** "How Pulitzer Board Often Overruled Juries' Selections," *Newsday*, Special reprint, 1975, p. 2.

243   **The Pulitzer Prizes were announced...** The Knight team's expectation that its Pulitzer entry would be successful may have been elevated by the announcement in mid-February that it won the George Polk Memorial Award. The citation for this distinguished award credited the work of staff members from the *Detroit Free Press, Miami Herald* and *Akron Beacon Journal.* The award describes the Knight Newspapers report as an example of "remarkable teamwork … that produced a major close-up report on what happened at Kent State University before, during and after the violence there."

CHAPTER TWENTY-TWO

246   **The names now number 58,276 and include eight women.** According to a *Washington Post* story published May 22, 2019, a study by the Vietnam Veterans Memorial Fund showed that while there are 58,390 names on the Wall, they represent 58,276 people, including eight women.

248   **After years of contentious debate and discussion...** Craig S. Simpson and Gregory S. Wilson, *Above the Shots, An Oral History of the Kent State Shootings.* (The Kent State University Press, Kent: 2016), pp 201-213.

248   **After years of contentious debate and discussion...** Ast's original design called for a memorial that would have cost more than $1 million. "After 20 Years, Apologies for Kent State Dead," E.J. Dionne Jr., *The Washington Post*, May 5, 1990.

The Song That Changed a Nation

From Clara Bingham's interview with Greil Marcus, Rolling Stone music critic, for her book *Witness to the Revolution: Radicals, Resisters, Vets, Hippies, and the Year America Lost Its Mind and Found Its Soul.* (New York: Random House, 2016.)

CHAPTER TWENTY-THREE

253   **Scranton was appointed…** Robert D. McFadden, "William W. Scranton, 96, G.O.P. Prodigy Who Led Pennsylvania Is Dead." *The New York Times,* July 23, 2013.

The members of *The President's Commission on Campus Unrest* were: William W. Scranton, former governor of Pennsylvania (chairman)
James F. Ahern, chief of police, New Haven, Conn.
Erwin D. Canham, editor-in-chief, *Christian Science Monitor*
James E. Cheek, president, Howard University
Lt. Gen. Benjamin O. Davis Jr., U.S. Air Force (retired); director, Civil Aviation Security, U.S. Department of Transportation
Martha A. Derthick, emerita professor, University of Virginia
Bayless Manning, dean, Stanford Law School
Revius O. Ortique Jr., attorney-at-law, New Orleans, La.
Joseph Rhodes Jr., junior fellow, Harvard University

256   **White was followed as a witness by Del Corso.** "Sylvester Del Corso, 85, Head of Guard at Kent State Attack." Obituary, *The New York Times,* April 11, 1998.

258   *The President's Commission on Campus Unrest* relied, in part, on stories and editorials published by the *Akron Beacon Journal.* The Commission's report was published by Arno Press, a publishing library service of The New York Times in 1970. The report mentions the *Beacon Journal* 34 times.

261   **Legal actions did follow…** "The campus and the Vietnam War: protest and tragedy." Lyle Denniston, *Constitutional Daily,* National Constitution Center: Philadelphia, Sept. 26, 2017. Denniston is an American legal journalist, professor, and author, who began reporting on the Supreme Court of the United States in 1958; he has contributed to numerous books and journals, and is the author of *The Reporter and the Law: Techniques for Covering the Courts* (Columbia University Press, 1992).

His summary of other legal actions focusing on a quest for justice from the Kent State shootings: "A group of students from Kent State filed a lawsuit against the Ohio National Guard, seeking to have the courts order reforms in the way the Guard used lethal force. They lost in the Supreme Court in a 5-to-4 decision in 1973 (*Gilligan v. Morgan*). The Justices in the majority concluded that they could not constitutionally put the judiciary in charge of military policy.

The families of three of the four Kent State students who had been killed fared better in the Supreme Court. In a ruling in 1974, the Justices held unanimously that they could go ahead with their claims that the governor and National Guard had violated the students' rights by actions at Kent State. The decision rejecting claims of state government immunity under the Eleventh Amendment was named for the Scheuer family, but also involved the Krause and Miller families. Eventually, in January 1979, the three families' civil lawsuits along with separate claims by the Schroeder family and by the wounded students were settled for $675,000 and a statement of regret by state officials. The most seriously wounded student, Dean Kahler, received $350,000. Other wounded students received between $15,000 and $42,500. The Krause, Scheuer, Miller and Schroeder families whose children had been killed each received $15,000. A series of criminal charges against eight National Guardsman ended without any guilty verdicts. Criminal charges for alleged roles in the burning of the campus ROTC building were filed against the group that came to be called the "Kent 25" — 24 students and one professor — but resulted in only one conviction and two guilty pleas."

262   **Therein is a message for today's activists, where a rise in reports of hate crimes...** "Bias-response Teams Criticized for Sanitizing Dissent." Center for Public Integrity, Aug. 27, 2018.

CHAPTER TWENTY-FOUR

266   **Soon to follow these investigations...** Thomas R. Hensley and Jerry M. Lewis, eds., *Kent State & May 4th.* (Kent: The Kent State University Press, 2010), pp. 63-86. Hensley and Lewis have provided a deeply researched and thoughtfully analyzed account of the Kent State shootings. Their valuable insights and accurate accounts were extraordinarily useful to the author in recalling the chronology of events during the period of April 30-May 4, 1970, and for a decade afterward.

Hensley and Lewis write that one important source for their analysis of the court cases has been a "thorough compilation of articles from the *Akron Beacon Journal* from May 4, 1970, through March 1979." The *Beacon Journal's* reporting on the 1970 shootings and "its continuing coverage of the legal aftermath of the shootings has been excellent."

274   **According to a story in The New York Times,
        Canterbury...** Agis Salpukas, "Kent Trial Hears Ex-Guard
        Leader." *The New York Times*, July 24, 1975, p. 41.

274   **The statement was signed by 28 defendants.** Text of the
        statement issued by defendants in the Kent State civil suits, as
        published in the Akron Beacon Journal, Jan. 4, 1979.

In retrospect, the tragedy of May 4, 1970, should
not have occurred. The students may have believed
that they were right in continuing their mass
protest in response to the Cambodian invasion,
even though this protest followed the posting and
reading by the university of an order to ban rallies
and an order to disperse. These orders have since
been determined by the Sixth Circuit Court of
Appeals to have been lawful.

Some of the Guardsmen on Blanket Hill, fearful
and anxious from prior events, may have believed
in their own minds that their lives were in danger.
Hindsight suggests that another method would
have resolved the confrontation. Better ways must
be found to deal with such confrontations.

We devoutly wish that a means had been found to
avoid the May 4 events culminating in the Guard
shootings and the irreversible deaths and injuries.
We deeply regret those events and are profoundly
saddened by the deaths of four students and
wounding of nine others which resulted. We hope
that the agreement to end this litigation will help
assuage the tragic memories regarding that day.

CHAPTER TWENTY-FIVE

280   **Kent State had a direct influence on national politics.** H.R.
        Haldeman, *The Ends of Power*. (New York: Times Books,
        1978.)

Jerry M. Lewis and Thomas R. Hensley, *The May 4 Shootings
at Kent State University: The Search for Historical Accuracy.*
The Special May 4 Collection, Kent State University Libraries.

281   **John Filo's photograph of anguished Mary Ann Vecchio...** R. Hariman and J.L. Lucaites, *No Caption Needed.* (Chicago: University of Chicago Press, 2007), p. 27.

280   **In June 1973, Congress passed legislation to prohibit the use...** Julian E. Zelizer, professor of history at Boston University, "How Congress Got Us Out of Vietnam." *The American Prospect*, Washington, DC, Feb. 17, 2007.

284   **The paper's local news dominance matches the findings...** John Sands, "Local News Is More Trusted Than National News — But That Could Change." John S. and James L. Knight Foundation, Miami, Fla., Oct. 29, 2019.

288   **Objectivity was the ultimate discipline of journalism...** Louis M. Lyons, The Business of Writing, Nieman Reports, October 1954. Reporting the News: Selections from Nieman Reports, Louis M. Lyons (The Belknap Press of Harvard University, Cambridge, Mass., 1965), p. 295. Lyons was the curator of the Nieman Fellowship program at Harvard. He invented the Nieman Program and directed it for 25 years. This article is from a lecture he gave at the Bread Loaf Writers Conference in Vermont in August 1954.

288   **Conspiracy theorists were quick to contend...** Craig S. Simpson and Gregory S. Wilson, *Above the Shots: An Oral History of the Kent State Shootings.* (Kent: The Kent State University Press, 2016), pp. 61, 153, 159.

290   **A roster of those Guardsmen has been published.** Peter Davies and the Board of Church and Society of the United Methodist Church, *"The Truth About Kent State: A Challenge to the American Conscience."* (New York: Farrar Straus Giroux, 1970), pp. 225-228.

290   **In 2010, the family of Allison Krause organized the Kent State Truth Tribunal.** Laurel Krause, *About the Kent State Truth Tribunal, Kent State Truth Tribunal: Seeking Truth and Justice at Kent State:* 2010, mendocoastcurrent.wordpress.com.

References and Suggested Additional Resources

Bates, J. Douglas. *The Pulitzer Prize: The Inside Story of America's Most Prestigious Award.* New York: Birch Lane Press, 1991.

Barbato, Carole A., and Laura L. Davis. *Democratic Narrative, History & Memory:* Kent: The Kent State University Press, 2012.

Barbato, Carole A., Laura L. Davis, and Mark F. Seeman. *This We Know: A Chronology of the Shootings at Kent State, May 1970.* Kent: The Kent State University Press, 2012.

Bills, Scott L., ed. *Kent State/May 4: Echoes Through A Decade.* Kent: The Kent State University Press, 1990.

Bingham, Clara. *Witness to the Revolution: Radicals, Resisters, Vets, Hippies, and the Year America Lost Its Mind and Found Its Soul.* New York: Random House, 2016.

Burgan, Michael. *Death at Kent State: How a Photograph Brought the Vietnam War Home to America.* North Mankato, Minn.: Compass Point Books, 2017.

Caputo, Phillip. *13 Seconds: A Look Back at the Kent State Shootings.* New York: Chamberlain Brothers, 2005.

Casale, Ottavio M., and Louis Paskoff, eds. *The Kent State Affair: Documents and Interpretations.* Boston: Houghton Mifflin, 1971.

Charles River Editors. *The Kent State Massacre: The History and Legacy of the Shootings that Shocked America.* Louisville, Ken., 2019.

Davies, Peter, and the Board of Church and Society of the United Methodist Church. *The Truth about Kent State: A Challenge to the American Conscience.* New York: Farrar Strauss Giroux, 1973.

Eszterhas, Joe, and Michael D. Roberts. *Thirteen Seconds: Confrontation at Kent State.* Cleveland: Gray & Company, publishers, 1970.

Feinstein, Anthony. *Dangerous Lives: War and the Men and Women Who Report It.* Toronto: Thomas Allen Publishers, 2003.

Feinstein, Anthony. *Journalists Under Fire: Psychological Hazards of Covering War.* Baltimore: The Johns Hopkins University Press, 2006.

Foreman, Gene. *The Ethical Journalist: Making Responsible Decisions in the Pursuit of News.* West Sussex, United Kingdom: John Wiley & Sons, 2010.

Fry, Hal. *"Print It!" 150 Years of the Akron Beacon Journal.* Akron: The Summit County Historical Society, 1989.

Gajda, Amy. *The First Amendment Bubble: How Privacy and Paparazzi Threaten a Free Press.* Harvard University Press, 2015.

Gelb, Arthur. *City Room.* New York: P.G. Putnam's Sons, 2003.

Giles, Robert H. *Newsroom Management: A Guide to Theory and Practice.* Detroit: Media Management Books, 1990.

Gordon, William A. *Four Dead in Ohio: Was There a Conspiracy at Kent State?* Laguna Hills, Calif.: North Ridge Books, 1995.

Grace, Thomas M. *Kent State: Death and Dissent in the Long Sixties.* Boston: The University of Massachusetts Press, 2016.

Grant, Edward, and Michael Hill. *I Was There: What Really Went On at Kent State.* Lima, Ohio: CSS Publishing Company, 1974.

Hall, Simon. *Rethinking the American Anti-War Movement.* New York: Routledge, 2012.

Hamilton, John Maxwell. *Journalism's Roving Eye: A History of American Foreign Reporting.* Baton Rouge: Louisiana State University Press, 2009.

Harris, Roy J. Jr. *Pulitzer's Gold: Behind the Prize for Public-Service Journalism.* Columbia, Mo.: University of Missouri Press, 2007.

Hassler, David. *May 4th Voices: Kent State, 1970, a Play.* Kent: The Kent State University Press, 2013.

Hedges, Chris. *War Is a Force That Gives Us Meaning.* New York: Public Affairs, 2002.

Hensley, Thomas R., and Jerry M. Lewis, eds. *Kent State & May 4th: A Social Science Perspective.* Kent: The Kent State University Press, 2010.

Hersh, Seymour M. *Reporter, a Memoir.* New York: Alfred A. Knopf, 2018.

Hohenberg, John, ed. *The Pulitzer Prize Story: News Stories, Editorials, Cartoons, and Pictures from the Pulitzer Prize Collection at Columbia University.* New York: Columbia University Press, 1959.

Hohenberg, John. *The Pulitzer Prizes: A History of the Awards in Books, Drama, Music, and Journalism Based on the Private Files Over Six Decades.* New York: Columbia University Press, 1974.

Hohenberg, John. *The Pulitzer Diaries: Inside America's Greatest Prize.* Syracuse, N.Y.: Syracuse University Press, 1997.

Jones, Alex S. *Losing the News: The Future of News That Feeds Democracy.* New York: Oxford University Press, 2009.

Kakutani, Michiko. *The Death of Truth: Notes on Falsehood in the Age of Trump.* New York: Tim Duggan Books, 2018.

Kelner, Joseph, and James Munves. *The Kent State Coverup.* New York: Harper and Row, 1980.

Knightly, Phillip. *The First Casualty: The War Correspondent as Hero and Myth-Maker from the Crimea to Iraq.* Baltimore: The Johns Hopkins University Press, 2004.

Lyons, Louis M., ed. *Reporting the News.* Cambridge, Mass.: The Belknap Press of Harvard University Press, 1965.

McCraw, David E. *Truth In Our Times: Inside the Fight for Press Freedom in the Age of Alternative Facts.* New York: All Points Books, 2019.

Means, Howard. *67 Shots: Kent State and the End of American Innocence.* Philadelphia: Da Capo Press, 2016.

Michener, James A. *Kent State: What Happened and Why.* New York: Fawcett Crest, 1971.

Patterson, Thomas E. *Informing the News: The Need for Knowledge-Based Journalism.* New York: Vintage Books, 2013.

Perlman, Sandra. *Nightwalking: Voices from Kent State.* Kent: Franklin Mills Press, 1995.

Pfeiffer, Dan. *Yes We (Still) Can: Politics in the Age of Obama, Twitter, and Trump.* New York: Hachette Book Group, 2018.

Pisor, Robert. *The End of the Line: The Siege of Khe Sanh.* New York: W.W. Norton & Company, 1982.

Prochnau, William. *Once Upon a Distant War, Young War Correspondents and the Early Vietnam War.* New York: Times Books, 1995.

Reporters of The Associated Press. *Breaking News: How The Associated Press Has Covered War, Peace, and Everything Else.* New York: Princeton Architectural Press, 2007.

Ruffner, Howard. *Moments of Truth: A Photographer's Experience of Kent State 1970.* Kent: The Kent State University Press, 2019.

Rusbridger, Alan. *Breaking News: The Remaking of Journalism and Why It Matters Now.* New York: Farrar, Straus and Giroux, 2018.

Simpson, Craig S., and Gregory Wilson. *Above the Shots: An Oral*

History of the Kent State Shootings. Kent: The Kent State University Press, 2016.

Stone, I.F. *The Killings at Kent State: How Murder Went Unpunished.* New York: Vintage Books, 1971.

The President's Commission on Campus Unrest. The Kent State Tragedy. New York: Arno Press, 1970.

Tucker, Paula Stone. *Surviving: A Kent State Memoir.* Mechanicsburg, Penn.: Sunbury Press, 2019.

Wahl-Jorgensen, Karin. *Journalists and the Public: Newsroom Culture, Letters to the Editor and Democracy.* Cresskill, N.J.: Hampton Press, Inc., 2007.

Whited, Charles. *Knight, A Publisher In The Tumultuous Century.* New York: E.P. Dutton, 1988.

Zaidan, Abe, with John C. Green. *Portraits of Power: Ohio and National Politics, 1964-2004.* Akron: The University of Akron Press, 2007.

Index

Addendum — The Ayers Sketches

These sketches by *Akron Beacon Journal* artist Chuck Ayers show the sequence of events on May 4, 1970. An editor had asked him to do the sketches. "I remember minute details of most of what I did and saw for about five days around May 4, but much of those five or six hours at the newspaper as I sketched are a blur." Six of Ayers' illustrations re-creating the turmoil were spread across the front of the local news section on Tuesday, May 5. He completed the drawings within hours of the shooting. His images came from his memory; he had not yet seen any of the scenes captured by the famous photographs that came to define the tragedy.

Soldiers standing ready near the burned out ROTC building.

Ohio Highway patrolmen arriving after the shooting.

Reprinted with permission of *The Akron Beacon Journal*

A Guardsman firing teargas grenades.

Reprinted with permission of *The Akron Beacon Journal*

Students throwing rocks at soldiers.

Reprinted with permission of *The Akron Beacon Journal*

Students tending to a student who had been shot

Reprinted with permission of *The Akron Beacon Journal*

Faculty pleading with students to disperse.

Editorial cartoons from Ayers' Beacon Journal portfolio.

CPSIA information can be obtained
at www.ICGtesting.com
Printed in the USA
LVHW091058211121
704030LV00004B/132